Macroeconomic Dynamics

Macroeconomic Dynamics

KEIZO NAGATANI

Professor of Economics
University of British Columbia

CAMBRIDGE UNIVERSITY PRESS

CAMBRIDGE

LONDON   NEW YORK   NEW ROCHELLE

MELBOURNE   SYDNEY

Published by the Press Syndicate of the University of Cambridge
The Pitt Building, Trumpington Street, Cambridge CB2 1RP
32 East 57th Street, New York, NY 10022, USA
296 Beaconsfield Parade, Middle Park, Melbourne 3206, Australia

First published 1981

Printed in the United States of America

Library of Congress Cataloging in Publication Data
Nagatani, Keizo.

Macroeconomic dynamics.

Includes bibliographical references and index.
1. Macroeconomics.   2. Capital.   3. Statics and
dynamics (Social sciences)   I. Title.
HB172.5.N33   339   80-28883
ISBN 0 521 23515 4 hard covers
ISBN 0 521 28015 X paperback

Contents

v

viii   **Contents**

Preface

Macroeconomics is greatly in fashion today. Soaring gold prices, the U.S. banks' prime rates approaching 20 percent per annum, a worsening gasoline shortage, and Canada's floating bank rate – these have been much in the headlines of North American newspapers during the first three months of the new decade. Eight percent inflation and high unemployment rates excite no one anymore. The performances of most industrialized economies in the past decade have been very unsatisfactory by historical standards. Conventional wisdom has proved to be simply inadequate to combat the maladies of combined inflation and unemployment. Macroeconomics has lost its credibility.

The decade-long economic difficulties have, on the other hand, greatly stimulated research in macroeconomics, both inside academia and outside it. Within academia, more and better doctoral theses are being produced than ever before. The quality of macroeconomics textbooks has markedly improved at all levels during the last several years. Two books published recently by Cambridge University Press (one by Professors Robert Barro and Herschel Grossman and the other by Professor Stephen Turnovsky) are prominent examples of quality macroeconomics textbooks. Adding another textbook to this list therefore calls for some rationalization.

Macroeconomics has a fairly long history if we take Quesnay's *Tableau Economique* (1759) as the starting point. During these years, many macroeconomic problems have arisen and received attention from economists. The result is a massive volume of studies dealing with the issues of the time; these studies cover almost any query one might have about macroeconomics. Although one can argue that the problems faced nowadays are never quite the same as those of the past, it seems fair to say that any macroeconomic problem one might conceive of is likely to have a history and that the past studies are likely to be of value to the current researcher. On the basis of such a recognition, this book takes a historical approach, though not so much by way of documentation as in spirit.

Ever since Quesnay, or even since the time of mercantilism, which

ix

preceded physiocracy, the central question of macroeconomics has been the prosperity of the economy – how to achieve and maintain it. To answer this question, classical economists formulated bold dynamic models of capital and growth in which the rate of capital accumulation held the key to prosperity, but the rate of capital accumulation depended in turn on the (expected) rate of return on investment. Keynes's major contribution in this context lay in his perceptive characterization of a "monetary economy," a name he gave advanced capitalist economies of our time, and of its investment behavior. Today there appears to be a common belief that macroeconomics should be concerned with short-run problems rather than the long-run problems of growth and prosperity. However, most of the short-run problems, such as unemployment, inflation, and exchange-rate variations, are closely related to the long-run prospect of the economy through investment.

This book is based on the lecture notes I have used in the second half (one semester) of the graduate macroeconomics course at the University of British Columbia from 1976 to 1980. It presupposes a knowledge of macroeconomics that prior use of textbooks such as Professor Branson's might be expected to provide. In teaching this material, I have developed a somewhat nonstandard approach, both in content and in orientation. In particular, I place emphasis on the capital-theory approach to macroeconomics. Although the manuscript went through a few rounds of polishing, I am not certain that it has settled into long-run equilibrium.

Many friends have helped me in preparing this book. Ernie Berndt, now of MIT, Clem Boonekamp, now of the IMF, Erwin Diewert, Robert Eastwood of the University of Sussex, Larry Epstein of the University of Toronto, John Foster of the University of Glasgow, Robert Jones, Yoshi Kanemoto, now of the University of Tsukuba, Philip Neher, Peter Sturm of the OECD, and Jim Wilen of the University of California at Davis read parts of the manuscript and offered useful comments. But my greatest debt is to the students who endured my course during the past several years. Not only were they patient enough to read the manuscript in various stages, they were also kind enough to convey their reactions, sometimes explicitly and sometimes by facial expression, and to point out many mistakes. Ragnar Arnason and Chris Boyd assisted me in editing. Mr. Arnason also contributed some of the questions that follow the chapters. For these services I am very grateful. Finally, I thank Mrs. May McKay and Miss Hilary Wilson for their efficient typing of the manuscript.

KEIZO NAGATANI

CHAPTER 1

A historical review

The highest ambition an economist can entertain who believes in the scientific character of economics would be fulfilled as soon as he succeeded in constructing a simple model displaying all the essential features of the economic process by means of a reasonably small number of equations connecting a reasonably small number of variables. Work on this line is laying the foundations of the economics of the future and should command the highest respect of all of us.

J. A. Schumpeter

1.1   The prosperity question

How to achieve and maintain the prosperity of a nation has always been the focal point of macroeconomics. This problem has, of course, been with mankind for a very long time, and so has macroeconomic thought.[1] However, the beginnings of modern macroeconomic analysis can be traced to the early sixteenth century. The first two hundred years in the history of macroanalysis constituted the era of mercantilism. By the expedient of applying the businessman's objectives to a nation, the mercantilists advocated maximization of net exports and consequently increased inflow of standard money as the key to national prosperity. As a means to accomplish this goal, they favored state intervention.

The eighteenth century was characterized by increasing sophistication in macroeconomic thinking, culminating in what can be called the Quesnaysian Revolution (1759). F. Quesnay (1694–1774) and his disciples are usually referred to as physiocrats because of their assertion of agriculture's unique ability to yield "produit net." As a political movement, physiocracy emerged as a reaction to the mercantilist (antiagricultural) policies of Colbert during the reign of Louis XIV. In hindsight, however, Quesnay's most important contribution was his schematization of the circular flow of the economy in terms of monetary expenditures. His *Tableau Economique* indeed contained what proved to be the building blocks of classical economics, and for that matter, even modern-day macroeconomics. First, it contained the no-

1

tion of (working) capital and the period-analytic dynamics. Second, it defined three classes of agents assuming distinct roles: proprietors, artisans, and farmers, who were later replaced by capitalists, laborers, and landlords in the classical scenario to suit a more advanced capitalist system. But Quesnay's notion of capital as constituting advances by proprietors was retained in the classical literature. Third, Quesnay's book was the origin of aggregate-demand analysis. For Quesnay, the key to prosperity was to secure an adequate level of aggregate expenditure forthcoming from the spending plans of the three classes of agents. The idea that expenditures constituted the limiting factor for production and employment, which was a commonplace among practitioners, also found support from such economists as J. J. Becher (1635–82), S. Boisguillebert (1646–1714), G. Ortes (1713–90), and T. R. Malthus (1766–1834). However, this type of aggregate analysis, which Schumpeter called Monetary Analysis, failed to gain much support among professional economists. The analytical rigor with which D. Ricardo (1772–1823), J. S. Mill (1806–73), and K. Marx (1818–83) carried out their "Real Analysis" had by the late nineteenth century completely overpowered Monetary Analysis. Thus Real Analysis became the orthodox classical economics.

Ricardo borrowed the first two of these building blocks from Quesnay, but he focused his attention on the distributive shares among the three classes in the long run. Because disturbances from the demand side are nonexistent in the long run, he concentrated on the supply side, or the technology of production. On the basis of several strong assumptions (e.g., an exogenously given subsistence wage, a single-variable factor of production, fixed input coefficients, and a uniform production period for all products), Ricardo was able to derive an extremely powerful causal (as against simultaneous) theory of relative prices and distribution in the long run. As for the long-run destination of a national economy, Ricardo predicted that a continuing application of increasing amounts of the capital–labor mix to a limited amount of land would eventually drive profits and wages down to their respective subsistence levels. The beauty of the Ricardian theory is compelling,[2] but it must be recognized that his results are crucially dependent on his powerful assumptions and that the simplicity of his logic tends to break down with the slightest relaxation of these assumptions.

The decade of the 1870s saw the Marginal Revolution initiated by W. S. Jevons (1835–82), C. Menger (1840–1921), and L. Walras (1834–1910), marking the opening of the neoclassical era. The Marginal Revolution laid a firm basis for the theory of choice, and it provided, in Walras's formulation, a multicommodity general-equilibrium framework suited for study of the structure of equilibrium prices. In retrospect, at least, one of the great accomplishments of Walras was his intuitive grasp of the viability of competitive markets, in other words, the ability of the competitive system to solve the society's allocations problem, a proposition that was only much later formally established by sophisticated existence proofs and demonstrations of the normative nature of competitive allocations. In a word, neoclassical economics is a more elaborate Real Analysis with its focus on static equilibrium.[3]

Elegant as it is, neoclassical general-equilibrium theory has severe limitations as a framework for macroanalysis. These limitations stem from its static-equilibrium character. To see this, consider the central results of the theory, which are the equilibrium-price relationships. The equality between the price of a factor and the value of its marginal product, the equality between the rental price of an asset and the interest times the price of the asset, the purchasing-power parity theory of exchange-rate determination, and so forth, are examples of such relationships. These relationships are deduced from the assumed rationality of individuals and competition (which equals perfect arbitrage) using the argument proceeding by way of contradiction. The deductive process does not in any way rely on or concern itself with knowledge of the actual price-formation process. In this sense the theory is not a very constructive one. However, in macroeconomics, where it is crucial to understand the dynamic processes of price and quantity variations, this type of equilibrium-price relationship is manifestly inadequate. Actual prices often turn out to be too irresponsive to important changes in the data (and, conversely, too sensitive to false signals) for them to maintain the system close to equilibrium. The reason for this is that along a dynamic path there are, in addition to the price variables, many other factors exerting their influences, the most important of which is probably the inertia caused by stock adjustments. By concentrating on equilibrium, which, by definition, is a state free from such inertia, static theory overstates the importance of prices in equilibrating the economy.

The Keynesian Revolution (1936) contained a major criticism of the neoclassical mentality just mentioned.[4] Keynes's achievements have been described variously in the literature, but his basic philosophy toward economic policy may be summarized as follows: Keynes was a man of great practical mind, although in the intuitive sense rather than in the econometrician's sense (Harrod 1951, pp. 145–6, 324; Patinkin 1976). He looked at macroeconomic problems from the stand-

point of the entrepreneur. His unreserved (and, in all fairness, unde-
served) praise of mercantilism in the *General Theory* (Chapter 23) is
evidence of this attitude. In his view, the key to prosperity was the
entrepreneur's state of mind, which revolved around the notion of
liquidity. We may recall the debate during the seventeenth and
eighteenth centuries whether "dearness and plenty" or "cheapness
and plenty" should spell prosperity. Keynes would have said that
"cheapness of liquidity and plenty" was the condition for prosperity.
Prosperity was a flow concept. It was not a stock concept in the sense
of wealth. It meant a satisfactory level of flow activities, with capital
turning over smoothly. For a given productive capacity it required a
sufficiently high level of aggregate demand. Thus, his theory re-
turned to the Malthusian tradition of aggregate-demand analysis
(*General Theory*, p. 32; see also Malthus 1836, Book II, Chapter 1).
The aggregate demand was broken down into consumption and investment. As for the consumption component, its "cheapness" might
be desirable, but its real value, Keynes postulated, was largely determined by the level of real income. Once consumption was made
dependent on income, investment assumed the key role in determining aggregate income, and it is here that the notion of liquidity
comes into the picture. Inadequate liquidity chokes investment and
results in a deficient aggregate demand. Moreover, according to
Keynes's theory of the consumption function, the richer the economy
is, the greater the requisite volume of investment, and hence the
greater the danger of inadequate liquidity resulting in "poverty in
plenty." How to keep entrepreneurs optimistic and willing investors is
the *sine qua non* of macroeconomic policy.

The importance of this problem was later schematized by one of his
students, R. F. Harrod (1948), in a growth context. Harrod depicted
the dynamics of the economy as an interaction between three growth
rates: the natural growth rate (the growth rate of income required to
maintain full employment of the labor force), the warranted growth
rate (the growth rate of income required to maintain full employment
of capital), and the actual growth rate of income. In his model, the key
determinant of investment is the output-capital ratio, which is a measure of the turnover rate of capital as a fund.[5] Entrepreneurs tend to
entertain a notion of some normal output-capital ratio, and if the
actual ratio falls short of (exceeds) this normal ratio, the rate of investment will decline (rise). This, by reducing (increasing) aggregate demand, results in a further decline (increase) in the actual output-
capital ratio, suggesting a serious instability. Since Solow's *Contribution*
(1956), it has become customary to view the Harrodian dynamic

model as a special case of neoclassical growth models in which the elasticity of factor substitution is zero. But such a mechanical interpretation must be judged unfair to Harrod, because Harrod's problem was one of disequilibrium in the goods and other markets, whereas neoclassical growth models were concerned with the pure resource dynamics under the condition of continuous full employment of resources.

At any rate, Keynes's theory has a number of elements signaling a return to the classical economics. Among these are the revival of the Malthusian aggregate-demand theory, the "fundist" notion of capital and its turnover rate as the key determinant of investment, and, perhaps most significantly, a renewed concern about the old problem of how to attain and maintain prosperity. However, this is not to say that the neoclassical economics ignores this question altogether. Indeed, the neoclassical welfare economics is directly concerned with it. But comparing alternative allocations of given resources and identifying the best within a static context is a very limited answer to the problem. Prosperity is a much more inclusive dynamic concept than that, and it cannot be separated from the problem of economic growth. Two centuries ago, Smith correctly identified prosperity with the state of progress. Today's data show a very close negative correlation between the investment–income ratio and the unemployment rate. The so-called Okun's law also points to the essentiality of growth in improving the condition of employment. As will be shown in Chapter 7, firms' employment decisions depend on the same set of factors as that determining their investment decisions.

1.2   Modern business cycles

Our emphasis thus far has been on growth and development in the long run. We now turn our attention to short-run fluctuations. Although it is no longer fashionable to speak of business cycles with regular periodicity, problems caused by fluctuations in the levels of economic activities and prices continue to be matters of major concern. But what causes these fluctuations? This subject has intrigued economists for the last century and a half, at least, although the meager theoretical results hardly reflect this.

Business cycles are a product of modern capitalist economies. This does not mean, of course, that they are or would be nonexistent under different systems. But it does mean that their emergence coincided with the sophistication in the mode of production, commerce, and credit arrangements that the capitalist system accomplished. One may identify the beginning of the nineteenth century with such a critical date. (For some reason, crises in the first part of the nineteenth century occurred very regularly, i.e., 1815, 1825, 1836–9, 1847–8, 1857, 1866, etc.) The causes of these fluctuations were then not as clearly identifiable as the causes of those in the past. It nevertheless became recognized that the sequences of events that took place during these cycles had a certain common pattern. This recognition prompted economists to search for a theory that could explain the cause and progression of business cycles in a unified manner. This marked the beginning of modern business-cycle theories.

The earliest forms of business-cycle theories were those of "overproduction" or "underconsumption" explanations of crises. As theorists became impressed by the hardships experienced during crises (bankruptcies, unemployment, collapse of credits, unsalability of commodities), versions of such theories flourished. In criticizing these theories, J. B. Say (1767–1832) rightly argued that overproduction was hardly the cause of crises, but rather a phenomenon of crises, and he insisted that the cause should be sought. But in the process of further investigations, he went astray. He argued, on the basis of what is now known as Say's law or Say's identity, that general overproduction was impossible: If there was overproduction of one good, there had to be underproduction of some other good or goods. He was thus led to a disproportionality theory of crises. Although Say's business-cycle theory was not successful (for, once money and financial assets are introduced, his argument breaks down), he is to be remembered for his introduction of analytical ideas into the field of business cycles.

The gradual advance in economists' understanding of the general-equilibrium structure of the economy established a convention of viewing economic fluctuations as the outcome of "real" and "monetary" interactions. According to the monetarist view, which follows the Quantity Theory tradition, the real part of the system is stable, and hence the principal causes of fluctuations must be the monetary factors. Monetarists tended to believe that the monetary and credit systems had some inherent weaknesses giving rise to occasional collapses. More recently, Friedman and other modern monetarists have argued that monetary policy is the major cause of the misbehavior of money. The reasons for money's misbehavior are multiple. Some, notably Friedman, stress the lags in monetary policy. According to this view, the monetary authority may fiddle with the money supply with the intention of stabilizing the economy, but because of various lags (e.g., recognition lag, lags in policy implementation, lags in the working out of the monetary effects into the system), the actual effects of such a well-meant policy are more often destabilizing than stabilizing. Others take the view that the actual money-supply mechanism, which relies heavily on commercial bank credit creation, has a strong tendency to passively adapt to the demand rather than counteract it. Either of these alleged monetary characteristics can therefore generate instability even if the real forces are proceeding smoothly.

In contrast, the "realist" view holds that booms and depressions are caused primarily by irregular investment patterns reflecting random spurts of technological innovations and other major structural changes. Money might modify the path of the economy, but it would never be the instigating force of fluctuations. Keynes's stand in the *General Theory* was that of the realist.

One name that must be mentioned in this context is that of K. Wicksell (1851–1926). Although Wicksell is usually classified as a monetarist, he accomplished a (potential) synthesis between the monetarist and realist views by placing the relationship between the real or "natural" rate of interest and the money or market rate of interest at the center of his dynamic theory, which has become known as the Wicksellian cumulative process (1934, Volume II, pp. 190–208). Letting these rates be r_n and r_m, respectively, his dynamics (modified as a business-cycle theory) can be described as follows:

$r_n > r_m \rightarrow$ investment $\uparrow \rightarrow$ distortion in the time structure of production $\rightarrow$ liquidity drain $\rightarrow r_m > r_n \rightarrow$ investment undertaken at low r_m proves to be the source of losses $\rightarrow$ depression $\rightarrow r_m \downarrow$

The cause of the initial divergence between r_n and r_m can be real or monetary. However, throughout his analysis of the cumulative process, Wicksell maintained the real side fixed. As a result, his theory became exclusively a theory of price dynamics. It has been noted (e.g., by Hicks 1965, pp. 121–2) that there are certain common features or dual relationships between the Wicksellian cumulative process and the Harrodian growth process (which includes the Keynesian multiplier process). Wicksell took r_n to be stable and r_m to be the cause of disturbances. Keynes and Harrod took r_n (or the marginal efficiency of capital) to be the main source of disturbances rather than r_m. Keynes's idea of the behavior of the monetary authority of the banking system was that it regards the interest rate as the instrument and that r_m tends to adapt to r_n, but with a long lag. Wicksell fixed the real part and stressed the price dynamics. Keynes and Harrod, in contrast, fixed prices[6] and stressed the quantity dynamics. But, in general, we expect the two types of dynamics to interact with each other.

1.3   Macroeconomics and capital theory

As this brief sketch of its history shows, macroeconomics has proceeded rather cyclically. In a sense, macroeconomics is constantly reworking old issues and ideas. As Schumpeter put it (1954, p. 1127), "all the essential facts and ideas about business cycle analysis had emerged by 1914." But a satisfactory model for macroanalysis is yet to be built. In light of the important role played by durable goods in an advanced economy, the key to successful model building seems to be the specification of the laws of motion of two dynamic variables: capital and expectations. Recent general-equilibrium studies have rightly stressed the role of capital markets in macrodynamic analysis (e.g., Hahn 1960; Tobin 1965). These studies have focused on the asset-market general equilibrium, which may be expressed as

$$r_1 + (\dot{p}_1/p_1)^e = r_2 + (\dot{p}_2/p_2)^e = \dots$$

across assets. Here r_j is the contractual or technological rate of return on asset j; p_j is the price of asset j, and $\dot{p}_j$ is its rate of change. The superscript e denotes expectation, so that $(\dot{p}_j/p_j)^e$ represents in percentage terms expected capital gains from holding asset j for another "period." The preceding chain of equations represents a state of perfect arbitrage, a necessary condition for a competitive equilibrium. Suppose the asset-market equilibrium were disturbed by a rise in, say, $(\dot{p}_1/p_1)^e$. This would make asset 1 temporarily more attractive than, say, asset 2. The price of asset 1 would rise and the price of asset 2 would fall because of market forces. If expectations were "adaptive," they would tend to endorse the initial shift in expectations, and it would be quite possible that $(\dot{p}_1/p_1)^e$ would be maintained high because of speculative demands. Whether or not $(\dot{p}_1/p_1)^e$ would be raised further as a result of market forces would depend on the speed and the magnitude of the investor switch to asset 1. The more efficient the asset markets are (in the sense of fast dissemination of market information, availability of many close substitutes, low transaction costs), the easier are such switches. In this sense the asset-market equilibrium contains an inherent element of instability. What the analyses of Hahn and Tobin capture is precisely this kind of instability. Note that the possibility just described never applies to perishable goods.

The instability inherent in these models of capital and growth is disturbing, for the preceding equalities among the rates of return across assets are a fundamental efficiency condition that an efficient competitive market is expected to achieve, and yet this same efficiency condition is a potential cause of instability. The central theme of Keynes's *General Theory* (of which the IS-LM model is indeed a sad representation) was to highlight this fundamental role of asset markets in a macroeconomy. Later we shall pursue this theme in order to reformulate Keynes's theory and to improve our understanding of macroeconomic issues in general.

CHAPTER 2

Dynamic optimization

2.1 Static versus dynamic optimization

The purpose of this chapter is to give a simple and more or less intuitive account of the techniques of optimal-control theory and to illustrate their use in economics in terms of a simple model of economic growth. We shall begin with a brief review of the elements of the conventional static-optimization theory in the hope that its parallels with its dynamic counterpart, which we shall attempt to highlight, will facilitate an understanding of the latter. The terminology employed here is that of Intriligator (1971).

Let us first consider the following classical static programming problem:

$$\max_{x} F(x) \text{ subject to } g(x) = 0 \qquad [g(x) = g_1(x),...,g_m(x)] \qquad \text{(C)}$$

where F and g are real-valued continuously differentiable functions defined over some subset $X \in R^n$ $(n > m)$. According to the method of Lagrange, we set up the Lagrangian function

$$L(x,y) \equiv F(x) + y \cdot g(x) \qquad (2.1)$$

where $y \in R^m$ is the set of Lagrangian multipliers. We then look for a pair (x^*,y^*) at which the Lagrangian function is maximized. Suppose we found such a pair. Letting small (but arbitrary) variations around that point be $(\Delta x, \Delta y)$, and computing the corresponding variation in L, we obtain

$$\Delta L \equiv L(x^* + \Delta x, y^* + \Delta y) - L(x^*,y^*)$$

$$= \left(\frac{dF}{dx} + y^* \frac{dg}{dx}\right) \Delta x + g(x^*) \cdot \Delta y$$

$$= 0 \qquad [\text{by the definition of } (x^*,y^*)] \qquad (2.2)$$

In order for (2.2) to hold for arbitrary $(\Delta x, \Delta y)$, their coefficients must vanish identically; that is,

$$\frac{dF(x^*)}{dx} + y^* \frac{dg(x^*)}{dx} = 0 \qquad [g(x^*) = 0] \qquad (2.3)$$

10

In a dynamic-optimization problem, time adds another dimension. Suppose the time horizon is given by an interval $[t_0, t_1]$. At each point of time t in the interval, one has a decision problem to solve. The instruments in such decisions are called *control variables* or *controllers* and are denoted by $u(t)$ defined over some subset $\Omega(t) \in R^r$. Solving a dynamic-optimization problem means, therefore, to choose a *time path* for the controllers $u(t)$ over the interval $[t_0, t_1]$, denoted by $\{u(t)\}$, or $\{u\}$ for short, such that a given objective functional $J\{u\}$ attains a maximum. We shall take $J\{u\}$ to be of the form

$$J\{u\} = \int_{t_0}^{t_1} I(x,u,t)dt \tag{2.4}$$

where I is generally assumed to be real-valued and continuous in all its arguments. In economic terms, $I[x(t),u(t),t]dt$ measures some benefit accruing in an interval $[t, t + dt]$, such as profits, utility of consumption, and so forth. The specific form in which $I(\ )$ enters into (2.4) implies that the benefits are *additive*. This seems reasonable in the case of profits, but for other problems, and even in the case of the utility of consumption, it is by no means obvious why the objective functional should have this form.

The variable $x(t)$ in $I(\ )$, generally a vector in R^n and central in dynamic-optimization problems, is called the *state variable*. It embraces all the durable or capital goods in the system, namely, all the variables that have a lasting influence on the dynamic-choice problem in hand. But for x, there would be no need to even consider dynamic optimization. In economic problems, the value of x at t_0 is typically given.

$$x(t_0) = x_0 \quad \text{given} \tag{2.5}$$

The values of x at subsequent dates, given x_0, are to be determined by the choice of the controllers. This relationship is usually expressed as

$$\dot{x} = f(x,u,t) \tag{2.6}$$

where f is again a vector of real-valued continuous functions of its arguments.

Let us now consider the following (classical) dynamic-optimization problem:

$$\max_{\{u\}} J\{u\} = \int_{t_0}^{t_1} I(x,u,t)dt \tag{D}$$

subject to

$$\dot{x} = f(x,u,t)$$
$$x(t_0) = x_0, \quad x(t_1) = x_1 \quad \text{given}$$

and $u \in \Omega$, where Ω is the set of admissible values of the controllers. By analogy to the static problem, define the Lagrangian

$$L(\{u\},\{f\}) \equiv J\{u\} + \int_{t_0}^{t_1} y[f(x,u,t) - \dot{x}]dt$$

$$= \int_{t_0}^{t_1} \{I(x,u,t) + y[f(x,u,t) - \dot{x}]\}dt \qquad (2.7)$$

where $\{y\}$ is the time profile of an n-dimensional Lagrangian multiplier or co-state variable. As before, we look for a pair $[\{u^*(t)\},\{y^*(t)\}] = (\{u^*\},\{y^*\})$ at which the Lagrangian is maximized. Let small but arbitrary deviations from $(\{u^*\},\{y^*\})$, supposing this exists, be $[\{\Delta u(t)\},\{\Delta y(t)\}] = (\{\Delta u\},\{\Delta y\})$, and consider the resulting variation in L. Considering first only $\{\Delta y\}$, we find

$$\Delta L_y = \int_{t_0}^{t_1} \Delta y[f(x^*,u^*,t) - \dot{x}^*]dt = 0 \qquad (2.8)$$

For (2.8) to hold for any arbitrary $\{\Delta y\}$, we must have

$$\dot{x}^* = f(x^*,u^*,t) \qquad (2.9)$$

for all t in $[t_0,t_1]$. Next consider $\{\Delta u\}$, holding $\{\Delta y\} = \{0\}$. To work this out, we write the last term of (2.7) as follows:

$$\int_{t_0}^{t_1} y\dot{x}dt = (yx)\Big|_{t_0}^{t_1} - \int_{t_0}^{t_1} \dot{y}xdt$$

$$= y(t_1)x(t_1) - y(t_0)x(t_0) - \int_{t_0}^{t_1} \dot{y}xdt$$

Substituting this into (2.7), we obtain

$$L(\{u\},\{y\}) = \int_{t_0}^{t_1} \{[I(x,u,t) + yf(x,u,t)] + \dot{y}x\}dt$$
$$- y(t_1)x(t_1) + y(t_0)x(t_0) \qquad (2.7')$$

The terms in square brackets constitute the *Hamiltonian function*, which we write as $H(x,y,u,t) \equiv I(x,u,t) + yf(x,u,t)$.

Let us now compute the variation in L due to a small variation in $\{u\}$, which (assuming H is continuously differentiable) becomes

$$\Delta L_u = \int_{t_0}^{t_1} \{H_u^*\Delta u + (H_x^* + \dot{y}^*)\Delta x\}dt - y(t_1) \cdot \Delta x(t_1) + y(t_0) \cdot \Delta x(t_0) \qquad (2.10)$$

where $\{\Delta x\}$ is the variation in the profile of the state variables caused by the variation $\{\Delta u\}$ in the controllers and $H^* = H(x^*,y^*,u^*,t)$. Noting from the end-point conditions in (D) that $\Delta x(t_1) = \Delta x(t_0) = 0$, ΔL_u reduces to the integral part, and by the same reasoning as before, we get

$$H_u^* = 0, \qquad H_x^* + \dot{y}^* = 0 \tag{2.11}$$

where, of course, $H_u^* = \partial H(x^*,y^*,u^*,t)/\partial u$ and $H_x^* = \partial H(x^*,y^*,u^*,t)/\partial x$.

To summarize: The first-order conditions for the classical dynamic-optimization problem (D) are

$$H_u^* = 0 \tag{a}$$

$$\dot{x}^* = f(x^*,u^*,t) = H_y^* \tag{b}$$

$$\dot{y}^* = -H_x^* \tag{c}$$

2.2   On the existence of a solution to (D)

Applicable to the existence problem in static cases, there is the fundamental existence theorem of Weierstrass, which states that a real-valued continuous function $F(x)$ defined over a compact subset Ω of R^n attains a global maximum (and a global minimum, for that matter) at some $x^* \in \Omega$. This result follows from the fact that if F is continuous and Ω is compact, then the image set [i.e., the set of real numbers $\{F(x): x \in \Omega\}$] is also a compact set in R^1. The image set is therefore a closed and bounded interval on the real line that clearly possesses a global maximum and a global minimum.

The same idea can be applied to the dynamic case under consideration. In the dynamic case, the control trajectory $\{u(t)\}$, $t \in [t_0, t_1]$, takes the place of x, and $J\{u\}$ takes the place of $F(x)$. But we have already assumed the functional $J\{u\}$ to be continuous in $\{u\}$, which corresponds to the continuity of $F(x)$. Thus, if the set of admissible functions $\{u(t)\}$ is compact, the existence of a solution is assured. Indeed, the following straightforward generalization of the preceding fundamental theorem is possible.

The generalized Weierstrass existence theorem

If the set M of functions u defined on $[t_0, t_1]$ is compact in itself, and if $J\{u\}$ is a continuous functional, then $J\{u\}$ attains a global maximum and a global minimum on M.

But what does it mean to say that a set of functions is compact? And . how does one find an appropriate set of functions that is compact?

Generally speaking, a set M lying in an abstract space X is said to be compact in itself if every infinite subset of this set contains a convergent sequence and if these limits belong to M. Because the compactness of a set means the self-containedness of the set with respect to limiting processes, the broader the set of functions one chooses, the better the chance that the set will be compact. In optimal-control problems, the set of control functions is defined on the interval $[t_0, t_1]$, with its value at t lying in a compact and usually convex set $\Omega(t) \in R^r$. This "tube," with length $t_1 - t_0$ and cross section $\Omega(t)$, is referred to as the control set U. Of all the vector-valued functions contained in U, the largest set relevant to our problem is the set of Lebesgue integrable functions (i.e., the set of functions u for which $J\{u\}$ exists). In optimal-control problems, admissible controllers are usually taken to be the set of piecewise continuous functions (i.e., functions that are continuous everywhere except possibly at a finite number of points in $[t_0, t_1]$ and that take finite jumps at these points of discontinuity). Graphically, an admissible controller looks like a string in the tube U with possibly a finite number of breaks. As a simple exercise with linear models will show, the set of continuous u is too narrow and often fails to possess a solution to an optimal-control problem. But even the set of piecewise-continuous functions is not large enough to guarantee its compactness without some additional conditions. The nature of the problem is illustrated by the following examples.

Example 1: Minimize $J\{u\} = \int_0^1 (x^2 + u^2)dt$, $\Omega(t) = [-1,1]$, $\dot{x} = u$, $x(0) = x(1) = 0$. This problem has a solution $u^* = 0$ for all t with $J\{u^*\} = 0$. But consider Example 2.

Example 2: Minimize $J\{u\} = \int_0^1 [x^2 + (1 \times u^2)^2]dt$, $\Omega(t) = [-1,1]$, $\dot{x} = u$, $x(0) = x(1) = 0$. This problem has no solution in the set of piecewise-continuous controllers. The reason is as follows: The function $(1 - u^2)^2$ is a bell-shaped function with minima in Ω occurring at the boundaries $u = \pm 1$. It therefore pays to choose these boundary values as far as the second term in the integrand is concerned. But the end-point condition on x requires that u alternate between $+1$ and -1, for otherwise $x(1) \neq 0$. Consider a feasible program in which the interval $[0,1]$ is split into $2r$ equal portions and in which u takes on the values $+1, -1, +1, -1,...$ in these intervals. The value of the program corresponding to this control is given by $J\{u^r\} = 1/12r^2$. Consider a sequence of programs $\{u^1, u^2,...,u^r,...\}$. As r increases (i.e., as the number of switches of the controllers increases), the value of the program declines, and in the limit it approaches zero, which is clearly the minimum of all feasible programs. But such an infinitely switching controller is not piecewise-continuous. That is, although there is a sequence of piecewise-continuous controllers tending toward the minimum of zero, its limit does not belong to the set of piecewise-continuous functions. [This example is taken from Fleming and Rishel (1975, p. 61).]

The difference between the two cases is that the $I(x,u,t)$ function is convex in u in example 1 but not so in example 2. Such a convexity implies that the I-minimizing u occurs at a fixed point (which generally depends on the state variable x), which yields a continuous optimal controller $u(t)$ as against an infinitely fluctuating one. A similar difficulty may arise when the I function is not convex in the state variable x. In such a case it may be desirable for x to oscillate rather than to stay put. But because x is an integral of u, this means that u must also oscillate. In the preceding examples, the function $f(x,u,t)$ was simply equal to u (i.e., linear in u). When it is nonlinear and more complex, similar convexity conditions on f are generally required to ensure the existence of a solution. Needless to say, in a maximization problem, the word "convexity" in the preceding discussion should be replaced by "concavity." In applied control problems these conditions are usually met by assumption.

One other small problem arising out of the compactness of $\Omega(t)$ is the possibility of "corner solutions." The condition (a) that appeared earlier should read more generally:

$$\max_{u \in \Omega(t)} H(x,y,u,t) \quad \text{for all } t, \quad t \in [t_0, t_1] \text{ and at given } (x,y) \qquad (a')$$

the result known as the Maximum Principle.

2.3   Sufficient conditions

In (C) we know that the pair (x^*,y^*) satisfying (2.3) is a local maximum if the Hessian matrix of second-order partial derivatives of the Lagrangian $|\partial^2 L/\partial x^2|_{x=x^*}$ is negative definite subject to $[dg(x^*)/dx]\Delta x = 0$. Sufficient conditions for a local maximum to be a global maximum are given by a theorem known as the local-global theorem, which states that if the opportunity set Ω is a nonempty compact convex set and if the objective function $F(x)$ is a concave function over Ω, then a local maximum is a global maximum. In a general nonlinear programming problem,

$$\max F(x) \text{ subject to } g(x) \geqq 0$$

the set of constraints $g(x) \geqq 0$ forms a convex set if $g(x) = [g_1(x),...,g_m(x)]$ are all concave functions. If, in addition, $F(x)$ is concave over such a convex set, then a local maximum is also a global maximum.

In dynamic-optimization problems things go in parallel. In the classical calculus of variations the second-order conditions were derived by taking the second variation of L in (2.7) with respect to $\{u\}$, which produces

$$\Delta^2 L_u = \int_{t_0}^{t_1} (\Delta u, \Delta x) \begin{bmatrix} H_{uu}{}^* & H_{ux}{}^* \\ H_{xu}{}^* & H_{xx}{}^* \end{bmatrix} \begin{bmatrix} \Delta u \\ \Delta x \end{bmatrix} dt$$

This leads to the Legendre-Clebsch conditions for a local maximum. In order to go from a local maximum to a global maximum, one needs a dynamic counterpart of the static local-global theorem. The classical theory proceeds to establish sufficient conditions under which no "conjugate points" exist. In the modern control-theory context, they are given by the following theorem.

Theorem (Mangasarian 1966, p. 141): Let $I(x,u,t)$ and each component of $f(x,u,t)$ be differentiable and concave in x and u for $t \in [t_0,t_1]$. If there exist vectors $u^*(t)$, $x^*(t)$, and $y^*(t)$ satisfying

$$\dot{x} = f(x,u,t) \tag{i}$$

$$u(t) \in \Omega(t) \tag{ii}$$

$$x(t_0) = x_0 \text{ given} \tag{iii}$$

$$x(t_1) = x_1 \text{ given} \tag{iv}$$

with $x^*(t), y^*(t)$ continuous and such that (a'), (b), (c), and

$$y^*(t) \geqq 0 \tag{v}$$

hold, then $u^*(t), x^*(t)$ will maximize the functional (2.4) globally subject to the conditions (i) through (iv). Condition (v) need hold only for those components of $f(x,u,t)$ that are nonlinear in x or u or both.

Proof: Let $J\{u^*\}$ be the value of the objective functional corresponding to the controller $\{u^*\}$, and let $J\{u\}$ be the similar value associated with any feasible controller $\{u\}$. Then

$$J\{u^*\} - J\{u\} = \int_{t_0}^{t_1} \{I(x^*,u^*,t) - I(x,u,t)\} dt$$

$$= \int_{t_0}^{t_1} \{I(x^*,u^*,t) - I(x,u,t)$$

$$+ y^*[f(x^*,u^*,t) - f(x,u,t) - \dot{x}^* + \dot{x}]\} dt$$

by condition (b)

$$\geqq \int_{t_0}^{t_1} \{H_x^* (x^* - x) + H_u^* (u^* - u) - y^*(\dot{x}^* - \dot{x})\} dt$$
by the concavity of H

$$\geqq \int_{t_0}^{t_1} \{H_x^* (x^* - x) - y^*(\dot{x}^* - \dot{x})\} dt \quad \text{by condition (a$'$)}$$

$$= \int_{t_0}^{t_1} \{H_x^* (x^* - x) + \dot{y}^* (x^* - x)\} dt$$
$$+ y^*(t_1)[x(t_1) - x^*(t_1)] - y^*(t_0)[x(t_0) - x^*(t_0)]$$

$$= \int_{t_0}^{t_1} (H_x^* + \dot{y}^*)(x^* - x) dt = 0 \quad \text{by condition (c)}$$

Note that the comparison path $\{u\}$ can be any feasible path and need not be close to $\{u^*\}$; that is, $\{u^*,x^*,y^*\}$ yields a global maximum.

2.4   Transversality conditions

According to the procedure described earlier, we first choose $\{u^*(t)\}$ so as to maximize the Hamiltonian function for given (x,y) at each t [see condition (a) or (a$'$)]. In this process, u is "maximized out," so that $H(x,y,u^*,t) = M(x,y,t)$; that is, the maximized Hamiltonian is a function only of x, y, and t. Using this M function, we derive a pair of differential equations as given by conditions (b) and (c). If the dimension of x is n, (b) and (c) provide a system of differential equations of size $2n$. To determine a unique solution to these equations, we therefore need $2n$ boundary conditions. Of these, n are given naturally by $x(t_0) = x_0$. What about the remaining n conditions? In the preceding problem we supplied these remaining conditions by specifying the terminal values of x at t_1. With $[t_1,x(t_1)]$ so specified, the problem is called a *fixed-end-point problem*. But there is no reason that $[t_1,x(t_1)]$ should always be fixed. More generally, we may assume that $[t_1,x(t_1)]$ should lie on some prescribed manifold $T[t_1,x(t_1)] = 0$. If $n = 1$, this will be a curve in the (t_1,x_1) space, and our optimal program must land on it. But exactly where on the curve?

This problem can best be handled if we start with a fixed-end-point problem. Suppose we solve the problem for an arbitrarily prescribed pair $[t_1,x(t_1)] = (\bar{t}_1,\bar{x}_1)$. Then the maximal "benefits" (i.e., the maximal value of the functional J) can be thought of as a function of $(\bar{t}_1,\bar{x}_1)$. We write it as $J^*(\bar{t}_1,\bar{x}_1)$. It is obvious that the problem of finding the optimal landing spot on the manifold is equivalent to solving the following problem:

$$\max J^*(\bar{t}_1,\bar{x}_1) \text{ subject to } T(\bar{t}_1,\bar{x}_1) = 0 \tag{2.12}$$

which is formally a separate static-optimization problem. If both J^* and T functions are differentiable, we would expect the first-order conditions to be the familiar equality between the two "marginal rates of substitution," or the tangency between the two curves. It is of some interest to know what $J_{\bar{t}_1}^*$ and $J_{\bar{x}_1}^*$ are. It can be easily shown that

$$J_{\bar{t}_1}^* = M[x^*(\bar{t}_1), y^*(\bar{t}_1), \bar{t}_1] \tag{2.13}$$

the value of the Hamiltonian function at $\bar{t}_1$, and

$$J_{\bar{x}_1}^* = -y^*(\bar{t}_1), \quad \text{that is,} \frac{\partial J^*}{\partial \bar{x}_{1j}} = -y_j^*(\bar{t}_1) \quad (j = 1,2,...,n) \tag{2.14}$$

Problem (2.12), of course, implies that $J_{\bar{t}_1}^*$ and $J_{\bar{x}_1}^*$ are to be set proportional to $T_{\bar{t}_1}$ and $T_{\bar{x}_1}$, respectively, for an optimum.

A special case that appears frequently in both theory and application is the case in which t_1 is given but $x(t_1)$ is completely unspecified. This problem is called a *free-end-point problem*. In this case $T(\bar{t}_1, \bar{x}_1) = 0$ reduces to $t_1 - \bar{t}_1 = 0$, and the preceding proportionality conditions become simply

$$y^*(t_1) = 0 \tag{2.14'}$$

or, if the constraints are of inequality type such that $x(t_1) - \bar{x}_1 \geqq 0$,

$$y^*(t_1)[x(t_1) - \bar{x}_1] = 0, \quad y^*(t_1) \geqq 0, \quad x(t_1) - \bar{x}_1 \geqq 0 \tag{2.14''}$$

The word "transversality" suggests that something cuts something else at a right angle. The terminal condition is so called because the preceding tangency condition can be stated alternatively in the form that the normal or the gradient of the curve $J^*(\bar{t}_1, \bar{x}_1)$ intersects $T(\bar{t}_1, \bar{x}_1)$ at a right angle at the point of optimal landing. As may be seen, the existence of a unique solution to a variable-end-point problem requires that the second-order conditions for the additional static problem (2.12) be satisfied.

2.5   A simple growth model

For the purpose of illustration, let us consider the following simple model of optimal economic growth. We write $t_0 = 0$, $t_1 = T$,

$$\max_{[c]} J\{c\} = \int_0^T e^{-\delta t} u(c) dt \quad (\delta \geqq 0) \tag{G}$$

subject to

$$\dot{k} = f(k) - nk - c \quad (n > 0)$$

$$c \in [0, f(k)]$$

$$k(0) = k_0 > 0, \quad k(T) = k_1 \geqq 0 \quad \text{given}$$

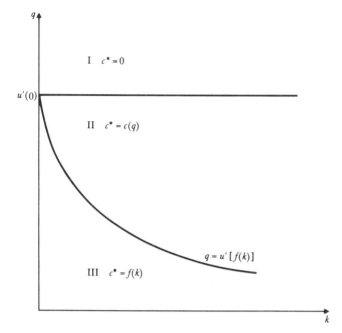

Figure 2.1. Optimal consumption as a function of (k,q).

The utility function $u(c)$ and the production function $f(k)$ are both assumed to be increasing, concave, and twice continuously differentiable in their arguments. In addition, we assume $f(0) = 0, f'(0) > n$, and $f(\bar{k}) - n\bar{k} = 0$ at some positive but finite $\bar{k}$. Needless to say, k is the state variable and c is the controller.

Recalling our previous discussion, we first set up the Hamiltonian function

$$H(k,\lambda,c,t) \equiv e^{-\delta t}u(c) + \lambda[f(k) - nk - c] \tag{2.15}$$

and maximize this with respect to c for given $k(t),\lambda(t)$ at each t; that is,

$$\max_{0 \leq c \leq f(k)} H(k,\lambda,c,t) \text{ or } \max_{0 \leq c \leq f(k)} [e^{-\delta t}u(c) - \lambda c] \tag{2.16}$$

from which we obtain

$$c^* = \begin{cases} 0 & \text{if } u'(0) \leq q \\ c(q) & \text{if } u'[f(k)] < q < u'(0) \\ f(k) & \text{if } u'[f(k)] \geq q \end{cases} \quad (q \equiv \lambda e^{\delta t}) \tag{2.17}$$

where $c(q)$ is the solution of $u'(c) = \lambda e^{\delta t} = q$. Because $u''(0) < 0, c'(q) < 0$.

Graphically, the optimal c^* takes three different forms in the (k,q) space, as shown in Figure 2.1.

In economic terms, $q(t)$ measures the imputed or shadow price (in utility terms and undiscounted) of the capital stock $k(t)$. At any point of time $t \in [0,T]$, the current output $f(k)$ can either be invested or be consumed at a one-to-one ratio. The shadow price of an additional unit of consumption is $u'(c)$, and the shadow price of an additional unit of capital is q. Hence the three phases. Phase I will disappear if $u'(0) = +\infty$, whereas phase III will be nonexistent if capital stock can be consumed.

Having obtained the optimal controller c^*, we can obtain the dynamic motion of the state variable k and the co-state variable q from the formula

$$\dot{k} = \frac{\partial M}{\partial \lambda}, \quad \dot{\lambda} = -\frac{\partial M}{\partial k} \quad \text{where } M(k,\lambda,t) \equiv H(k,\lambda,c^*,t) \tag{2.18}$$

Written out in full, they are

$$\text{I} \begin{cases} \dot{k} = f(k) - nk \\ \dot{q} = [n + \delta - f'(k)]q \end{cases}$$

$$\text{II} \begin{cases} \dot{k} = f(k) - nk - c(q) \\ \dot{q} = [n + \delta - f'(k)]q \end{cases}$$

$$\text{III} \begin{cases} \dot{k} = -nk \\ \dot{q} = (n + \delta)q - u'[f(k)] \cdot f'(k) \end{cases}$$

The phase diagram in Figure 2.2 describes the family of (infinitely many) optimal notions. Once k_0, k_1, and T are given, we can pick a portion of one of these curves as the solution of our problem (G). One must study the construction of the diagram closely. A few remarks are in order. First, the existence of a solution is assured. If the program begins with a finite positive k_0, k will never increase without limit, for it is too costly to do so (recall our assumption about $\bar{k}$). With k staying finite, the control region $[0,f(k)]$ is compact. The functions u and f are, of course, continuous. Hence $J\{c\}$ is a continuous functional. Second, with u and f concave and with $q \geqq 0$, the sufficient conditions are clearly met. Furthermore, the strict concavity of these functions means that the solution is unique. The proof of the sufficiency and the uniqueness is really unnecessary, but it is given in (2.19) because of its other uses. In (2.19), $\{c\}$ is again any feasible program.

$$J\{c^*\} - J\{c\} = \int_0^T e^{-\delta t}[u(c^*) - u(c)]dt$$

$$= \int_0^T e^{-\delta t}[u(c^*) - u(c) + q^*[f(k^*) - nk^* + c^* - \dot{k}^*$$

$$- f(k) + nk\,c + \dot{k}]\}dt$$

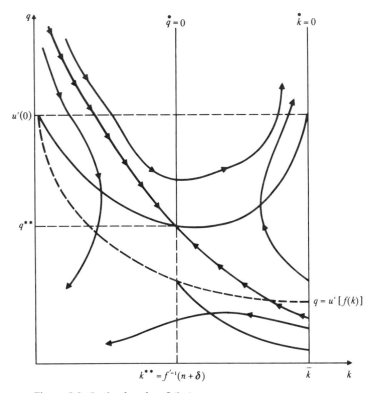

Figure 2.2. Optimal paths of (k,q).

$$\geq \int_0^T e^{-\delta t} q^*\{[f'(k^*) - n](k^* - k) - (\dot{k}^* - \dot{k})dt\}$$

$$= \int_0^T e^{-\delta t}[(\delta q^* - \dot{q})(k^* - k) - q^*(\dot{k}^* - \dot{k})]dt$$

$$= q^*(0)[k^*(0) - k(0)] - e^{-\delta T}q^*(T)[k^*(T) - k(T)] = 0$$

$$(2.19)$$

In (2.19), the inequality is strict if $k \neq k^*$ at some $t \in (0,T)$. This equation (2.19) shows some other things. Suppose we have the same optimal-growth problem as previously, except for the fact that the initial capital stock is slightly larger. All other parameters (i.e., δ, T, k_1) remain unchanged. Now let the preceding $\{c\}$ be the optimal-control trajectory for the new problem. Then, reading the inequality as an approximate equality, we get

$$J\{c\} - J\{c^*\} = q^*(0)[k(0) - k^*(0)] = q^*(0)[k_0 + \Delta k_0 - k_0]$$
$$= q^*(0)\Delta k_0 \qquad (2.20)$$

Dividing both sides by Δk_0 and letting $\Delta k_0 \to 0$, we have

$$\frac{\partial J\{c^*\}}{\partial k_0} = q^*(0) \tag{2.21}$$

Namely, the marginal contribution of the initial capital to the maximized benefits is $q^*(0) = \lambda^*(0)$. It is in this sense that q is called the shadow price of capital. Similarly, the effect of a small increase in the terminal capital requirement k_1 is given by

$$\frac{\partial J\{c^*\}}{\partial k_1} = -e^{-\delta T}q^*(T) = -\lambda^*(T) \tag{2.22}$$

In the absence of any evaluation of the terminal stock, an increase in it means some welfare loss.

Third, and finally, when T goes to infinity, it seems logical to conclude that the optimal path is the curve with multiple arrowheads. Why? Because, for any given k_0 and k_1, as T is increased, the optimal path bulges more and more toward the point E or the point (k^{**}, q^{**}). More specifically, we interpret the $\{c^*\}$ in (2.19) as the path that converges to (k^{**}, q^{**}) over an infinite horizon and the $\{c\}$ in (2.19) as any other feasible path. Then $q^*(T) \to q^{**}$ and $k^*(T) \to k^{**}$, and clearly $\lim_{T \to \infty} e^{-\delta T}q^*(T)k^*(T) = 0$. Thus

$$J\{c^*\} - J\{c\} \geq \lim_{T \to \infty} e^{-\delta T}q^*(T)k(T) \geq 0$$

for any other feasible path. Indeed, the right-hand inequality can be ruled out because the domain of k is bounded. For this reason, the transversality condition for the infinite-horizon problem is customarily written as

$$\lim_{T \to \infty} e^{-\delta T}q^*(T)k^*(T) = 0 \tag{2.23}$$

A better way (in anticipation of the case in which $\delta = 0$) might be

$$\lim_{T \to \infty} e^{-\delta T}[q^*(T) - q^{**}][k^*(T) - k^{**}] = 0 \tag{2.23'}$$

2.6   Problems with infinite horizons

When T goes to infinity, the control set U ceases to be compact, and an optimal solution may not exist. Broadly speaking, there are two types or cases of nonexistence. One is the nonexistence "at zero," and the other is the nonexistence "at infinity," as it were. Let us begin with the first and simple case of nonexistence at zero. Suppose we have one apple to eat over our infinite time horizon, and suppose our benefits are additive without discounting; $J\{c\} = \int_0^\infty u(c)dt$, $k_0 = 1$, $\dot{k} = -c$, where $u(c)$ is assumed to be increasing, concave, and time-invariant. Because there is no discounting, the optimal-marginal-allocation rule is to consume a constant amount. We call this constant amount $\bar{c}$. Then $\bar{c} = 1/T$, and hence as $T \to \infty$, $\bar{c} \to 0$. It looks as if $\{c*\} = \{0\}$. But clearly we can do better than that by eating the whole apple on the first "day," for $u(1) > u(0)$. But by the nature of $J\{c\}$, a better way of consuming the apple is to eat half on the first day and the remaining half on the second, because by the concavity of the u function, $u(1) + u(0) \leq u(\frac{1}{2}) + u(\frac{1}{2})$. An even better way is to consume $\frac{1}{4}$ per day for four days. A still better way is to consume $\frac{1}{8}$ per day over eight days, and so forth, whose limit is again zero consumption for all t.

The more interesting and more important case is the nonexistence at infinity. This case is so called because $J\{u*\}$ explodes to infinity. If $J\{u*\}$ explodes for some feasible $\{u*\}$, there generally are many neighboring paths of $\{u\}$ for which $J\{u\} = +\infty$ also. If so, no comparison will be possible.

Three solutions have been offered to handle this problem. The first solution was the trick employed by Frank Ramsey in a celebrated article (1928). Ramsey's trick was to postulate a utility function $u(c)$ such that it is concave and such that $u(c) \leq 0$ for all $c \geq 0$ and $u(c**) = 0$ at some unique positive $c**$, called the "bliss point" (Figure 2.3). In this way, $J\{c*\}$ was guaranteed to converge. The second solution was to employ an "overtaking criterion." According to this criterion, an infinite program $\{u^1\}$ is said to overtake another infinite program $\{u^0\}$ if there exists a finite $T > 0$ such that $J^t\{u^1\} \geq J^t\{u^0\}$ for all $t \geq T$. Here $J^t\{u\}$ is the cumulative benefit from time zero to time t. Using this method, Koopmans (1965) arrived at the following generalization of the Golden Rule theorem. As Phelps had shown, the maximal sustainable per-capita consumption is attained at the level of k at which $f'(k) = n$. We denote this value by k_{GR}. Consider the following infinite-horizon problem:

$$\max J\{c\} = \int_0^\infty u(c)dt \tag{K}$$

subject to

$$\dot{k} = f(k) - nk - c$$
$$c \in [0, f(k)]$$
$$k(0) = k_0 > 0 \quad \text{given}$$

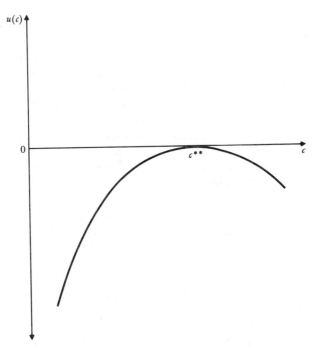

Figure 2.3. The bliss point in consumption.

Here $u(c)$ is any increasing concave utility function free from Ramsey-type restrictions. For concreteness, we assume $k_0 < k_{GR}$. Koopmans first showed that any path of k that failed to reach k_{GR} was not optimal. Consider a path that starts at k_0, rises monotonically to k_1 ($k_0 < k_1 < k_{GR}$) at time t_1, and then stays at k_1 forever. We call this program 1. Let program 2 be a path that is identical with program 1 up to $t = t_1$ but that continues to rise to k_2 ($k_1 < k_2 < k_{GR}$) by $t = t_2$ and then becomes stationary. In comparing these two programs we see that program 2 yields less utility than program 1 between t_1 and t_2 because of its heavier investment requirement. But because t_2 is finite, so is the difference in utilities. The sustainable utility level at $k = k_2$ [$u(\bar{c}_2) = f(k_2) - nk_2$], on the other hand, is definitely greater than the corresponding utility at $k = k_1$, which is $u(\bar{c}_1) = f(k_1) - nk_1$. Thus the utility loss incurred by program 2 between t_1 and t_2 will be offset by its steady-state utility in excess of that under program 1 within some finite interval, say $t_3 - t_2$. It is then plain that the cumulative utility under program 2 is greater than that under program 1 for all $t > t_3$. In other words, program 2 overtakes program 1. Program 2 will, in

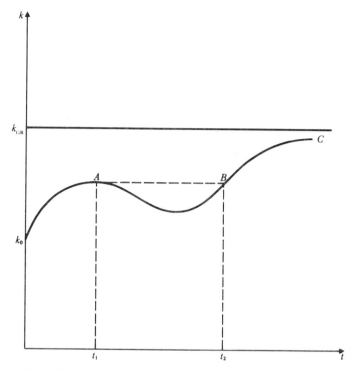

Figure 2.4. Nonoptimality of fluctuating path.

turn, be overtaken by program 3, which reaches a steady level k_3 ($k_2 <$ $k_3 < k_{GR}$), and so forth.

Next, Koopmans showed that an optimal path cannot have a "bulge" (Figure 2.4). Consider a feasible path as shown in this figure. Along this path,

$$k(t_2) - k(t_1) = \int_{t_1}^{t_2} \dot{k}\,dt = \int_{t_1}^{t_2} [f(k) - nk - c]\,dt = 0$$

so that

$$\int_{t_1}^{t_2} c\,dt \doteq \int_{t_1}^{t_2} [f(k) - nk]\,dt$$

But the preceding equation is true for another feasible path $k_0 ABC$ that maintains a constant capital stock between t_1 and t_2. In other words, the total consumption between t_1 and t_2 is the same for the two paths. Then, by the concavity of $u(c)$, the latter path yields a higher cumulative utility between t_1 and t_2 than the former. Namely, the latter path overtakes the former path by $t = t_2$. Combining these results, we conclude that an optimal path must raise k monotonically toward k_{GR} over time. The final question: At what speed does this occur? To determine this, Koopmans rewrote the problem as follows:

$$\max \int_0^\infty u(c)dt \Leftrightarrow \min \int_0^\infty [u(c_{GR}) - u(c)]dt$$

$$\Leftrightarrow \min \int_{k_0}^{k_{GR}} \frac{u(c_{GR}) - u(c)}{dk/dt} \, dk$$

$$= \min \int_{k_0}^{k_{GR}} \frac{u(c_{GR}) - u(c)}{f(k) - nk - c} \, dk$$

because $\dot{k} > 0$ along an optimal path, this change of variable is acceptable. Differentiating the integrand with respect to c, we get

$$u(c_{GR}) = u(c^*) + u'(c^*) \cdot \dot{k}^* \tag{2.24}$$

along an optimal path. Needless to say, $c_{GR} \equiv f(k_{GR}) - nk_{GR}$. Graphically, the optimal-consumption rule at any k_t is shown in Figure 2.5.

The third solution is to introduce a positive discount rate, or time preference. But the idea of discounting the future was immoral by Benthamite standards. Irving Fisher (1907; 1930) called it impatience and made it one of the fundamental causes of interest rates. But when it came to justifying its existence, he had to rely on human frailty due to poverty, lack of education, and so forth, all of which were signs of imperfections so alien to the stylized neoclassical theory. More recently, however, Koopmans (1960) proved that if the intertemporal utility function $u(c^1, c^2, \ldots, c^t, \ldots)$ satisfies the conditions of stationarity (preferences unaffected by passage of time), independence (the absence of intertemporal complementarity), and boundedness (the value of u bounded, i.e., the existence of an optimum), then the existence of impatience is logically implied. In this sense, "conditions hardly stronger than those that appear needed to define impatience in a meaningful way are sufficient to prove that there are zones of impatience" (Koopmans 1960, p. 288). This is a fairly forceful, if not pleasing, argument. We note also that the preceding apple problem can be solved with a positive discounting.

2.7   Problems of intertemporal planning

The problem of optimal growth can be thought of as a straightforward extension of the familiar static problem in welfare economics. Just as there are the market approach and the planning approach in

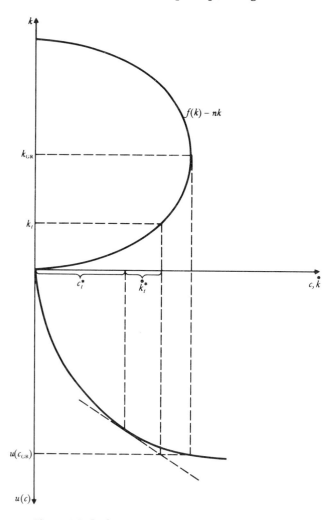

Figure 2.5. Optimal rate of capital accumulation.

statics, so are there the same two approaches in dynamics. But there is an important difference. The concept of dynamic optimality or efficiency is a much more inclusive concept than that of static optimality or efficiency. The latter is just a part of the former.

To illustrate the difference, we take the following simple production problem. We start at $t = 0$ with some given initial stocks $[k_1(0), k_2(0)]$. These stocks reproduce themselves through some technological relations with a one-period lag. Our goal is to attain largest

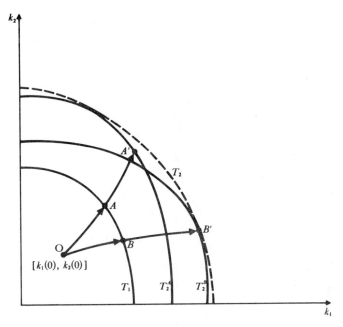

Figure 2.6. Static efficiency and dynamic efficiency.

stocks at the end of period T (Figure 2.6). Starting at $[k_1(0),k_2(0)]$ in period zero, the economy can reach the period-one transformation curve T_1, provided static-efficiency conditions are met. If the economy lands on T_1 at A, it can land on T_2^A in period two, which is all that static efficiency requires. If the economy lands on T_1 at B, it can proceed to a point on T_2^B. In other words, the sequences OAA' and OBB' satisfy the static-efficiency conditions. But the true transformation curve for period two is the outer envelope of infinitely many $T_2^A,T_2^B,T_2^C,...$ denoted by T_2. The two-period dynamic efficiency requires that the economy be on T_2. The figure shows that whereas the sequence OBB' is dynamically efficient, the sequence OAA' is not.

It is thus plain that the accomplishment of optimal growth, whether we rely on planning or on market mechanism, is a very difficult task. And the greatest source of difficulty is information about the future. For concreteness, suppose we have the infinite-horizon optimization problem defined earlier by problem (G). We know that the path shown by the curve with multiple arrowheads is the optimal one. All other paths eventually lead $q(t)$ to either plus infinity or minus infinity, with consumption converging toward zero. In either case the eventual consequence is ridiculous. But why do the sophisticated techniques of optimal-control theory not provide us with a warning system? The answer is that the differential equations describing optimal motions are only "marginal" conditions prescribing the directions of motion to be taken over a very short time slice; they lack the capacity to allow us to assess, from a global standpoint, where we stand. Consider, in particular, the differential equation for q:

$$\dot{q} = q[n + \delta - f'(k)] \quad \text{or} \quad \dot{q}/q = n + \delta - f'(k)$$
$$\text{or} \quad \dot{q}/q + f'(k) = n + \delta \tag{2.25}$$

In the last equation, the term $n + \delta$ represents the (social) interest or carrying cost of k–this is the rate at which capital depreciates. The term $f'(k)$ is, of course, the marginal productivity rate of return on capital, and, finally, the term $\dot{q}/q$ represents the instantaneous capital gain on k. Therefore equation (2.25) states that along an optimal path the net return on capital (i.e., the rate of return over cost) is zero. There is an inherent element of myopia in this pricing rule. At any point in time, $n + \delta$ and $f'(k)$ are given, and so an optimal rate of price change $\dot{q}/q$ is uniquely determined. But this rule does not tell us what the level of q should be. Indeed, a high q requires a large $\dot{q}$, whereas a low level of q calls for a small $\dot{q}$. The ability to follow the optimal trajectory requires constant review of the level of q in relation to k and an enormous amount of foresight. Suppose a planner wants to follow the optimal path (described by the curve with multiple arrowheads in Figure 2.2) but makes a slight mistake at the beginning. Sooner or later the path he has chosen will lead him into either phase I or phase III. In both of these phases the relative price of investment goods to consumption goods, $p \equiv q/u'(c)$, deviates from a value of unity. In phase I, $p > 1$, whereas in phase III, $p < 1$. But because the marginal rate of transformation between the two goods is always unity, the fact that $p \neq 1$ should make him realize that an error has been made and that he should take corrective measures. Of course, ideally the error should have been detected sooner. But the cost of constant vigilance can be very high.

The market interpretation of equation (2.25) would be to view it as the capital-market equilibrium condition. As such, it has two features. First, it incorporates myopic expectations (the expected rate of price change is always equal to the current actual rate). Second, it represents only the market-clearing condition for the current spot tradings. This latter point is particularly important, for it points to the role of futures markets. Indeed, it is not difficult to show that if a complete set of futures markets existed, they would be able to tell us when an errant path has been chosen. For example, if a path diverging upward were selected, p would rise above unity. But if p rose above unity, there would not be enough demand for ownership of the stock of capital existing then, and hence a signal would be received right away that would work to lower the initial or current price of capital goods. Likewise, if an errant path diverging downward were picked, p would fall to zero in finite time. But at a zero price, the demand for capital would be very high, and the market would not clear unless the price were raised. Such a signal would push up the initial price of capital goods. The only price path that could clear the whole sequence of futures markets would be the one that prevailed along the stable optimal path.

2.8   A practical solution to the intertemporal planning problem

Before concluding Chapter 2, let us take a look at an illuminating article by Goldman (1968). The idea of the article is roughly as follows: The informational requirements for an optimal intertemporal planning are extremely high, as we saw earlier. But if this is so, would it not be sensible to take a more modest attitude of learning by doing? Specifically, Goldman's strategy is to confine the time horizon of the planning at t to a time interval over which information is reasonably reliable, but, on the other hand, to retain flexibility by changing plans continuously in the light of the new information. Goldman illustrated the working of his continuously revised sequence of plans using a simple growth problem like problem (G), which shows that the sequence succeeds in hunting down the long-run equilibrium $(k**,q**)$ without, at any time t, relying on any information beyond the short planning horizon.

The planning problem at time t is specified as follows:

$$\max_{\{c\}} J^T\{c\} = \int_t^{t+T} e^{-\delta(\tau-t)} u[c(\tau)] \tag{G'}$$

subject to

$$\dot{k} = f(k) - nk - c$$

$$c \in [0, f(k)]$$

$$k(t) = k(t + T) = k_t > 0 \quad \text{given}$$

Notice the stationarity built in by the equality between the initial (current) stocks and the terminal stocks. T is, of course, the (short) plan-

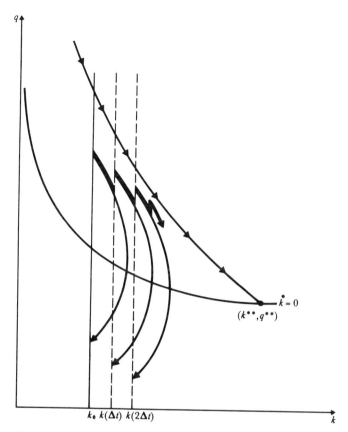

Figure 2.7. Continually revised optimal path.

ning horizon. If the planner has a four-year term, T may be set at four years. The important idea here is that any plan laid down at t will not be followed until the end of T years. Rather, the plan will be followed only for ΔT years, at which point a similar but new plan will be worked out using $k(t + \Delta T)$ as the initial stock, in accordance with (G'). This second plan will again be followed from time $t + \Delta t$ to $t + 2\Delta t$, at which point a third plan will take over. If there are any changes in various parameters of the system (tastes, technology, demography, etc.), they will be incorporated in the revisions.

The diagram in Figure 2.7 illustrates the working of such a sequence of plans. We assume $k_0 < k^{**}$ for concreteness. Figure 2.7 depicts only the relevant portion of the phase diagram. The bold zigzag path is the Goldman path. Two things are to be noted. First, the zigzag path always lies between the infinite optimal path (curve with multiple arrowheads) and the $\dot{k} = 0$ curves, and as long as $k < k^{**}$, it will keep moving to the right. So it will eventually converge to k^{**}, at which point k will actually become stationary. The path never diverges upward or downward without bound. It is also "robust" to parametric changes. Second, the zigzag path generally differs from the first best path. In this sense, constant welfare losses are incurred. The shorter the planning horizon T, the farther away (down) will be the Goldman path from the first best path. But, as we argued earlier, how long a T we can confidently pick is itself an informational problem.

The preceding analysis suggests that in a democratic society where T is fixed at four or six years, and where a single plan tends to be followed for the entire term of T years, the economy may be subjected to cycles generated by the political process. The resulting dynamic inefficiencies can be quite significant, especially in a society where two opposing political parties alternate in government.

Before concluding this chapter, let us mention one severe limitation of the highly aggregative model as a means of understanding and prescribing for realistic economies. The preceding model assumes that the two factors of production are perfectly homogeneous and malleable. These assumptions are useful in bringing out certain essential choice problems involved in long-term economic planning or policy, but at the same time, they preclude some of the fundamental difficulties faced by the planner. One such difficulty is that of choosing the industrial pattern of the economy. In reality, capital goods are heterogeneous and, once installed, are not shiftable. Even labor is not very shiftable. In order to deal squarely with the problem of long-term planning or policy, it is therefore necessary to study a model with heterogeneous factors. What heterogeneous factors do is to drastically increase the chance of making errors and thereby the chance of fluctuations of the economy. Nagatani and Neher (1977) studied a simple two-capital model and showed that the optimal path would generally oscillate (in the space of capital goods) and that per-capita real income would also exhibit cycles along the optimal path.

Questions

2.1 Prove that if $g(x) = [g_1(x),...,g_m(x)]$, $x \in R^n$, is the vector of real-valued concave functions, then $S = \{x \mid x \in R^n, g(x) \geqq 0\}$ is a convex set if it is not empty.

2.2 Show that if the state variables are nonexistent, the dynamic-optimization problem, such as (D), is equivalent to a static-optimization problem.

2.3 (a) Prove that along an optimal path, $\partial H/\partial t = dH/dt$.

(b) Give an economic interpretation of this result. (Hint: Recall Hotelling's lemma or "Envelope Relations" in static-optimization problems.)

2.4 Solve the problem (2.12) and illustrate the solution graphically for the case $n = 1$. Where in the graph is the transversality condition shown?

2.5 (a) Prove equalities (2.13) and (2.14). (Hint: Make good use of the kind of operation presented at the end of Section 2.3.)

(b) Give an economic interpretation of these results.

2.6 The dynamic-optimization problem (D) is said to be autonomous if the Hamiltonian function does not depend explicitly on t.

(a) Prove that if the problem is autonomous, then the Hamiltonian maintains a constant value over time along an optimal path.

(b) Prove that if the problem is nonautonomous, but time enters only through a discount factor, as in the problem (G), then $H(t) - \delta J(t,t_1)$ maintains a constant value over time along an optimal path.

2.7 (a) Explain Figure 2.5.

(b) If $k_t > k_{GR}$, how does the figure work?

2.8 Find the shortest curve that starts from the origin in the (x,y) space and terminates on the circle $(x - 4)^2 + (y - 2)^2 = 4$. [Hint: The length of a curve $y(x)$ is given by $L = \int_0^{x_1} [1 + (dy/dx)^2]^{1/2}dx$. Use dy/dx as the controller. Be sure to explain how to choose between the two points of intersection.)

2.9 Consider the growth problem (G) with $\delta = 0$, $u(c) = c$, $f(k) = \min [(k/a),(1/b)]$ and fixed k_0, T, and k_1.

(a) Under what conditions will the optimal program head for a positive long-run equilibrium k^{**}? (Hint: the productivity of capital.)

(b) Assuming the conditions in (a), calculate $J^*(k_0,T,k_1)$ explicitly. What are $J_{k_0}^*$, J_T^*, and $J_{k_1}^*$?

(c) For concreteness, consider the special case in which $k_0 = k_1 < k^{**}$ Study how the optimal trajectory shifts with an increase in T. From this, deduce the optimal program with $T = \infty$. (Hint: the turnpike theorem.)

2.10 Suppose the T in Section 2.8 were a choice variable. Construct a sensible model that determines an optimal T.

2.11 Referring to Figure 2.7, for any given level of k, the society saves less along the Goldman path than along the infinite-horizon optimal path. Can one conclude from this that the lack of foresight is synonymous with a greater rate of time preference?

CHAPTER 3

Hicksian temporary equilibrium and comparative dynamics

3.1 The concept of temporary equilibrium

A temporary equilibrium is a snapshot of a dynamic economy evolving through time. A temporary equilibrium is different from a static equilibrium for two reasons: (1) each "period" is not self-contained; it is constrained by past history and by the state of expectations about the future; (2) it is generally not a position of rest but is subject to certain dynamic forces; if x_t denotes the position of a temporary equilibrium, it has, within it, certain systematic forces $\dot{x}_t$, so that a temporary equilibrium can be properly understood only in terms of the pair $(x_t, \dot{x}_t)$.

A temporary equilibrium is also different from an intertemporal equilibrium in that a temporary equilibrium does not generally imply any consistency among a sequence of plans over time. A temporary equilibrium can be identical with an intertemporal equilibrium only when prohibitively high informational requirements are met.

In any case, the term "temporary" is readily understandable. But "equilibrium" is not, although we tend to associate it with the Walrasian notion of equilibrium, in which a set of flow markets clear simultaneously. The Hicksian temporary equilibrium we take up in this chapter is indeed one such equilibrium. However, in this chapter we adopt a much broader concept of equilibrium. We shall call any snapshot of a dynamic economy a temporary equilibrium regardless of the clearance or nonclearance of the flow markets in the sense of Walras. The reason is as follows: Temporary equilibrium is the weakest or broadest of the several equilibrium concepts in economics. As an equilibrium, it must possess a minimum structure, but at the same time it must be broad enough to encompass virtually all possible states the economy may occupy at a given time. Otherwise, we would be left with many states of the economy that would not belong to any equilibrium, and consequently we would have to face the difficult task of dealing with disequilibrium states about which we knew next to nothing. The Hicksian temporary equilibrium is manifestly too strong, and it leaves out many states as disequilibrium states. The

34

actual economy is seldom in equilibrium in the Hicksian sense, as evidenced by continual wide fluctuations in business inventories (which reflect the gap between aggregate supply and aggregate demand for goods). Economists have conventionally employed tâtonnementlike dynamic equations to describe such disequilibrium states, but the validity of such an ad hoc formulation is very much in doubt. In Chapter 7 we shall define a broader and yet workable concept of temporary equilibrium and analyze it. But, for now, we confine our attention to the Hicksian temporary equilibrium.

3.2   Hicksian temporary equilibrium

The first systematic treatment of temporary equilibrium was provided by Hicks (1946, Part IV). Hicks defined a time period, which he called "week," long enough for all the existing flow markets to clear but short enough for stocks and expectations to be constant. In this framework, a temporary equilibrium is characterized by a vector of prices (including interest rates) that, during the course of "week," clears these markets at given levels of stocks and expectations. Symbolically,

$$p_t^* = p(k_t, \{p^e\}_t; \theta) \tag{3.1}$$

where p_t^* is the equilibrium price vector, k_t is the vector of existing stocks, $\{p^e\}_t$ are the time profiles of prices expected at time t for all time from t onward, and θ is the set of parameters exogenous to the model.

Hicks's analysis of temporary equilibria proceeds by comparing them with their static counterpart. A static equilibrium is thought of as a special case of (3.1) in which k has settled down to its steady-state value and $\{p^e\}$ has become a constant profile equaling p, the current price vector. In other words, a static equilibrium is a special kind of temporary equilibrium in which stocks are at desired levels and the elasticities of price expectations are unitary. On the basis of this observation, the tâtonnement stability of temporary equilibrium is compared with that of static equilibrium. Hicks concluded that a temporary equilibrium tends to be less stable the more elastic are the price (excluding interest rates) expectations, whereas the similar elasticities on interest rates exert an opposite (i.e., stabilizing) effect. Hicks went on to a comparative static analysis of (3.1) when there is some exogenous shift in demand (one of our θ values). Adopting the commodities-securities-money triad, he investigated how an increase in demand for one of these three goods affects the money prices of the other two goods. To keep the analogy to the static case tight, he began by taking expectations as unitary elastic. The results were then subjected to modifications in terms of elastic expectations.

The method of dynamic analysis Hicks presented in *Value and Capital* was strongly Walrasian in spirit and was quasi-static. First, his concern was primarily to determine the extent to which static methods were applicable to dynamic problems. Second, he did not have a complete theory to determine the dynamic behavior of stocks and expectations. Thus capital accumulation, for example, was viewed as a parametric increase in stocks.

Hicks's theory of temporary equilibrium has since met criticism from both neoclassicists and Keynesians. The neoclassicists have complained about the lack of rationality in the Hicksian formulation. Their idea of macrodynamics is to work out precise models of optimal capital accumulation along with models of rational (i.e., consistent) expectations and regard macrodynamics as the study of the paths generated by such precise models. In a word, their strategy is to eliminate "errors" from macrodynamics.

The Keynesian complaints have been directed at the assumptions of flexible prices and full employment. Putting aside the naive fixed-money-wage variant of the Keynesian tradition, the following two ideas seem to have been expressed in the literature: One is to introduce the quantity constraints in disequilibrium situations into individual-choice problems with a view to accommodating unemployment equilibrium. Despite the obvious differences in results, this theory is completely Walrasian in its conception of the market mechanisms, as will be shown in Chapter 5. The second idea is a more fundamentalist Keynesian theory stressing the role of stocks and denying the existence of stable relationships among a set of flow markets. This latter idea will be presented in Chapter 7.

Despite these criticisms, the Hicksian temporary-equilibrium theory, and especially the version with fixed or constant expectations, has been used extensively in both theoretical and empirical applications because of its handiness. For examples, see the work of Diewert (1974; 1977) and Nagatani and Neher (1976).

The two articles by Diewert dealt with models of temporary equilibrium. The first (1974) discussed a temporary-equilibrium model for consumers, whereas the second (1977) provided an existence proof of Walrasian temporary equilibrium with capital formation. The novel part of Diewert's formulation in both articles was his general treatment of durable goods, a formalization of the idea expressed in Walras's *Elements of Pure Economics* (1926), but somehow forgotten in the later formulations by Hicks and Patinkin and by many other mathematical general-equilibrium theorists.

According to Walras, any good, whether it is a consumer good or a producer good, is generally capable of producing "service d'approvisionnement" (the service of availability). This fact calls for a distinction between the price of such flow services of a good and the price of the same good as an asset. The two prices will be the same only if the good is "perishable."

In the first article, Diewert explained the relationship between the two prices of a good as follows: Let p_t^* ($1 \leq t \leq T$) be the spot purchase price of a good expected to prevail in period t (standing at the beginning of period one), and let $R_1^*,...,R_{T-1}^*$ be the expected one-period interest rates associated with the holding of a financial asset. Also let δ ($0 \leq \delta \leq 1$) be the physical depreciation rate per period of the good in question. If $\delta = 1$, the good is a perishable good. Now let the price of the flow services of the good during period t be p_t. How is p_t related to p_t^* and R_t^*? If we interpret p_t as the discounted rental price at $t = 1$, it can be expressed as the decline during period t in the discounted asset value of the good; that is,

$$p_t = \frac{p_t^*}{(1 + R_1^*) \dots (1 + R_{t-1}^*)} - \frac{(1 - \delta)p_{t+1}^*}{(1 + R_1^*) \dots (1 + R_t^*)}$$

In particular, setting $t = 1$,

$$p_1^* - p_1 = \frac{1 - \delta}{1 + R_1^*} p_2^*$$

The meaning of this equation is as follows: When a consumer purchases one unit of this good at the price p_1^*, one can say that he consumes part of the good in the form of flow services (the part corresponding to p_1) and saves (invests) that part of the good corresponding to the term $[(1 - \delta)/(1 + R_1^*)]p_2^*$. Using this distinction, the act of purchase by a consumer is divided between consumption and investment. Diewert's article then applied this framework to household data. The model was otherwise Hicksian. Price expectations were assumed static, and capital markets were assumed to be perfect. The second article provided a rigorous proof of the existence of this type of temporary equilibrium. Because the object was an existence proof, expectations were generalized to be continuous functions of current prices.

The report by Nagatani and Neher (1976) explored, in a highly aggregated model, the growth potential of the world economy in the presence of an exhaustible resource (i.e., oil). The model assumes the

OPEC to monopolize the world petroleum supplies, fixing the oil price (relative to non-oil goods) and investing its saving in physical capital to be used to produce non-oil goods. On the other hand, the rest of the world, called the PIC, is assumed to be the price-taker.

Under certain standard assumptions about technology, the temporary equilibrium is obtained as the pair (p,r), where p is the relative price of oil and r is the interest rate. More specifically, if k is the world capital stock and b is the stock of oil, the temporary equilibrium is characterized by

$$p_t^* = p(k_t,b_t) \qquad (p_k > 0,\ p_b < 0)$$

$$r_t^* = r(k_t,b_t) \qquad (r_k < 0,\ r_b > 0)$$

As b is run down, it causes p to rise (increasing cost) and the interest rate (the marginal productivity of capital) to fall. In this sense, the existence of an exhaustible resource acts to produce technological regression. The long-run solution from the global standpoint is therefore continual technological progress to offset the downward pressure coming from exhaustible resources. The serious problem from the PIC point of view, in the meantime, is the fundamental negative relationship between the growth rate of its economy and the oil price. A sufficiently high oil price precludes growth of the PIC economy.

The model is primitive in a number of respects. First, the naive monopoly-competitor assumption may be unrealistic. Second, it depends on the static-expectations assumption, which probably is unrealistic. These shortcomings, however, did not seriously impede the main purpose of the report, which, besides offering a rigorous temporary-equilibrium analysis, was to show that any growth-and-development program cannot ignore the global constraints imposed by exhaustible resources.

The reader who is interested in the oil problem is referred to several articles published in the *Journal of Development Economics* (December 1975) and the *European Economic Review* (August 1976). Some of these articles presented models that were more sophisticated than that of Nagatani and Neher.

3.3   Comparative dynamics

How would the position of temporary equilibrium shift if k or $\{p^e\}$ or another parameter changed? The answer to this question calls for an analytical method known as comparative dynamics. The analytical techniques involved are quite general and applicable to any dynamic system, not just to the Hicksian model. But we bring this subject up now because of its special relevance to the analysis of temporary equilibrium.

The idea of comparative dynamics can be conveyed as follows: In comparative statics we ask how the optimal values of choice variables change in response to a change in the value of a parameter. Symbolically, we have the problem

$$\max_{x \in \Omega} f(x;\theta)$$

where x is the vector of choice variables, θ is the parameter, and Ω is the opportunity set. If f is continuously differentiable with respect to x over Ω, and if a maximum exists in the interior of Ω, then the optimal values of x (x^*) are found as a solution of $f_x(x^*;\theta) = 0$. The comparative-statics analysis is concerned with the effect of a change in θ on such an x^*. If f_x is continuously differentiable with respect to x and θ in a neighborhood of $[x^*(\theta^0),\theta^0]$, say, then such an effect can be evaluated as

$$\frac{\partial x^*}{\partial \theta} = - \left[f_{xx}[x^*(\theta^0),\theta^0] \right]^{-1} \cdot f_{x\theta}[x^*(\theta^0),\theta^0]$$

provided $|f_{xx}[x^*(\theta^0),\theta^0]| \neq 0$.

In dynamic-optimization models the solutions are time profiles of the variables. Comparative dynamics is concerned with the problem of how such a profile or path changes with a change in (the profile of) the parameter.

Take, for example, the investment function. One derives such a function as a solution to an optimal-capital-accumulation problem. Namely, the investment function describes the optimal rate of change in the capital stock implied by such a solution. What will happen to such a program when the interest rate undergoes a specific pattern of change? The optimal program, which can be depicted as a curve in the capital-stock – investment space, will shift up or down in response to the change in the interest rate. What we usually call the interest sensitivity of investment is nothing but the "impact effect," that is, the effect of a change in the interest rate (profile) on investment at the time of the interest-rate change.

It should be stressed that the impact effect derived from a comparative-dynamics analysis is not the same as the short-run effect derived from the usual comparative-statics analysis. According to the latter, the capital stock is given for the moment, and thus it drops out of the set of choice variables. But according to the comparative-dynamics method, the fact that the capital stock is given does not mean that the firm will accept it just as given; rather, unless it is already at a desired level, the firm will take immediate action to change it. As we stated earlier, a temporary equilibrium can be fully described only by the pair $(x_t, \dot{x}_t)$. To capture the latter component $\dot{x}_t$ (i.e., the motion of the economy in a given position), we need the method of comparative dynamics.

In what follows, we intend to describe the use of the comparative-dynamics technique. Our exposition will rely on the work of Oniki (1973). One thing we shall omit from his analysis is the possibility of "switches" in the controllers and the comparative statics on the switching times.

We assume the following type of optimal-control problem:

$$\max \int_{t_0}^{t_1} I(x,u,\theta)dt$$

subject to

$$x(t) = f[x(t),u(t),\theta], \qquad x(t_0) = x_0 \quad \text{given}$$

$$u(t) \in \Omega[x(t),\theta] \qquad (t_0 \leq t \leq t_1)$$

$$\zeta^i[x(t_i),\theta] = 0 \qquad (i = 0,1)$$

where the last equations specify the boundary conditions. We assume the following: that $f_x, f_u, f_\theta, I_x, I_u, I_\theta, f_{xx}, f_{xu}, f_{x\theta}, I_{xx}, I_{xu}$, and $I_{x\theta}$ exist and are continuous; that the optimal controller $u^*(t) = u[q(t),x(t),\theta] \in \Omega[x(t),\theta]$ is continuously differentiable with respect to all its arguments and for all t; that an optimal solution $[x^*(t),q^*(t)]$ exists and is unique. The optimal solution satisfies the differential equations

$$\dot{x} = \frac{\partial}{\partial q} M(x,q,\theta) \tag{3.2}$$

$$\dot{q} = -\frac{\partial}{\partial x} M(x,q,\theta) \tag{3.3}$$

where $M(x,q,\theta) \equiv H[x,q,u(x,q,\theta),\theta]$, the maximized Hamiltonian. In addition, the optimal solution satisfies the transversality conditions

$$\psi^0[x(t_0,\theta),q(t_0,\theta),\theta] = 0 \tag{3.4}$$

$$\psi^1[x(t_1,\theta),q(t_1,\theta),\theta] = 0 \tag{3.5}$$

We assume that the functions ψ^0 and ψ^1 are also continuously differentiable with respect to the three arguments.

3.4   An example

In order to facilitate an understanding of the idea of comparative dynamics, we shall reverse the usual order of stating the general results first and illustrating by examples afterward.

Let us consider a now-familiar problem encountered in growth theory:

$$\max \int_0^T u(c)e^{-\delta t}dt \tag{3.6}$$

subject to

$$\dot{k} = f(k) - nk - c$$

$$c \in [0, f(k)]$$

$$k(0) = \bar{k}_0 \quad \text{given}$$

$$k(T) = \bar{k}_1 \quad \text{given}$$

By the Maximum Principle, and by the assumption that c^* is an interior solution, we have

$$u'(c^*) = q \quad \text{or} \quad c^* = c(q) \qquad [c'(q) < 0] \tag{3.7}$$

and the differential system becomes

$$\dot{k} = f(k) - nk - c(q) \tag{3.8}$$

$$\dot{q} = [n + \delta - f'(k)]q \tag{3.9}$$

The general solutions of these differential equations can be written as

$$k(t;k_0,q_0;n,\delta) \quad \text{and} \quad q(t;k_0,q_0;n,\delta) \tag{3.10}$$

where (k_0,q_0) are arbitrary initial values in terms of which the entire family of solutions of the system (3.8) and (3.9) is represented. Of this family, the solution of the current maximization problem is the one that satisfies the prescribed boundary conditions.

$$k(0;k_0,q_0;n,\delta) - \bar{k}_0 = 0 \tag{3.11}$$

$$k(T;k_0,q_0;n,\delta) - \bar{k}_1 = 0 \tag{3.12}$$

Assume that these two equations yield solutions (k_0^*,q_0^*) as functions of the parameters n, δ, $\bar{k}_0$, and $\bar{k}_1$ (and T, for that matter, if T is a choice variable, although we do not consider T as a variable parameter). These (k_0^*,q_0^*) are the "right" initial values with which to start the present accumulation program. The solution of the program is therefore given by the pair

$$\{k(t;k_0^*,q_0^*;n,\delta),q(t;k_0^*,q_0^*;n,\delta)\} \qquad (0 \leqq t \leqq T) \tag{3.13}$$

Formally stated, the comparative-dynamics exercise proceeds in three steps. The first step is to perform the comparative-statics exercise on the system (3.11) and (3.12) for the pair (k_0^*,q_0^*) with respect to the parameter in question. We shall use δ for illustration. We denote the original value of δ by δ_0 and the new value by $\delta_1 = \delta_0 + d\delta_0$. From (3.11) and (3.12), we get

$$\begin{bmatrix} \dfrac{\partial k(0;k_0^*,q_0^*;n,\delta_0)}{\partial k_0} & \dfrac{\partial k(0;k_0^*,q_0^*;n,\delta_0)}{\partial q_0} \\ \dfrac{\partial k(T;k_0^*,q_0^*;n,\delta_0)}{\partial k_0} & \dfrac{\partial k(T;k_0^*,q_0^*;n,\delta_0)}{\partial q_0} \end{bmatrix} \begin{bmatrix} dk_0^* \\ dq_0^* \end{bmatrix} = - \begin{bmatrix} \dfrac{\partial k(0;k_0^*,q_0^*;n,\delta_0)}{0\delta} \\ \dfrac{\partial k(T;k_0^*,q_0^*;n,\delta_0)}{\partial \delta} \end{bmatrix} \tag{3.14}$$

or, more concretely,

$$\begin{bmatrix} 1 & 0 \\ \dfrac{\partial k(T;k_0^*,q_0^*,n,\delta_0)}{\partial k_0} & \dfrac{\partial k(T;k_0^*,q_0^*;n,\delta_0)}{\partial q_0} \end{bmatrix} \begin{bmatrix} dk_0^* \\ dq_0^* \end{bmatrix} = - \begin{bmatrix} 0 \\ \dfrac{\partial k(T;k_0^*,q_0^*;n,\delta_0)}{0\partial\delta} \end{bmatrix} d\delta \tag{3.14'}$$

which yields

$$\begin{cases} \dfrac{\partial k_0^*}{\partial \delta} = 0 \\ \dfrac{\partial q_0^*}{\partial \delta} = - \dfrac{\partial k(T;k_0^*,q_0^*;n,\delta_0)}{\partial \delta} \Big/ \dfrac{\partial k(T;k_0^*,q_0^*;n,\delta_0)}{\partial q_0} \end{cases} \tag{3.15}$$

provided the Jacobian determinant $\partial k(T;k_0^*,q_0^*;n,\delta_0)/\partial q_0$ does not vanish. But this is the fundamental "controllability condition," and we naturally assume this. Moreover, in this example we shall show that this condition is met.

The second step is to actually evaluate the terms on the right-hand side of (3.15), but before doing so, let us briefly consider the meaning of these terms. The term $[\partial k(T;k_0^*,q_0^*;n,\delta_0)/\partial q_0]dq_0$ measures by how much the value of k at $t = T$ will change if the initial price is raised from q_0^* to $q_0^* + dq_0$ at unchanged k_0^* and δ_0. The term $[\delta k(T;k_0^*,q_0^*;n,\delta_0)/\partial \delta]d\delta$ measures a similar response in the value of the terminal stock to a small change in the discount rate from δ_0 to δ_1, at unchanged k_0^* and q_0^*. Because any optimal program must realize the given $\bar{k}_1$ at $t = T$, the sum of these two variations must be zero for any optimal program. Hence the second equation in (3.15). Figure 3.1 illustrates the first variation. In this figure, the curve labeled $WF_T(q_0)$ is

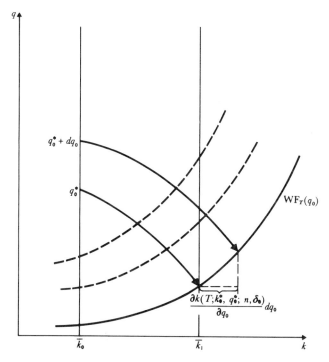

Figure 3.1. The effect of q_0 on $k(T)$.

the locus of points $[k(T),q(T)]$ corresponding to various choices of q_0. WF stands for wave front. The broken curves are similar wave fronts for different values of t. That all of these wave fronts have positive slopes is one of the things we are about to prove.

Now, in order to evaluate the two partial derivatives in (3.15), we introduce the concept of *variational differential equations*. In general, given a differential system

$$\dot{z} = F(z;\theta) \tag{3.16}$$

its solution is of the form $z(t;\theta)$. When this solution is substituted back into (3.16), we get the following identity:

$$\dot{z}(t;\theta) \equiv F[z(t;\theta);\theta] \tag{3.17}$$

If the function F has a sufficient amount of differentiability, this equation can be differentiated with respect to (any one of) the parameters θ to yield

$$\dot{z}_\theta(t;\theta) = F_z[z(t;\theta);\theta] \cdot z_\theta(t;\theta) + F_\theta[z(t;\theta);\theta] \tag{3.18}$$

where $\dot{z}_\theta(t;\theta) \equiv \partial^2 z(t;\theta)/\partial t\partial\theta$, $z_\theta(t;\theta) \equiv \partial z(t;\theta)/\partial\theta$, etc. The equation system (3.18) is called a variational differential system. In our present example, equations (3.8) and (3.9) correspond to (3.16), and θ represents the collection (k_0, q_0, n, δ).

According to (3.15), we must study two variational systems, one for q_0 and the other for δ. Consider first q_0 as the parameter in question. Equations (3.8) and (3.9) then yield the following variational differential system:

$$\begin{bmatrix} \dot{k}_{q_0} \\ \dot{q}_{q_0} \end{bmatrix} = \begin{bmatrix} f' - n & -c' \\ -qf'' & n + \delta - f' \end{bmatrix} \begin{bmatrix} k_{q_0} \\ q_{q_0} \end{bmatrix} + \begin{bmatrix} 0 \\ 0 \end{bmatrix} \tag{3.19}$$

Because q_0 is the initial value of q, $q_{q_0}(0) = 1$, and in view of (3.11), $k_{q_0}(0) = 0$. In other words, we consider the differential system (3.19) in the variational variables (k_{q_0}, q_{q_0}) with the initial values

$$k_{q_0}(0) = 0, \qquad q_{q_0}(0) = 1 \tag{3.20}$$

The question is the kinds of paths that (k_{q_0}, q_{q_0}) follow, given the initial condition (3.20) and the coefficient matrix

$$\begin{bmatrix} f' - n & -c' \\ -qf'' & n + \delta - f' \end{bmatrix} \quad \text{whose sign pattern is} \quad \begin{bmatrix} ? & + \\ + & ? \end{bmatrix}$$

The answer to this question can be found easily through the graphic method employed by Oniki (Figure 3.2). Let the motion of (k_{q_0}, q_{q_0}) start at $(0,1)$ at time zero. Substituting these initial values in the right-hand side of (3.19), and taking the sign pattern of the coefficient matrix into account, we see that k_{q_0} must initially move to the right. The initial direction of motion of q_{q_0} is not clear; it may rise or fall. This information is shown by the arrows on the vertical axis. In either case, the pair (k_{q_0}, q_{q_0}) moves into the first orthant. What we want to know is whether or not the pair stays in the first orthant. To see this, consider the behavior of (k_{q_0}, q_{q_0}) along the horizontal axis. Taking (k_{q_0}, q_{q_0}) to be $[(+), 0]$, and studying (3.19) again, we discover that whereas the direction of motion of k_{q_0} is indeterminate, that of q_{q_0} is definitely positive; that is, q_{q_0} is on the rise. Hence we conclude that the pair (k_{q_0}, q_{q_0}) must stay in the first orthant for all $t > 0$. This means that

$$k_{q_0}(t) > 0, \qquad q_{q_0}(t) > 0 \quad \text{for all } t > 0 \tag{3.21}$$

This proves the positivity of the slopes of the wave fronts in Figure 3.1. Because (3.21) holds for any solution path of the differential system (3.8) and (3.9), and because it holds for all $t > 0$, the same

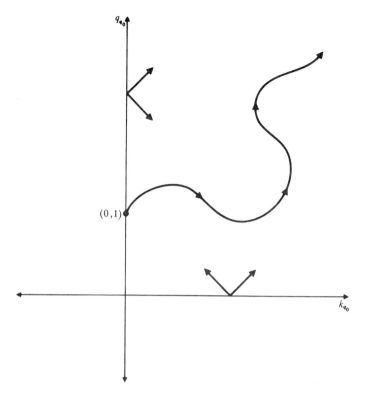

Figure 3.2. The effects of q_0 on $k(t)$ and $q(t)$.

must be true of the optimal path and at $t = T$; that is,

$$\frac{\partial k(T;k_0^*,q_0^*;n,\delta_0)}{\partial q_0} > 0 \tag{3.22}$$

which is the denominator of the second equation in (3.15).

Turning to the numerator, the parameter to be studied is δ. The variational differential system is

$$\begin{bmatrix} \dot{k}_\delta \\ \dot{q}_\delta \end{bmatrix} = \begin{bmatrix} f' - n & -c' \\ -gf'' & n + \delta - f' \end{bmatrix} \begin{bmatrix} k_\delta \\ q_\delta \end{bmatrix} + \begin{bmatrix} 0 \\ q \end{bmatrix} \tag{3.23}$$

with the initial condition

$$k_\delta(0) = 0, \qquad q_\delta(0) = 0 \tag{3.24}$$

By applying the same reasoning as before, we find (Figure 3.3) that

$$k_\delta(t) > 0, \qquad q_\delta(t) > 0 \quad \text{for all } t > 0 \tag{3.25}$$

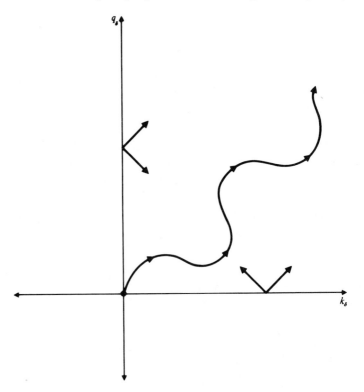

Figure 3.3. The effects of δ on $k(t)$ and $q(t)$.

From (3.25) we obtain

$$\frac{\partial k(T;k_0^*,q_0^*;n,\delta_0)}{\partial \delta} > 0 \tag{3.26}$$

We have thus found that

$$\frac{\partial q_0^*}{\partial \delta} = -\frac{[+]}{[+]} < 0 \tag{3.27}$$

What we call the "impact effect" is summarized in (3.27). This shows what will happen to the optimal program at $t = 0$ when the discount rate undergoes a once-and-for-all change. It is precisely this knowledge that we need in a temporary-equilibrium analysis.

We are at the third step at long last. What we have discovered thus far is the response of the optimal program at $t = 0$ to a given parametric change. What about the response at subsequent dates? To this question we now turn. Remembering that the parameter in question

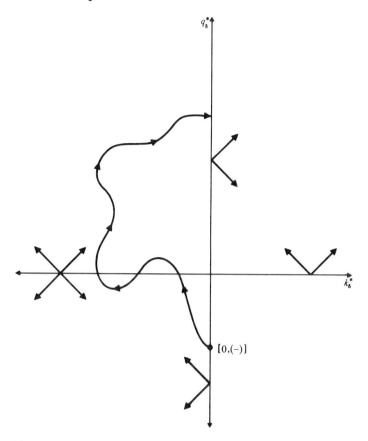

Figure 3.4. The effects of δ on $k^*(t)$ and $q^*(t)$: fixed-end-point case.

is still δ, the relevant variational system is given by

$$\begin{bmatrix} \dot{k}_\delta^* \\ \dot{q}_\delta^* \end{bmatrix} = \begin{bmatrix} f' - n & -c' \\ -q^*f'' & n + \delta_0 - f' \end{bmatrix} \begin{bmatrix} k_\delta^* \\ q_\delta^* \end{bmatrix} + \begin{bmatrix} 0 \\ q^* \end{bmatrix} \tag{3.28}$$

which is essentially the same as (3.23), except that we are now study-ing an optimal program (and hence the asterisks on the variables). From (3.15) and (3.27), the initial condition is given by

$$k_\delta^*(0) = 0, \qquad q_\delta^*(0) < 0 \tag{3.29}$$

The results of the analysis are summarized in Figure 3.4. The pair (k_δ^*, q_δ^*) stays to the left of the vertical axis. This means that an increase in δ reduces the size of the capital stock at all intermediate dates. But, of course, the prescribed level of terminal stock must be attained at $t = T$. Hence the path must land on the vertical axis. The price variable, on the other hand, starts negative and ends positive; that is, an increase in δ lowers the optimal shadow price first but eventually raises it.

The economics of the preceding result are fairly straightforward. Suppose the problem (3.6) has a unique optimal solution for a constant profile of the discount rate δ_0. Denote it by the pair $[k^*(t;\delta_0),q^*(t;\delta_0)]$, with $0 \leqq t \leqq T$. Take another constant profile of the discount rate $\delta_1 = \delta_0 + d\delta$ and suppose the problem (3.6) has a unique optimal solution for δ_1 also. Denote this solution by $[k^*(t;\delta_1),q^*(t;\delta_1)]$, with $0 \leqq t \leqq T$. When the difference $\delta_1 - \delta_0 = d\delta$ is small, the difference between the two solutions can be presented by derivatives such as

$$\lim_{(\delta_1 - \delta_0) \to 0} \frac{k^*(t;\delta_1) - k^*(t;\delta_0)}{\delta_1 - \delta_0} \equiv k_\delta^*(t) \quad \text{at each } t \quad (0 \leqq t \leqq T)$$

(In order for these operations to be valid, we need a sufficiently "smooth" structure. The previously mentioned differentiability assumption ensures that.)

According to Figure 3.4, a once-and-for-all uniform increase in δ (i.e., $\delta_1 > \delta_0$) immediately reduces the price q^*. This means that consumption is increased and investment is reduced immediately. This leads to a smaller capital stock at the next instant. Indeed, the figure shows that this is true for the entire planning horizon (except at the terminal). The interesting question is whether or not the "fiesta" can be maintained throughout. The answer is negative, as is shown by the fact that q_δ^* moves up to positive values at some intermediate time point. The early fiesta must be made up for by "mucho trabajo" later.

This completes the example. A few additional aspects of comparative dynamics are discussed in the next two sections.

3.5   Infinite programs and comparative dynamics

Continuing with the simple growth example, suppose the planning horizon is infinite. Then the optimal solution, if it exists, is characterized by the following conditions:

$$\dot{k} = f(k) - nk - c(q) \tag{3.8}$$

$$\dot{q} = [n + \delta - f'(k)]q \tag{3.9}$$

$$k(0) = \bar{k}_0 > 0 \quad \text{given} \tag{3.29}$$

$$\lim_{T \to \infty} e^{-\delta T} q(T) \cdot k(T) = 0 \tag{3.30}$$

Our problem is to perform a comparative-dynamics exercise on such an optimal solution.

According to the method described in the previous section, we should first examine the boundary conditions (3.29) and (3.30). But we encounter a difficulty here. Because the condition (3.30) is in a limiting form, it is just too vague to be of use. The alternative is to look at the stationary pair defined by (3.8) and (3.9), the pair we denoted as (k^{**}, q^{**}) earlier. We have learned that for given technology and taste and for proper ranges of parameters, such a pair exists and is finitely positive, and the optimal solution in fact converges to the stationary point. This means that if we confine ourselves to such cases we may take (k^{**}, q^{**}) as the terminal position of an optimal path.

The comparative-dynamics exercise in the infinity case may be broken down into two steps. The first step is to do the comparative-statics exercise on the stationary or the long-run pair (k^{**}, q^{**}). Using δ as the parameter, this part of the exercise is quite straightforward. We set the left-hand sides of (3.8) and (3.9) at zero and derive

$$\begin{bmatrix} f' - n & -c' \\ qf'' & n + \delta - f' \end{bmatrix} \begin{bmatrix} dk^{**} \\ dq^{**} \end{bmatrix} = - \begin{bmatrix} 0 \\ q^{**} \end{bmatrix} d\delta \qquad (3.31)$$

In (3.31), all the terms in the coefficient matrix are, of course, evaluated at the stationary point. Its determinantal value is given by $J = -q^{**} \cdot f''(k^{**}) \cdot c'(q^{**}) < 0$. Note that $n + \delta - f'(k^{**}) = 0$ and $f'(k^{**}) - n = \delta$. From (3.31) we obtain

$$\frac{\partial k^{**}}{\partial \delta} = \frac{1}{f''(k^{**})} < 0, \qquad \frac{\partial q^{**}}{\partial \delta} = \frac{\partial}{f''(k^{**})c'(q^{**})} > 0 \qquad (3.32)$$

The second step is to completely spell out the effect of a change in δ on the entire optimal path, that is, to work out an analysis comparable to that contained in Figure 3.4, knowing (1) that the trajectory of the variational variables must start from somewhere along the vertical axis at $t = 0$ and (2) that the trajectory must end in the second orthant after a very long time. See equation (3.32). Alternatively, we may let time run in reverse and state the problem as follows: Starting with an "initial" position given by (3.32), find a trajectory of the variational variables that lands on the vertical axis after an infinite recession of time.

Whichever method we follow, the answers are the same, and the result is depicted in Figure 3.5. One must convince oneself that the trajectory could not have started above the origin, that is, $q_\delta^*(0)$ could not have been positive.

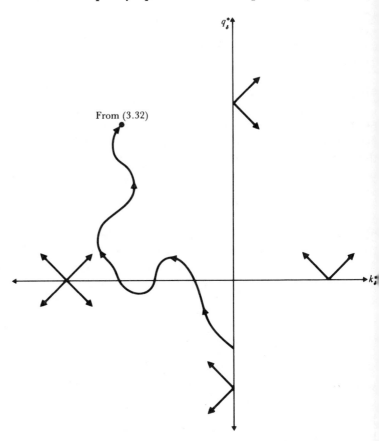

Figure 3.5. The effects of δ on $k^*(t)$ and $q^*(t)$: infinite-horizon case.

3.6   Long-run versus short-run effects

According to Figure 3.5, the long-run effect of an increase in δ is to reduce the steady-state level of the capital stock. Its short-run effect (or, better still, its impact effect) is to reduce the rate of investment. There is perfect agreement between the two responses: Investment is immediately reduced because less capital is needed in the long run. This is the type of reasoning we economists employ constantly (but implicitly) in predicting impact responses. But are we correct in doing so?

It is our common practice to use the comparative-statics results in predicting the future. The model used is often a static model, which in our present context may be interpreted as the long-run model. In terms of our illustrative model, our usual practice boils down to inferring from (3.32) that

$$\frac{\dot{k}*(0)}{\partial \delta} < 0 \tag{3.33}$$

without any analysis. In our simple model this inference turns out to be right, as we have just seen. But such an inference is not valid in general. In the following appendix we shall present a general formula that relates the impact effect to the long-run effect and that indicates the degree to which the two effects move in the same direction.

Appendix

The purpose of this appendix is to provide a general formula relating the impact effect to the long-run effect. Let us consider the following optimal motion:

$$\dot{k} = F(k,q;\theta)$$

$$\dot{q} = G(k,q;\theta), \qquad k(0) = k_0 \quad \text{given} \tag{3.A1}$$

or, combining the two sets of equations,

$$\dot{z} = A(z;\theta), \qquad k(0) = k_0 \quad \text{given} \tag{3.A1'}$$

where $z \equiv (k,q)$. We assume that this equation has a unique solution, given an appropriate terminal condition, and that the solution depends continuously on k_0 and the parameters θ. We further assume that it is stable; that is, the solution $z*(t;k_0;\theta) \rightarrow z*(\theta)$ as $t \rightarrow \infty$. Finally, we assume enough differentiability of the function A.

We begin with an infinite program. By the long-run effect of a once-and-for-all change in (any member of) θ, we mean the usual comparative-statics results on the equilibrium values; that is,

$$z_\theta^* = \partial z*(\theta)/\partial\theta - -\{\partial A[z*(0);0]/\partial z\}^{-1} \cdot \{\partial A[z^*(\theta);\theta]/\partial\theta\}$$
$$= -A_z^{*-1} \cdot A_\theta^* \tag{3.A2}$$

In a well-designed optimal problem, such an equilibrium is a saddle point; that is, the $2n$ eigenvalues of the matrix A_z^* are real and come in pairs with opposite signs, so that n of them are negative and the remaining n eigenvalues are positive. (To be precise, it is possible that some of the eigenvalues become complex conjugates. In such cases, the real parts of these eigenvalues still come in pairs with opposite signs.) At any rate, the matrix A_z^* is nonsingular, and the sign of its determinant is $(-1)^n$.

Turning to the impact effect, let us assume that the dynamic motion of the system (3.A1′) can be approximated by the following linear differential system with constant coefficients, where we write A for A_z^* for simplicity.

$$\dot{z}(t;\theta) = A[z(t;\theta) - z^*(\theta)] \tag{3.A3}$$

whose solution is of the form

$$z(t;\theta) = z^*(\theta) + VE_{mt}c \tag{3.A4}$$

where $c \equiv (c_1,...,c_{2n})$ is a vector of constants of integration, $m \equiv (m_1,...,m_{2n})$ is the set of eigenvalues of A, V is a $2n \times 2n$ matrix consisting of columns of eigenvectors associated with m, and E_{mt} is a diagonal matrix with $e^{m_j t}$ $(j = 1,...,2n)$ along its main diagonal. By an appropriate reordering of m, we can make the first n eigenvalues negative and the remaining n eigenvalues positive. Also, writing z by components, we arrive at the following partition of (3.A4):

$$\begin{bmatrix} k(t) \\ g(t) \end{bmatrix} = \begin{bmatrix} k^*(\theta) \\ q^*(\theta) \end{bmatrix} + \begin{bmatrix} V_{11} & V_{12} \\ V_{21} & V_{22} \end{bmatrix} \begin{bmatrix} E_{m^1t} & 0 \\ 0 & E_{m^2t} \end{bmatrix} \begin{bmatrix} c^1 \\ c^2 \end{bmatrix} \tag{3.A5}$$

where $m^1 = (m_1,...,m_n) < 0$ and $m^2 = (m_{n+1},...,m_{2n}) > 0$.

Because we are presently interested in the stable path toward equilibrium, the coefficients c_j associated with positive m_j must be zero (i.e., $c^2 = 0$). This condition determines the values c^1 and the optimal initial prices q_0^* from (3.A5) as

$$k_0 - k^*(\theta) = V_{11}c^1, \quad \text{i.e., } c^1 = V_{11}^{-1}[k_0 - k^*(\theta)] \tag{3.A6}$$

$$q_0^* - q^*(\theta) = V_{21}c^1 = V_{21}V_{11}^{-1}[k_0 - k^*(\theta)] \tag{3.A7}$$

It is useful here to recall the fact that in a maximization problem the function $J^*(k_0)$ is a concave function of k_0, with $\partial J^*(k_0)/\partial k_0 = q_0^*$. (See Question 3.4 following.) This means that the matrix $(\partial q_0^*/\partial k_0)$ is a negative definite matrix. Referring to (3.A7), this means that the matrix $V_{21}V_{11}^{-1}$ is negative definite. It turns out that this concavity condition is quite important for our purpose.

Partitioning (3.A3) into stocks and prices, we have

$$\begin{bmatrix} \dot{k}(t;\theta) \\ \dot{q}(t;\theta) \end{bmatrix} = \begin{bmatrix} A_{11} & A_{12} \\ A_{21} & A_{22} \end{bmatrix} \begin{bmatrix} k(t;\theta) - k^*(\theta) \\ q(t;\theta) - q^*(\theta) \end{bmatrix} \tag{3.A8}$$

Setting $t = 0$ and using (3.A7), the stock equation becomes

$$\dot{k}(0;\theta) = A_{11}[k_0 - k^*(\theta)] + A_{12}V_{21}V_{11}^{-1}[k_0 - k^*(\theta)] \tag{3.A9}$$

which, on differentiation with respect to θ, yields the formula we have been after:

$$\dot{k}_\theta(0;\theta) = -A_{11}k_\theta^* + A_{12}(-V_{21}V_{11}^{-1})k_\theta^*$$
$$+ [\partial(A_{11} + A_{12}V_{21}V_{11}^{-1})/\partial\theta][k_0 - k^*(\theta)] \tag{3.A10}$$

We call the first term on the right-hand side of (3.A10) the *quantity effect*, because $A_{11} = (\partial k/\partial k)$, and the second term the *price effect*, because $A_{12} = (\partial \dot{k}/\partial q)$. The sum of the quantity and price effects is called the *equilibrium effect*. The third term, in contrast, is called the *disequilibrium effect*, since it arises from the gap between the initial stocks and the equilibrium stocks. Because no general statement can be made about the disequilibrium effect, we shall concentrate on the equilibrium effect.

We consider the price effect first. We learned earlier that $-V_{21}V_{11}^{-1}$ is a symmetric positive definite matrix. Moreover, the matrix A_{12} is a symmetric positive definite matrix when the I and f functions are concave in x and u. Hence the price-effect portion of the impact effect is a positive definite matrix times the long-run effect. Thus the price-effect term has a considerable amount of structure in it that tends to make the impact effect qualitatively similar to the long-run effect. Unfortunately, the positive definiteness of a matrix does not imply the positivity of all its elements. In the relatively simple models encountered in applications, however, we frequently discover that the vector k_θ^* is one-signed for most parameters and that the matrix $A_{12}(-V_{21}V_{11}^{-1})$ is indeed semipositive. If so, the price effect is unambiguous.

Next, consider the quantity effect, $-A_{11}k_\theta^*$. Again, in most cases the matrix $-A_{11}$ turns out to be positive semidefinite. This arises from the nature of economic models such that the rate of accumulation of stocks is inversely related to the actual stock levels. But there are some known perverse cases (such as the neoclassical two-sector growth model with reversal of the capital-intensity condition) in which the elements on the main diagonal of $-A_{11}$ become negative. The quantity effect, like the income effect in the Slutsky equation, can work against the normal price effect. Apart from such pathologic cases, the quantity effect tends to reinforce the price effect. In any case, one can easily check these difficulties in advance by inspecting the coefficient matrix A.

Let us move on to the finite fixed-end-point case. We take the horizon to be $[0,T]$, and we denote the terminal stocks by k_T. In this case, the following two sets of equations determine the values of c^1 and c^2:

$$V_{11}c^1 + V_{12}c^2 = k_0 - k^*(\theta) \tag{3.A11}$$

$$V_{11}E_{m^1T}c^1 + V_{12}E_{m^2T}c^2 = k_T - k^*(\theta) \tag{3.A12}$$

Using this solution for c^1 and c^2, the initial optimal prices q^* are determined by

$$q_\theta^* - q^*(\theta) = V_{21}c^1 + V_{22}c^2 \tag{3.A13}$$

From (3.A13) we obtain another positive definite matrix C, again from the concavity of $J^*(k_0)$:

$$C \equiv -\partial q_\theta^*/\partial k_0$$
$$= (V_{21} - V_{22}V_{12}^{-1}V_{11})(V_{11}E_{m^1T} - V_{12}E_{m^2T}V_{12}^{-1}V_{11})^{-1}V_{12}E_{m^2T}V_{12}^{-1} - V_{22}V_{21}^{-1} \tag{3.A14}$$

On the other hand, because

$$\dot{k}_\theta(0) = -A_{11}k_\theta^* + A_{12}[q_\theta^*(0) - q_\theta^*]$$

and because $q_\theta^*(0) - q_\theta^* = V_{12}(\partial c^1/\partial\theta) + V_{22}(\partial c^2/\partial\theta)$ from (3.A13), it follows that

$$\dot{k}_\theta(0) = -A_{11}k_\theta^* + A_{12}[C - (V_{21} - V_{22}V_{12}^{-1}V_{11})$$
$$\times (V_{11}E_{m^1T} - V_{12}E_{m^2T}V_{12}^{-1}V_{11})^{-1}]k_\theta^* \tag{3.A15}$$

Comparing with the infinite case, equation (3.A10), the impact effect in the present case is complicated by the presence of the term $(V_{21} - V_{22}V_{12}^{-1}V_1)(V_1E_{m^1T} - V_{12}E_{m^2T}V_{12}^{-1}V_1)^{-1}$. This matrix turns out to be the inverse of Oniki's matrix $[\partial k(T)/\partial q_0]$. This matrix $[\partial k(T)/\partial q_0]$ measures by how much the stocks k will increase by time T if the initial prices are chosen slightly higher. Thus we may rewrite (3.A15) as

$$\dot{k}_\theta(0) = -A_1k_\theta^* + A_{12}\{C - [\partial k(T)/\partial q_0]^{-1}\}k_\theta^* \tag{3.A16}$$

Where $C = (-\partial q_\theta^*/\partial k_0)$ is a positive definite matrix. The matrix $[\partial k(T)/\partial q_0]$ explodes as $T \to \infty$, and hence its inverse disappears in the limit. This is the reason that such a term did not exist in the infinite case. But in a finite-time problem, it exerts its influence through the price-effect term. Because the nonsingularity of this matrix is a controllability condition, its inverse is assumed to exist. Moreover, it probably possesses some structure such as positive definiteness. But even so, it is much more difficult in our current finite-time fixed-end-point case to infer the direction of the impact effect from that of the long-run effect.[1]

Thus far we have examined the relationship between k_θ^* and $\dot{k}_\theta(0)$. There are other flow variables of importance, with respect to which similar comparisons can be made. One such example, a model of an inventory-managing firm, is considered in Chapter 7. The firm produces to and sells out of a stock of inventories, whose shadow price is q. In such a model, any parametric change that causes q_θ^* to rise produces as impact effects an increase in the rate of production and a decrease in the rate of sales of the product, despite the fact that the rate of sales is to increase (rather than decrease) in the long run. The implications of this type of model for the actual price-formation processes are studied in some detail in Chapter 7.

Questions

3.1 In what sense is the condition that the Jacobian in (3.14′) be nonsingular the fundamental controllability condition? What does it mean to say that this Jacobian vanishes?

3.2 Consider a competitive firm facing a given product price p and a given convex cost function $c(y)$, where y is the output. The firm carries an inventory of finished products because of various marketing costs. Let the rate of sales be s and the level of inventories be z. Then clearly

$$\dot{z} = y - s \tag{3.Q1}$$

Assume that at any given point in time, the maximum rate of sales $\bar{s}$ is determined by the inventory level z:

$$\bar{s} = \bar{s}(z), \qquad d\bar{s}/dz > 0 \tag{3.Q2}$$

Finally, assume that the firm's objective is given by

$$J \equiv \int_0^\infty [ps - c(y)]e^{-it}dt \tag{3.Q3}$$

(a) Study the optimal behavior of the firm starting at $t = 0$ with a given positive z_0.

(b) Suppose the product price rises (by a small amout) at $t = 0$ and is expected to stay high forever. How should the firm react to such a change in the long run? What will be the firm's immediate response? (Note: If you must make any additional assumptions, state them clearly.)

3.3 (a) Using the model of capital accumulation in the text, evaluate the effect of an increase in the terminal stock k_1 on the optimal program.

(b) Do the same for an increase in the planning horizon T. (This problem is slightly more complex than the previous one.)

3.4 Prove that the function $J^*(k_0)$ is a concave function for a maximization problem under suitable assumptions about the curvature of the functions involved. [Hint: The concavity of $J^*(k_0)$ is synonymous with the downward-sloping demand curve for k_0. In this sense, it should be fairly robust.]

CHAPTER 4

Rational-expectations models

4.1 The role of expectations in dynamic models

The Hicksian temporary equilibrium was determined relative to given stocks of capital and a given state of expectations. Because a temporary equilibrium is but a snapshot of the economy at a point in time, one must "animate" the snapshot in order to arrive at a dynamic model. In other words, one must specify laws of motion for the stocks of capital and the expectational variables. Hicks (1946) stopped short of providing these laws. Our concern in this chapter is the law or rule of expectations formation.

Despite its essential role in dynamic models and the long history of the latter, the theory of expectations formation is among the least explored subjects in economics. When economists have had to specify rules of expectations formation, they have traditionally resorted to a few very crude ones. The famous cobweb model, for instance, assumes that producers expect the last-period demand price to prevail in the current period. The Cournot-Bertrand oligopoly models and the accelerator models of business cycles in macroeconomics rely on similar assumptions. But, of course, very little justification for these crude rules can be provided. In the late fifties, however, some new ideas began to emerge. In conjunction with our improving knowledge about the structure of dynamic models, they have subsequently been further developed and refined. Our purpose here is to survey the central body of theory developed during this period, called the rational-expectations hypothesis.

It is plain that there are as many dynamic models as there are rules of expectations formation. There is little doubt that the lack of theory on expectations formation has resulted in a lot of ad hockeries in dynamic model building and that these have not been conducive to the progress of macroeconomic theory. In order to correct the situation, we must somehow narrow the range of indeterminacy by restricting expectations to a "sensible" class. But what should we mean by sensible? The following seem to be two reasonable criteria: The first criterion is consistency. Any rule of expectations formation that differs from the realized path systematically and widely is not a sensible rule. The second criterion may be termed efficiency. A sensible rule should utilize the available information fully and efficiently. By the word "efficiently" we typically mean wise use of economic theory. In what follows we shall see how these criteria are incorporated in the rational-expectations hypothesis.

4.2   Brock's equilibrium forecasting

We are all familiar with Walras's theory of tâtonnement. In this theory a set of agents engage themselves in trade in a marketplace. Given an arbitrarily cried initial price vector, each agent computes his excess demand for goods. If aggregate excess demands do not vanish at this price, another price vector is cried out, and the agents recompute their excess demands. If the aggregate excess demands still fail to disappear, yet another price vector is cried, and so on. Assuming this process is capable of hunting down an equilibrium-price vector, individual plans will finally be made consistent with the quantity restrictions for the market as a whole, and the tâtonnement process ends. In order to completely spell out such a tâtonnement process, one needs a price-adjustment rule that maps the current price vector into a new price vector. Symbolically, such adjustment rules can be expressed as

$$p_{t+1} = q(p_t) \tag{4.1}$$

Needless to say, such adjustment rules are not unique. Walras used what is known as the Gauss-Seidel iteration method to describe his adjustment process (1954, p. 172). Samuelson (1941) formulated a different adjustment rule. Another rule, informationally more centralized and hence probably more efficient than Samuelson's, might be Newton's gradient method. The dynamics of adjustment processes naturally vary from one rule to another. But if any one of these rules does indeed hunt down an equilibrium-price vector successfully, such an equilibrium-price vector must be a fixed point in the mapping of expression (4.1). Namely, if $p*$ is an equilibrium-price vector, then the following must hold:

$$p* = q(p*) \tag{4.2}$$

Assuming the existence of such a convergent-adjustment rule, one may pretend that the adjustment process has already been completed and that all tradings take place at the equilibrium price. This is what the static-equilibrium theory usually does.[1]

Brock's idea (1972) was to extend the same strategy to dynamics. Consider a market whose aggregate behavior depends in a known way on people's expectations about the future. Initiate the dynamics with a randomly chosen expectations rule at time zero, say. To be specific, let $x(t)$ $(0 \leqq t < \infty)$ denote a certain aggregate quantity, and let $x_t^e(s)$ $(t \leqq s)$ denote the expectations of x for time s formed at time t. Suppose we write the expectation formation rule as

$$x_t^e(s) = \bar{x} + f_t(s)[x(t) - \bar{x}] \tag{4.3}$$

where $\bar{x}$ is the equilibrium value of x (to be explained later) and the function $f_t(s)$ is the expectations function belonging to the set

$$F \equiv \{f_t(s) / f_t(t) = 1, \quad f_t(\infty) = 0 \quad \text{and} \quad f_t(s) \text{ is} $$
continuous and monotonically decreasing in s}

Suppose further that the behavior of the quantity is given by

$$\dot{x} = \phi\{x^e\}, \qquad x(0) = x^0 \quad \text{given} \tag{4.4}$$

where $\{x^e\}$ is generally the whole time profile of $x_t^e(s)$ $(s \geqq t)$. We assume that there is an $\bar{x}$ such that $\phi\{\bar{x}\} = 0$ and that $\lim_{t \to \infty} x(t) = \bar{x}$. Brock's aim was to investigate the existence of an equilibrium $f_t(s) = \bar{f}(s)$ in F such that if expectations were formed according to this $\bar{f}$, then the actual path of $x(s)$ generated by (4.4) would coincide with $x_t^e(s)$ for all $s \geqq t$. Suppose we start at time zero with an arbitrary expectations function $f_0 \in F$, but suppose that the forecasts generated by this f_0 are not consistent with actual observations. Then, at some time point (e.g., time 1), f_0 is revised to $f_1 \in F$ according to some formula: $f_1 = E(f_0)$. If f_1 is still not consistent, it will be further revised to $f_2 = E(f_1)$ at time 2, and so on. Precisely what kind of revision rule the map E represents depends on the nature of the problem. The question Brock asked was this: If such a process continues, will the sequence $\{f_n\}$ $(n = 0,1,...)$ eventually converge to $\bar{f}$? If so, will such an $\bar{f}$ be unique? In his view, if a unique $\bar{f}$, which is the fixed point of all the sequences in F generated by mapping rules like E, is found, it will be identified as the *equilibrium-expectations function*, which has the property that if expectations are formed with this $\bar{f}$ in (4.3), they will be perfectly consistent with the realized values of $x(t)$. Thus all ad hockeries and indeterminacies in expectations formation are removed exactly as the notion of Gauss-Seidel tâtonnement removes indeterminacies about the price-adjustment process and the notion of equilibrium prices removes the indeterminacy of prices in neoclassical general-equilibrium theory. A rigorous proof of the existence and the uniqueness of $\bar{f}$ is somewhat involved, but we can illustrate the idea by means of a simple example provided by Brock himself.

In this example, x is a continuous measure of industry size, and Brock postulated that the rate of entry, $\dot{x}$, is equal to the discounted sum of expected profits. Profits at any time depend on the price of the product, and the price, in turn, depends on the (expected) size of the industry. Thus equation (4.4) takes the form

$$\dot{x}(t) = \int_t^\infty e^{-\delta(s-t)}\, \pi[p\{\bar{x} + f_t(s)[x(t) - \bar{x}]\}]ds, \qquad x(0) = x_0 \qquad (4.4')$$

Brock assumed the profit function to be linear in x; that is,

$$\pi[p(x)] = mx + b \qquad (b > 0, m < 0) \qquad (4.5)$$

Under this additional assumption, (4.4') becomes

$$\begin{aligned}
\dot{x} &= \int_t^\infty e^{-\delta(s-t)} \{m[\bar{x} + f_t(s)(x - \bar{x})] + b\}ds, \qquad \bar{x} = -b/m \\
&= m(x - \bar{x}) \int_t^\infty e^{-\delta(s-t)} f_t(s)ds
\end{aligned} \qquad (4.6)$$

In this linear case, Brock noted that $f_t(s)$ may be written as $f(s - t)$. Putting $f_t(s) = f(s - t)$ and letting $s - t \equiv y$, (4.6) becomes

$$\dot{x} = m(x - \bar{x}) \int_0^\infty e^{-\delta y} f(y)dy \qquad (4.7)$$

For $f \in F$, the integral in (4.7), a Laplace transform of f, clearly exists. Integrating (4.7) yields

$$x(t) - \bar{x} = (x_0 - \bar{x}) \exp\left[mt \int_0^\infty e^{-\delta y} f(y)dy\right]$$

or

$$g(t) = \frac{x(t) - \bar{x}}{x_0 - \bar{x}} = \exp\left[mt \int_0^\infty e^{-\delta y} f(y)dy\right] \qquad (4.8)$$

What (4.8) means is the following: Given an arbitrary expectations function $f \in F$, it yields the ratio $[x(t) - \bar{x}]/(x_0 - \bar{x})$ as a function of f, as shown in (4.8). But this ratio is nothing but the f in (4.3), with the expected value replaced by the actual. [Put $s = t$ and set the current t at zero in (4.3).] It is also clear from (4.8) that $g(0) = 1$, $g(t)$ is continuous in t, $g(t)$ is decreasing in t, and $g(t) \to 0$ as $t \to \infty$. In other words, $g \in F$ also. This suggests that we put

$$E(f) = \exp\left[mt \int_0^\infty e^{-\delta y} f(y)dy\right] \equiv \exp\left[mtL(f)\right] \qquad (4.9)$$

An equilibrium-expectations function, if it exists, is then a fixed point of this map $E(f)$ of f; that is, $\bar{f} = E(\bar{f})$.

In order to find $\bar{f}$, we note from (4.9) that $\bar{f}$ has the form e^{Kt} $(K < 0)$ (since it must decrease with time). Substituting $\bar{f}(t) = e^{Kt}$ into $\bar{f} = E(\bar{f})$, we find

$$e^{Kt} = \exp\left[mt \int_0^\infty e^{-\delta y} e^{Ky} dy\right] = e^{mt/(\delta - K)}$$

Thus the value of K we were looking for is identified with the negative root of the quadratic equation $K^2 - \delta K + m = 0$; that is,

$$\bar{K} = \frac{\delta - \sqrt{\delta^2 - 4m}}{2} \qquad (m < 0)$$

The uniqueness of such a fixed point (though obvious in this case) and the actual convergence of the adjustment process $f_n(t) = e^{K_n^* t}$ to $\bar{f}(t) = e^{\bar{K}t}$ can be formally proved by appealing to the fact that the preceding $\bar{K}$ is the unique fixed point of the second iterate of the map $H(K) = m/(\delta - K)$,

$$H^{[2]}(K) = H[H(K)] \equiv G(K) = \frac{m(\delta - K)}{\delta^2 - \delta K - m}$$

and that $G(K)$ is a "contraction" mapping (i.e., a function having a flatter slope than unity). See Figure 4.1.

To summarize: Pick an arbitrary negative number K_0 and define $f_0(t) = e^{K_0 t}$. Then follow the adjustment rule (4.9):$f_n = E(f_{n-1})$. Then the sequence $\{f_0, f_1, f_2, \ldots\}$ eventually converges to a unique limit $\bar{f}(t) = e^{\bar{K}t}$ such that if this f is substituted into (4.3), it generates a self-fulfilling set of forecasts:

$$x_t^e(s) = \bar{x} + e^{\bar{K}(s-t)}\left[x(t) - \bar{x}\right] \equiv x(s) \qquad \text{(all } s \geqq t)$$

Not only does this $\bar{f}$ uniquely determine the dynamics of the model (4.6), it also removes all the ad hockeries from the dynamic model in the sense that whereas there may be many convergent-adjustment rules, $\bar{f}$ is the unique limit of all such rules. Brock went on to prove the existence and uniqueness of an equilibrium-expectations function under fairly general conditions.

The existence of a unique equilibrium forecast suggests that it can be used to build macrodynamics on firmer ground comparable to that for equilibrium statics. There is, indeed, a strict parallel between the two: Equilibrium forecasts are to dynamics what equilibrium prices are to statics. This parallelism also means that such a macrodynamic theory logically has the same set of problems as equilibrium statics, the central one being the informational feasibility of the tâtonnement process. If one doubts the workability of static tâtonnement processes

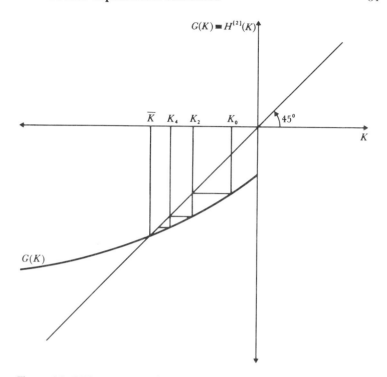

Figure 4.1. $G(K)$ as a contraction mapping and the existence of a unique $\bar{K}$.

(as Keynesians do), one has far better reason to denounce its dynamic counterpart. One might even argue that false expectations are an inherent part of economic fluctuations.[2] But at least the preceding analysis indicates that a perfectly consistent forecast does exist and that it depends on certain structural parameters of the system, which is nice to know.

4.3 Rational expectations illustrated

The term "rational expectations" was coined by John Muth (1961). In his article he argued that the major defect of dynamic economic models was their lack of theory on expectations formation. In his view, the not uncommon argument that the assumption of rationality in economics leads to theories inconsistent with observed phenomena was simply untrue. Rather, inconsistencies were due precisely to the fact that dynamic economic models did not assume enough rationality. Muth then advanced a theory of expectations that stated that "expectations were essentially the same as the predictions of the relevant economic theory." This hypothesis he called the "rational expectation hypothesis." "The prediction of the relevant economic theory" typically means predicting the equilibrium of the relevant economic model. Thus, in a word, his was an attempt to endogenize expectations and solve for them simultaneously with the current set of prices.

We have already studied Brock's notion of equilibrium forecasts, which may be regarded as the idealized solution under the rational-expectations hypothesis. But the concept of rational expectations need not be confined to such an idealized solution; it should, in principle, be applicable to more realistic "fuzzy" cases under informational constraints, for its concern is how best to assemble a given amount of information with the aid of economic theory. It is as much a positive theory as a normative one.

In a more realistic situation, Muth's idea may be formalized (Negishi 1964) as follows: Consider an agent who does business in good i. Then he may be supposed to possess fairly good knowledge of the market for i and a few other related markets. Specifically, he is assumed to have in mind the dynamic law

$$\dot{p} = E \tag{4.10}$$

where p is the vector of prices of goods belonging to his sub-general-equilibrium system and E is the corresponding vector of excess demands, which generally depends on the entire profiles of expected future prices. For simplicity (or plausibility), let us assume that he replaces such profiles by a vector of representative future prices q and that he is particularly interested in q_i. He thinks that there is a particular pair (p^*, q^*) $(p^* = q^*)$ at which his system is in equilibrium [i.e., $E(p^*, q^*) = 0$], and he approximates E_i in (4.10) by

$$E_i = \sum_j \left(\frac{\partial E_i}{\partial p_j}\right) (p_j - p_j^*) + \left(\frac{\partial E_i}{\partial q_i}\right) (q_i - q_i^*) \tag{4.11}$$

where the partial derivatives of E_i are all evaluated at equilibrium. In estimating (4.11), however, q_i is not available in the quantitative data. Hence the estimation must be the regression of E_i on p and $\dot{p}_i$.

$$E_i = \sum_j a_{ij} p_j + b_i \dot{p}_i + c_i \tag{4.12}$$

In (4.11) and (4.12), the dropping of the cross-effects of expected future prices or of the rate of change in prices means that the agent, because of lack of knowledge and interest, takes $q_j = p_j$ (all $j \neq i$) or $\dot{p}_j =$

0 (all $j \neq i$). This is not an essential assumption, but it may be a good approximation to reality, where agents are constrained by high costs of information and computation. A more complete estimation would be to estimate the whole vector of excess demands, allowing for all such cross-effects, which would naturally be more costly.

Now suppose (4.12) has been estimated. Then, recalling that the rational-expectations estimate is an equilibrium forecast, the expected p_i, $\hat{q}_i$, is obtained as a solution of the estimated equation (4.12) by setting $E_i = 0$ and $\dot{p}_i = 0$ and using $p^* = \hat{q}_i^*$:

$$0 = a_{ii}\hat{q}_i + \sum_{j \neq i} a_{ij}p_j + c_i \tag{4.13}$$

If the estimation is good (econometrically), E_i in (4.12) may be equated to that in (4.11). Replacing E_i in (4.12) with $\dot{p}_i$ from (4.10), transferring it to the right-hand side, and subtracting this equation from (4.13), we obtain

$$\hat{q}_i = p_i + \frac{b_i - 1}{a_{ii}} \dot{p}_i \tag{4.14}$$

Substituting (4.14) into (4.11) and comparing with (4.12), we identify the coefficients as follows:

$$a_{ii} = \frac{\partial E_i}{\partial p_i} + \frac{\partial E_i}{\partial q_i} \tag{4.15}$$

$$b_i = -\frac{\partial E_i / \partial q_i}{\partial E_i / \partial p_i} \tag{4.16}$$

Using (4.15) and (4.16), (4.14) becomes

$$\hat{q}_i = p_i - \left(\frac{\partial E_i}{\partial p_i}\right)^{-1} \dot{p}_i \tag{4.17}$$

which is the rational-expectations rule in the present simple model. Is this not what one would do as a back-of-envelope calculation?

The apparent simplicity of formula (4.17) should not be taken too seriously. This was largely a result of our assumption that the agent in market i disregarded possible changes in other related prices. Had he engaged himself in a full simultaneous estimation, he would have obtained a formula much more sophisticated than (4.17).[3] At any rate, in the spirit of the rational-expectations hypothesis, we can imagine all the agents in the economy forming expectations in the manner described. The end result is a conceptually solid behavioral model of price expectations, although informational constraints might produce some inconsistencies.

4.4   Rational expectations and Pareto optimality

The basic idea of the rational-expectations hypothesis, which is to determine expectations as equilibrium magnitudes, leads naturally to the use of markets. In the real world there are some forward markets where agents can make forward tradings now at prices at which these forward markets clear. To the extent that these markets determine forward prices, they serve as expected prices under the rational-expectations hypothesis. To put it another way, a realistic temporary equilibrium with a complete set of current spot markets and a subset of futures markets may be taken to be a prototype of rational-expectations models. If the Hicksian temporary equilibrium was uninteresting because of lack of normative implications, a temporary equilibrium with common equilibrium expectations (no matter how incomplete and tentative) is expected to possess some efficiency properties. Is an allocation achieved in a rational-expectations model as described earlier optimal in the sense of Pareto? Note that this is an allocation problem with incomplete contingent markets in the sense of Arrow (1964). The following is a brief survey of the literature on this subject.

Diamond (1967) studied the normative property of decentralized decisions under uncertainty. He considered an economy with one commodity and two periods (which means all the decisions are made at one time). The source of uncertainty is in production. The production function of firm j has the form $f^j(\theta, k_j)$, where k_j is the amount of inputs (e.g., labor) and θ represents the state of nature, which is unknown at the time of production decision. The inputs k are supplied by consumer households. The firms promise to pay the suppliers of k a fixed real wage that is a specified number of units of the homogeneous output. This wage is set in advance and is the same across the states of nature. There are two assets by means of which individuals can effect reallocation. One is bonds, which are promises to pay a fixed amount of the commodity. These bonds are issued and held by individuals. The other is equity shares or stocks issued by firms, and their yields are dependent on the state of nature. If a consumer owns x percent of firm j's equity, he receives x percent of firm j's profits $\pi_j(\theta) = f^j(\theta, k_j) - rk_j$; r is the fixed wage rate, whatever θ may turn out to be. At the very beginning, individuals are endowed with certain amounts of bonds and certain nonnegative numbers of shares. They also attach certain subjective probabilities to possible future states of nature. Consumption is assumed to take place after the realization of a particular state and after production and distribution.

An individual's performance criterion is the expected utility of consumption. The choice variables are the quantities of bonds and stocks to hold, and individuals adjust their holdings by trading their initial endowments in the bond and stock markets. Firms, on the other hand, choose the input levels so as to maximize their own equity value. Finally, it is assumed that all consumers and firms act competitively. When this economy attains an equilibrium, it is called a *stock-market equilibrium*.

Let us turn to the *centrally planned economy*. This economy is subject to the same technological uncertainty as the preceding stock-market economy, but it is endowed with a planner who has a certain redistributive power. Although such a power may be specified in many ways, a fair comparison between the two economies imposes a natural restriction. The restriction is that all the planner's directives be issued before the outcomes of particular states (its violation would, in effect, allow him to create additional securities). Diamond assumed that the planner controls the following: (1) the interfirm allocation of the input k (whose total is fixed); (2) the fraction of the output of each firm to be delivered to each individual (which is set independent of the state of nature); (3) the quantity of output each individual delivers to other individuals (which is fixed independent of the state of nature). In Diamond's analysis, the planner knows each individual's utility function and probabilities, as well as each firm's production function, and he attempts to maximize one individual's expected utility (using this individual's probabilities) subject to given levels of expected utilities of all other individuals and, of course, subject to the productive capacity of the economy. When the preceding three instruments are chosen to solve this problem, the resulting equilibrium is shown to be the same as the stock-market equilibrium. In this sense, the stock-market equilibrium is Pareto-optimal in the restricted sense we have described.

Hart (1975) has recently cast some doubt on Diamond's result, which was based on the analysis of a model with one commodity and two periods. In a more general model with many commodities and many periods, the (sequence of) stock-market equilibria might not, Hart argued, be Pareto-optimal. To make his point, Hart used Radner's sequential model and constructed examples in which rational-expectations models failed to reach Pareto-optimal equilibria. But the nature of the failures included (1) nonuniqueness of equilibria and (2) degeneracy of a certain kind (e.g., even when one starts out with a certain number of securities, it may so happen that the equilibrium payoff vectors of this set of securities become linearly dependent, so that the economy in effect has a smaller number of securities). These are rather pathologic cases.

To sum up: The temporary equilibria of rational-expectations models may be taken to be Pareto-optimal in an appropriately restricted sense. But this is not much more than a tautology. There is, indeed, very little we can say about such temporary equilibria from a normative point of view, for we are typically in a world of second best.

4.5   Rational expectations in macroeconomics

We have thus far studied rational expectations in a micro-type general-equilibrium framework. Recently, however, rational expectations have become fashionable in macroeconomics. In this section we shall consider this issue, relying on the article by Sargent and Wallace (1975). In this article they discussed the effectiveness of monetary policy (i.e., whether or not monetary policy can influence the levels of output and employment).

In the past, Friedman claimed that monetary policy could peg neither the (real) interest rate nor the unemployment rate for any sustained period of time (1968, p. 5). The reason, according to Friedman, is that although a rise in the rate of inflation due to an expansionary monetary policy may temporarily reduce the expected real factor costs and interest rates and hence stimulate production, people will sooner or later adjust their expectations to the new rate of inflation, and consequently these gains will disappear, reestablishing the old real interest rate and factor prices. Any effect monetary policy may have is therefore bound to be temporary, and the existence of such temporary effects depends on the time lags in the adjustments in people's expectations. But what if people's expectations are formed not adaptively but rationally? Suppose, in particular, that the public has the same knowledge of the structure of the economy and has access to the same information as the monetary authority. Can monetary policy under these circumstances affect the real variables in any systematic way?

Sargent and Wallace considered an economy whose structure is given by the following six equations:

$$y_t = a_1 k_{t-1} + a_2(p_t - {}_t p_{t-1}{}^*) + u_{1t} \qquad (a_1, a_2 > 0) \tag{4.18}$$

$$y_t = b_1 k_{t-1} + b_2[r_t - ({}_{t+1}p_{t-1}{}^* - {}_t p_{t-1}{}^*)] + b_3 Z_t + u_2 t \\ (b_1 > 0, b_2 < 0) \tag{4.19}$$

$$m_t = p_t + c_1 y_t + c_2 r_t + u_{3t} \qquad (c_1 > 0, c_2 < 0) \tag{4.20}$$

$$k_t = d_1 k_{t-1} + d_2[r_t - (_{t+1}p_{t-1}* - _t p_{t-1}*)] + d_3 Z_t + u_{4t}$$
$$(d_1 > 0, d_2 < 0) \quad (4.21)$$

$$Z_t = \sum_{j=1}^{q} \rho_j Z_{t-j} + \xi_t \quad (4.22)$$

$$u_{it} = \sum_{j=1}^{q} \rho_{ij} u_{i,t-j} + \xi_{it} \quad (4.23)$$

In these equations, y_t, p_t, and m_t are the natural logarithms of output, price level, and money supply, respectively; r_t is the nominal interest rate; Z_t is the vector of exogenous variables; $_{t+i}p_{t-j}*$ is the public's expectation in period $t - j$ of the logarithm of the price level to prevail in period $t + i$; k_{t-1} is a measure of productive capacity; u_{it} values are random variables whose serial dependence is specified by equation (4.23); ξ values are serially uncorrelated random variables. Equation (4.18) is a Phillips-Lucas type of aggregate supply function, and equation (4.19) is an aggregate-demand function. Equation (4.20) is an LM relation, and equation (4.21) specifies the manner in which productive capacity changes over time.

Let us consider the case in which the money supply is used as a policy instrument. In this case the first three equations yield solutions for (y_t, r_t, p_t) as functions of the values of $(m_t, k_{t-1}, p*)$ and Z and u. The solution for p_t becomes

$$p_t = A(_t p_{t-1}*) + B(_{t+1}p_{t-1}*) + Cm_t + X_t \quad (4.24)$$

where A, B, and C are certain constants determined by the parameters of the system and X_t is a linear function of k_{t-1}, Z_t, and the u_{it} values.

Now, suppose price expectations are formed adaptively; that is, they are given by

$$_{t+1}p_t^* = \sum_{i=0}^{q} v_{1i} p_{t-i}$$

$$_{t+2}p_t^* = \sum_{i=0}^{q} v_{2i} p_{t-1} \quad (4.25)$$

where the v values are fixed numbers. Then equation (4.24) implies that p_t depends on the past values of m. This means that the path of p_t is influenced by the history of monetary policy. The solutions of the same three equations for y_t have a form similar to that of equation (4.24), which implies that the path of y_t, too, is influenced by the monetary policy taken in the past. Thus the money-supply policy is effective when expectations are formed adaptively with lags.

Next, suppose expectations are formed rationally; that is, they are given by

$$_{t+i}p_{t-j}* = E_{t-j}p_{t+i} \tag{4.26}$$

where E_{t-j} denotes expectations taken at $t - j$ on the basis of observations up to and including the period $t - j$. Using (4.26), equation (4.24) is now written

$$p_t = A(E_{t-1}p_t) + B(E_{t-1}p_{t+1}) + Cm_t + X_t \tag{4.27}$$

from which

$$E_{t-1}p_t = A(E_{t-1}p_t) + B(E_{t-1}p_{t+1}) + CE_{t-1}m_t + E_{t-1}X_t \tag{4.28}$$

Subtracting (4.28) from (4.27),

$$p_t - E_{t-1}p_t = C(m_t - E_{t-1}m_t) + X_t - E_{t-1}X_t \tag{4.29}$$

If the money supply follows some deterministic feedback rule on the basis of all the observations up to and including period $t - 1$, then $m_t - E_{t-1}m_t = 0$, and (4.29) reduces to

$$p_t - E_{t-1}p_t = X_t - E_{t-1}X_t \tag{4.30}$$

But because $X_t - E_{t-1}X_t$ is a linear combination of ξ values in equations (4.22) and (4.23), it follows that $p_t - E_{t-1}p_t$ is an exogenous process that is independent of the rule chosen for the money supply. Also, from (4.18), (4.26), and (4.30),

$$y_t = a_1k_{t-1} + a_2(X_t - E_{t-1}X_t) + u_{1t} \tag{4.31}$$

If k_{t-1} is also an exogenous process, so is y_t. To see that this is indeed so, substitute (4.31) into (4.19) and express r_t as a function of k_{t-1} and an exogenous process. Using this relation in (4.21) yields a difference equation in k that shows that the dynamics of k are generated by exogenous processes. Hence, coming back to (4.31), we conclude that in this rational-expectations model, the path of y_t (and other endogenous variables) is determined by exogenous processes quite independently of the (deterministic) money-supply rule adopted by the authority.

Although the model manipulations appear complex, the message is quite plain. If the public has the same knowledge of the structure of the economy and has access to the same information as the monetary authority, including the authority's policy rule, and if the public forms expectations rationally in the sense of (4.26), no action by the authority can affect the path of the economy, for any such action and its potential effects will already have been taken into account by the public. Monetary policy will be totally ineffective in such a case, not only in the long run but also in the short run, and quite irrespective of the slope of the LM curve! In order for the monetary policy to be effective, the policy must have some element of surprise to the public. Within the framework of the discussion of Sargent and Wallace, such a surprise might arise because of an informational discrepancy between the authority and the public or because of a random element in the monetary rule itself. The former effect probably plays a significant role in real economies. As for the latter, it contradicts the conventional purpose of a monetary policy to insert randomness deliberately, although to the general public, ignorant of many of the facts, the policy may easily appear to be random.

Although never anything to stir the minds of the Chicago theorists, another and probably more important source of effectiveness of monetary policy in the short run is the variety of adjustment costs under which firms and households operate in the short run. The existence of binding contracts between suppliers and demanders, in terms of both prices and quantities, and the difficulties of altering the consumption/savings habits of households are, by themselves, sufficient for the monetary authority to trap the public as a whole, even though the public suffers from no informational barriers. Fischer (1977) and Phelps and Taylor (1977) argued that in the presence of such constraints, monetary policy will be effective, rational expectations notwithstanding. Fischer assumed that wage contracts are renewable only once "every two periods" and that in any period half of the workers are bound by the contracts made a period ago. Phelps and Taylor assumed that prices and wages must be determined "one period in advance." These lags imply that the economy is temporarily off the IS-LM intersection (all these authors use simple linear IS-LM models for analysis). More recently, Blinder and Fischer (1978) have shown that commodity inventories, too, act as a similar source of inertia. This is quite important. Expectations are not the only determinants of the effectiveness of policy. These lags are equally important, and we shall discuss them further in Chapter 7.

Apart from the showiness of the results of Sargent and Wallace, the concept of rational expectations, when carried to its extreme, is less interesting as a tool for macroeconomic analysis. The central goal of macroeconomics is to understand economic fluctuations. If all the agents were the competent general-equilibrium theorists, data collectors, and econometricians Sargent and Wallace assumed, monetary policy might be impotent, but first economic fluctuations would be eliminated (Arrow 1978). The original idea of Muth that agents use economic theory in forming expectations is an attractive and highly plausible hypothesis. But, as is often the case, its extreme version must be judged empirically unrealistic.

4.6   Rational expectations under uncertainty

It goes without saying that the very need for forming expectations arises from the uncertainty concerning future events. It is therefore time we considered the question of expectations formation in an explicit behavioral model of uncertainty.

In the real world we do not have means of resolving such uncertainty entirely and immediately, as in Arrow's complete contingent markets (1964), but we have developed various devices to resolve future uncertainty at least partially. To protect themselves against the contingencies of the future, individuals engage in various storage activities. More significantly, our economy has developed a set of forward markets in which an individual, if he so wishes, can now sell goods to be delivered at a future date at a certain price rather than at an uncertain future spot price. In order for him to be able to sell in the forward market, there must be someone who is willing to purchase his goods now at the fixed price and thereby bear the burden of uncertainty. In the real world there are actually a number of well-organized forward markets in which demands for and supplies of forward contracts are matched against each other, and the corresponding set of equilibrium forward prices is established.[4] Needless to say, these forward markets cannot resolve the future uncertainty completely. The future spot prices still remain more or less uncertain. However, the important fact is that the equilibrium forward prices do contain some valuable information about the future spot prices. That is, if q is the future spot price and θ are the stochastic determinants of q, so that $q = q(\theta)$, then the equilibrium forward price p^* generally allows the observer to gain some knowledge of the true values of θ. In other words, p^* itself is a function of θ. By inverting the equation $p^* = p(\theta)$, the observer may get an idea about the implied values of θ. Call them $\hat{\theta}$. This $\hat{\theta}$ then serves as an estimator of θ and hence of q. Clearly, how good a predictor $\hat{\theta}$ is of the true values of θ depends on the informational content of p^*. One can imagine, as an extreme case, the situation in which $\hat{\theta}$ predicts the true values of θ with perfect accuracy, so that the uncertainty about q is completely resolved by the forward markets. But in general, $\hat{\theta}$ leaves some degree of uncertainty (i.e., a white noise) about the true values of θ. Decision makers are therefore left with a probability distribution of θ conditional on $\hat{\theta}$. The point is that this distribution is in some sense less dispersed than the prior distribution of θ. Suppose a set of traders freely participate in the two sets of markets, spot markets and forward markets. What will be the common equilibrium forecast of q in such a situation? This is the problem of "noisy" rational expectations. There is a large and rapidly growing literature on various aspects of this problem; see, for example, the October 1977 issue of the *Review of Economic Studies* and the report by Grossman and Stiglitz (1978) and the references therein. But here we confine ourselves to the pioneering work by Lucas (1972), partly because of its elegance and partly because of its macroeconomic significance.

The setting of Lucas's model is the Samuelsonian intergenerational model.[5] Consider an economy in which there are overlapping generations of mortal individuals. Each generation consists of N identical individuals who live for two periods, the working period and the retirement period. In a given period, therefore, there are N young individuals and N old ones. Each young individual works n hours and produces a quantity n of output. The product does not keep, but there is a fiat money, so that the savings of the young may be held in it. Thus the young generation sells part of its product to the old and acquires cash in exchange, for which it buys goods during its retirement period.

Stochastic elements are introduced into the model in the following manner: First, the government makes transfer payments to the old in fiat money on their retirement in proportion to their cash balances. If the pretransfer cash balance of a retiree is m, his posttransfer balance is $m' = mx$. It is assumed that an old person has no desire to bequeath. Hence he simply spends this m' for consumption; in other words, the old generation has no decision problem to solve. By assumption, the young generation knows the old generation's pretransfer cash balance m but not the posttransfer balance m'. In this sense, the policy variable x constitutes a random monetary disturbance for the decision problem of the young. Namely, the young attempt to infer the value of x from the equilibrium price in the current consumption-goods market in order to form a sensible expectation about the future transfer-payment parameter x'.

Lucas then introduced another disturbance, this time of "real" nature. There are two physically separate markets for consumer goods over which the young are allocated stochastically, fraction $\theta/2$ going on one and fraction $1 - (\theta/2)$ to the other. The old, on the other hand, allocate themselves between the two markets in such a way that total monetary demand is the same in both.[6] Once individuals are allocated, there is no switching or communication between markets, and a single equilibrium price is established in each market. The allocation parameter θ serves as a "real" disturbance that, along with the monetary disturbance x, presents a stochastic optimization problem to the young. The young will learn of the actual values of x and θ after one period, but, being mortal, they will not have an opportunity to utilize this knowledge. Thus the economy proceeds in this manner period after period. To simplify matters, it is assumed that the distributions of the random variables x and θ are serially independent and identical over periods.

Turning to the decision problem of the young, each member attempts to maximize

$$U(c,n) + E[V(c')]\tag{4.32}$$

where c is the current consumption, n is the labor supply, c' is the future consumption, and U and V are strictly concave and twice continuously differentiable functions. The side constraints are, of course,

$$n - c - \lambda/p = 0\tag{4.33}$$

where λ is nominal cash balance to be carried forward by the young, and

$$c' = \lambda x'/p'\tag{4.34}$$

(primes denote variables in the next period). The expectation in (4.32) is taken over the distribution of x' and p' conditional on p and m. Assuming that individuals' preferences are such that an interior solution exists, the preceding problem can be first solved for (c,n) for a prescribed value of λ/p. If c and n (or rather $-n$) are normal goods, then an increase in λ/p reduces c and increases n. That is, the indirect utility function, $U[c(\lambda/p),n(\lambda/p)] = H(\lambda/p)$, is a decreasing function of λ/p. Furthermore, it is clearly concave in λ/p. Now, maximizing $H(\lambda/p) + E[V(\lambda x'/p')]$ with respect to λ, we obtain

$$H'(\lambda/p)/p + E[V'(\lambda x'/p')(x'/p')] = 0$$

or, in Lucas's notation,

$$h(\lambda/p)/p = \int V'(\lambda x'/p')(x'/p')dF(x',p'/m,p)\tag{4.35}$$

where $h(\lambda/p) = -H'(\lambda/p)$ is a positive increasing function of λ/p. Because h is increasing and V' is decreasing in λ, if a solution for λ exists, it is unique. If $\lim_{c'\to 0} V'(c') = \infty$ and $\lim_{c'\to\infty} V'(c') = 0$, a unique positive solution indeed exists.

Now the market equilibrium. Consider the market that received the fraction $\theta/2$ of the young generation. Because the old are allocated evenly between markets, the total supply of cash is $Nmx/2$. The total demand for cash, on the other hand, is $N\theta\lambda/2$. Hence, an equilibrium calls for $Nmx/2 = N\theta\lambda/2$, or $\lambda = mx/\theta$. Substituting this value of λ into (4.35), an equilibrium of this market is characterized by

$$h(mx/\theta p)/p = \int V'(mxx'/\theta p')(x'/p')dF(x',p'/m,p) \qquad (4.36)$$

From this equation, an equilibrium-price function is derived as follows: The current state of the economy is fully described by the three variables (m,x,θ). Thus it is justifiable to write the equilibrium current price as $p(m,x,\theta)$. But the problem at hand is one of intertemporal equilibrium. Lucas proposed that $p' = p(m',x',\theta')$ be the condition for such an intertemporal equilibrium; that is, the future spot price will have the same functional form as the current price, with the current data being replaced by those of the future. Using this function, the equilibrium condition (4.36) is rewritten as[7]

$$h[mx/\theta p(m,x,\theta)]/p(m,x,\theta)$$

$$= \int V'[mxx'/\theta p(m\xi,x',\theta')][x'/p(m\xi,x',\theta')]dG[\xi,x',\theta'/p(m,x,\theta)] \quad (4.37)$$

Certain properties of the equilibrium-price function can be inferred from (4.37). First, the variables x and θ enter only in the ratio form, x/θ. Second, an increase in m (i.e., a fully announced, distributionally neutral change in the money supply) causes an equiproportional change in the price level. These two facts imply that

$$p(m,x,\theta) = m\psi(x/\theta) \qquad (4.38)$$

where $\psi(x/\theta)$ is a positive increasing function. Lucas went on to prove the uniqueness of the price function in (4.38).

As a special case, consider the equilibrium-price function when the disturbances are purely monetary (i.e., x is random, but θ is fixed and known). The equilibrium-price function in this case takes the form

$$p(m,x) = mx/y^* \qquad (4.39)$$

where y^* is the level of real cash balances y satisfying $h(y) = V'(y)$. Equation (4.39) states that if disturbances are purely monetary, the equilibrium price changes in proportion to the rate of change in the money supply x, with per-capita real balances unaffected. That is, money is neutral even when the monetary change is not fully announced. This result is not surprising in itself in light of the nature of equilibrium forecasts, but it suggests that monetary policy affects real activities primarily because individuals do not know if the disturbance they experience is real or monetary. As equation (4.38) shows, the equilibrium price reveals to them only the value of the ratio x/θ. A given change in price is attributable to a change in this ratio, but individuals cannot identify the source of the disturbance. A given increase in the price may come from an increased money supply (an increase in x) or from a reduced supply of goods (a decrease in θ) or from both. In the absence of prior knowledge of the source of disturbance, individuals may mistake a monetary disturbance for real and react in real terms. The short-run effects of monetary policy may, in reality, be largely of this nature.

Lucas then addressed the question of why individuals tend to interpret periods of higher-than-average x values as "good times" in the sense of larger real output; that is, they believe in a positive correlation between the real output and the rate of increase in the price level. By construction, the real output Y is given by

$$Y = \tfrac{1}{2}\theta N\bar{n}(x/\theta) + \tfrac{1}{2}(2 - \theta)N\bar{n}(x/2 - \theta) \tag{4.40}$$

and the nominal income PY is given by

$$PY = \tfrac{1}{2}\theta N\bar{n}(x/\theta)m\psi(x/\theta) + \tfrac{1}{2}(2 - \theta)N\bar{n}(x/2 - \theta)m\psi(x/2 - \theta) \tag{4.41}$$

so that the "average" price level P is the ratio of (4.41) to (4.40). In these equations the function $\bar{n}(x/\theta)$ signifies the previously mentioned function $n(\lambda/p)$ evaluated at the equilibrium real balance, $(mx/\theta)/[m\psi(x/\theta)] = (x/\theta)/[\psi(x/\theta)]$. Think of the right-hand sides of (4.40) and (4.41) as functions of $\ln x$ and θ. Taking the logarithm of these equations and linearly approximating around $E(\ln x) = \mu$ and $\theta = 1$, the following equations are obtained:

$$\ln Y = \ln N + \ln \bar{n}(e^{\mu}) + \eta_{\bar{n}}(\ln x - \mu) \tag{4.42}$$

$$\ln P = \ln m + \ln \psi(e^{\mu}) + \eta_{\psi}(\ln x - \mu) \tag{4.43}$$

where $\eta_{\bar{n}}$ and η_{ψ} are the elasticities of the functions $\bar{n}$ and ψ evaluated at $(\mu, 1)$. By the definition of $\bar{n}$, its elasticity is related to the elasticity of the function n through

$$\eta_{\bar{n}} = \eta_n(1 - \eta_{\psi}) \tag{4.44}$$

From (4.43) it follows that

$$\ln P - \ln P_{-1} = \eta_{\psi}(\ln x) + (1 - \eta_{\psi})(\ln x_{-1}) \tag{4.45}$$

With this much preparation, consider the regression hypothesis

$$\ln Y = \beta_0 + \beta_1(\ln P - \ln P_{-1}) + \epsilon \tag{4.46}$$

where ϵ is a serially independent, identically distributed random variable. Using (4.42) and (4.45), the probability limit of the estimated coefficient β_1 is the ratio of covariance between $\ln Y$ and $(\ln P - \ln P_{-1})$ divided by the variance of the latter, which turns out to be

$$\text{Plim } \hat{\beta}_1 = \frac{\eta_\psi \eta_{\bar{n}}}{2\eta_\psi^2 - 2\eta_\psi + 1} \tag{4.47}$$

or, using (4.44),

$$\text{Plim } \hat{\beta}_1 = \frac{\eta_\psi \eta_n (1 - \eta_\psi)}{2\eta_\psi^2 - 2\eta_\psi + 1} \tag{4.48}$$

Lucas's argument (1972, p. 118) overlooks the difference between n and $\bar{n}$ functions and writes (4.48) as

$$\text{Plim } \hat{\beta}_1 = \frac{\eta_\psi \eta_n}{2\eta_\psi^2 - 2\eta_\psi + 1} \tag{4.49}$$

where η_n should be read as $\eta_{\bar{n}}$. Lucas's point is that the probability limit in (4.49) is positive; that is, there is a positive statistical relationship between the real output and the price increase, despite the fact that his model rules out any true or "usable" trade-off between them.

This result is counterintuitive. Why should the real output move with price changes in this illusionless rational-expectations model? In order to examine the validity of his conclusion, we must study the term $\eta_\psi \eta_n (1 - \eta_\psi)$ more closely. We know from the preceding analysis that both η_n and η_ψ are positive. But what about $1 - \eta_\psi$? Lucas showed (pp. 114–16) that this term is positive when the joint distribution of the two random variables x and θ (they are independently distributed by the way) satisfies the following conditions: (1) for any fixed $\bar{\theta}$, $\Pr\{\theta \leq \bar{\theta} \mid x/\theta = z\}$ is an increasing function of z; (2) for any fixed $\bar{x}$, $\Pr\{x \leq \bar{x} \mid x/\theta = z\}$ is a decreasing function of z. The intuitive justification for these conditions is as follows: An equilibrium price reveals to individuals the value $z = x/\theta$. Because it is a ratio, an increase in z can come from all sorts of variations in x and θ. For instance, z can increase when both x and θ increase or when both x and θ decrease, provided the relative magnitudes of variations in x and θ are right. In general, therefore, the informational content of z is not very high. What these two conditions do is to impose a degree of regularity, so that an increase in z is more likely to have come from a decrease in θ or an increase in x or both. What is crucial to the positivity of the term $1 - \eta_\psi$ is the first condition. It can be easily shown that if $\Pr\{\theta \leq \bar{\theta} \mid x/\theta = z\}$ is irresponsive to the level of z, $1 - \eta_\psi = 0$, and hence $\text{Plim } \hat{\beta}_1 = 0$. It is also easy to construct an example in which this is true.[8] But the fact remains that Lucas's conclusion is still quite plausible. This is an important point, for it suggests that some statistical relations such as the Phillips curve may not be "usable," despite their prevalence.

4.7   Applications of the rational-expectations hypothesis

The idea of rational expectations is usually expressed as

$$_t p_{t+1}{}^e = \underset{t}{E} \; (P_{t+1}/I_t)$$

where $_t p_{t+1}{}^e$ is the agents' subjective expectation of the variable p for period $t + 1$ held in period t, I_t is the set of available information in period t, and $E(P_{t+1}/I_t)$ is the conditional expectation of P_{t+1} given I_t. From this it is argued that

$$P_{t+1} = \underset{t}{E} \; (P_{t+1}/I_t) + \epsilon_t$$

where ϵ_t is a serially independent random variable with zero mean. By interpreting forward or futures prices as $E_t(P_{t+1}/I_t)$, the future spot price becomes the forward or futures price plus a white noise under rational expectations. In this sense, rational expectations are said to imply market efficiency. Numerous empirical studies have been done for stock markets, foreign-exchange markets, and other select commodity markets for which well-organized forward tradings take place. At the macro level, the same idea has been applied to the output–inflation trade-off problem, as suggested by Lucas. The policy implication of the hypothesis is that for a monetary policy to have an effect on real output, it must come as a random shock to the public, for its systematic part has already been fully taken into account by the public. Another related implication of the rational-expectations hypothesis is that in curbing inflation, monetary policy tools (e.g., the announced target growth rate of the money stock) can be altered drastically rather than gradually (which would be necessary if expectations were formed adaptively). Thus the rational-expectations hypothesis has strong implications for the behavior of the system as well as for policy effects.

But how do we know whether or not expectations are formed rationally? Notice that all the preceding applications rely on indirect evidence concerning the stochastic properties of the error term. Because of the efficient use of available information, it is argued, the error term ϵ_t in the earlier formula becomes a white noise. We do know, however, that an equilibrium forecast of a variable in a dynamic system depends, in general, on all the parameters of the system. To assume that the agents in the real world possess such extensive and accurate knowledge of their economic environment is difficult. The partial-equilibrium approach, on the other hand, inevitably introduces misspecification and leads to denial of the white-noise property of the error term, for the dynamics of the omitted variables could have their own trends and cycles. Take, for example, foreign-exchange markets. Suppose that the difference between the future spot rate and the corresponding forward rate were found not to be a white noise. Would this prove that expectations are not formed rationally? Or suppose that the difference were found to be a white noise. Would this prove that expectations are formed rationally? Neither inference is generally valid in a world in which many missing variables are exerting their sluggish influences. For the former case could be merely a consequence of a limited information set I_t. Similarly, the latter case could be produced accidentally by the interactions of many missing variables. In order to get out of this impasse, rational-expectationists employ stationarity assumptions. That is, although there are many variables influencing the variable in question, these variables are assumed to be stationary. The earlier model of Lucas is a good example. Population, tastes, and technology are all stationary and hence need not concern him or the inhabitants of his model economy. His sharp result rests on the liberal use of such stationarity assumptions. To use the dynamic model of Chapter 2 as an example, it is easy to see how the price variable q becomes a purely random variable if the state variables x are indeed stationary. From the formal point of view, however, to assume that these state variables are stationary is the same as ignoring these variables and the dynamics generated by them and, more important, ignoring the need to forecast the future paths of these variables. Unfortunately, we do not live on a South Pacific island, to which a model with a heap of stationarity assumptions would apply quite well, but in a capitalist economy with many durable assets. The current prices of these assets depend in an essential manner on the future course of events. The quantities of these assets, on the other hand, take a long time to alter. When such an economy is shocked, the effects tend to be distributed over many periods. The growth and fluctuations of a capitalist economy are the results of such sluggish adjustments on the part of capital goods. It is difficult to believe that the real-world agents would be capable (and the capital market so perfect) as to recognize fully the implications of future changes in capital goods and reduce the forecast error to a white noise.

The rational-expectations hypothesis is a very attractice and potentially useful concept. Considering the essential role of expectations in closing a dynamic model and the normative properties of rational expectations, it is clearly a good place to start (just as are stylized competitive equilibrium models in studying the static problems of resource allocations and welfare). Its message that agents make the best use of the available information in forming expectations and that their behavioral pattern tends to be affected by policy is, in principle, quite plausible. Such examples abound in the microeconomic area of public economics. But in applications, and especially in macroeconomic applications, one must be careful. Otherwise, there is the danger of the rational-expectations hypothesis becoming a pet idea in economic thinking (just as naive competitive models have). First, one must realize that the models intended to demonstrate the power of rational expectations are full of simplifying assumptions. The power of statistical tests based on crude models is naturally limited. Moreover, if the data during the seventies were favorable to the hypothesis, it is equally important to explain the success of the activist policies during the sixties. Second, the rational-expectations models are inherently equilibrium models. Although it is possible to produce cycles out of these models, one can argue that they have precluded the most important types of fluctuations that occur in capitalist economies.

At present we are witnessing an extensive rewriting of the Walrasian general-equilibrium theory to incorporate such realistic elements as durable goods, imperfect capital markets, uncertainty, and bargaining. In the light of this trend, what is needed is not an armchair lecture on a stylized model of rational expectations but an understanding of how expectations are actually formed (given that most economic agents intend to act rationally in the sense of Muth), what a realistic rational-expectations formula looks like, and what its macroeconomic consequences are.

Questions

4.1 Confirm for yourself that the previously presented expectations formula

$$x_t^e(s) = \bar{x} + e^{K(s-t)} [x(t) - \bar{x}] \qquad (s \geqq t)$$

indeed produces a path of self-fulfilling expectations.

4.2 Consider an industry composed of N identical firms. Each firm produces and sells a homogeneous output Y_j subject to a production function aK_j, where a is a positive constant. The firm's capital K_j can be augmented by investment, but there is an adjustment cost $\frac{1}{2}cI_j^2$ ($c > 0$). Thus the firm's problem may be stated as one of maximizing (dropping j subscripts):

$$J \equiv \int_0^\infty [p^e(t)aK - rK - \tfrac{1}{2}cI^2]e^{-it}dt \tag{4.Q1}$$

subject to

$$\dot{K} = I - \delta K \qquad (\delta > 0) \tag{4.Q2}$$

In equation (4.Q1) the parameter r measures the rate of return on capital available elsewhere. Suppose each of the N firms starts with a common capital stock K_0 at $t = 0$, and the market-demand curve for the product is given by

$$P(t) = A - B\left(\sum Y_j\right) = A - BaNK(t) \qquad (A,B > 0) \tag{4.Q3}$$

so that the initial price $P(0)$ is

$$P(0) = A - BaNK_0 \tag{4.Q4}$$

which is generally different from the long-run equilibrium price.

Now the problem: Assuming that the number of firms remains N, show that the unique self-fulfilling price-expectation function for the industry is given by

$$P_{(t)}^e = \bar{P} + [P(0) - \bar{P}]e^{mt} \qquad (t \geqq 0) \tag{4.Q5}$$

where

$$\bar{P} = \frac{c\delta(i + \delta)A + BNar}{c\delta(i + \delta) + BNa^2} \quad \text{and} \quad m = \frac{i - \sqrt{(i + 2\delta)^2 + 4BNa^2/c}}{2}$$

Notice the complex ways in which the rational-expectations function depends on the parameters of the system.

4.3 Investigate the "sensibility" of the adaptive-expectations rule

$$x_{t-1}^e(t) = x(t - 1) + a[x(t - 1) - x_{t-2}^e(t - 1)] \tag{4.Q6}$$

in terms of the following models of the economy:

$$x(t) - bx(t - 1) + cx_{t-1}^e(t) \tag{4.Q7}$$

$$x(t) = x(t - 1) + f[x(t - 1) - x_{t-2}^e(t - 1)] \tag{4.Q8}$$

$$x(t) = g \sin t \tag{4.Q9}$$

where the coefficients a, b, c, f, and g are positive constants. Assume in all instances that a is a maximum-likelihood estimate and that $x_0^e(1)$ is generated by some other rule. Determine the following for each of the three cases:

(a) What is the rational-expectations rule?

(b) Is the resulting economy stable?

4.4 Consider the model presented in Section 4.3 with N goods ($N + 1$, to be precise, but one is subsumed by Walras's law).

(a) Assuming that every trader takes the whole economy as his system and that he forms expectations according to equation (4.17), examine the stability of the economy.

(b) In contrast, assume that every trader forms expectations about the N prices simultaneously in the manner described in the last paragraph of Section 4.3. Show that in this case expectations have no effect on the stability of the economy. Why?

(c) On the basis of your results in parts (a) and (b), is it possible to infer that the more efficient use of information in the latter scheme always contributes to stability?

4.5 Prove equation (4.39).

4.6 Suppose the random variables x and θ are distributed according to the following beta distributions:

$$f(x) = \frac{6}{\bar{x}^3} x(\bar{x} - x) \qquad (0 \leq x \leq \bar{x}, \quad \bar{x} = \text{some positive constant})$$

$$g(\theta) = \frac{6}{8} \theta(2 - \theta) \qquad (0 \leq \theta \leq 2)$$

(a) Derive the joint density function for θ and $z \equiv x/\theta$ from the preceding f and g functions.

(b) Using the joint density function for z and θ obtained in part (a), compute $\Pr\{\theta \leq \bar{\theta} \mid x/\theta = z\}$. Show that this probability increases with an increase in z for all values of $\bar{\theta}$ and z.

CHAPTER 5

Equilibrium theories of Keynesian unemployment

5.1 The problem

In the *General Theory* (1936, p. 9), Keynes stated his problem as follows:

It is not very plausible to assert that unemployment in the United States in 1932 was due either to labour obstinately refusing to accept a reduction of money wages or to its obstinately demanding a real wage beyond what the productivity of the economic machine was capable of furnishing. Wide variations are experienced in the volume of employment without an apparent change either in the minimum real demands for labour or in its productivity. Labour is not more truculent in the depression than in the boom – far from it. Nor is its physical productivity less. These facts from experience are a *prima facie* ground for questioning the adequacy of the classical analysis.

So, in Keynes's view, labor's behavior was not the cause of the Depression. Labor was not asking too much. It was even receptive to some money-wage cuts. But it had no power to raise employment. If the supply side was not to blame, the attention naturally shifted to the demand side. On the demand side, Keynes (1936, p. 32) first recalled the long-neglected but important point made by Malthus that a deficient demand was a possibility. The analysis of demand led to his theory of effective demand and the notion of the aggregate-supply function (or rather its inverse, the employment function as a function of the expected proceeds). In this connection, the most important contribution of Keynes was his emphasis on the role of expectations. The importance of long-run expectations as a determinant of investment demand (his notion of the marginal efficiency of capital) is well known. The cost of financing investment projects, on the other hand, is given by appropriate interest rates to be determined in the asset markets, including the stock market. Here the psychology of the participating investors and speculators, which Keynes called the state of liquidity preference, plays the key role. To Keynes, an interest rate was the price of renting the liquidity services of money and hence was directly influenced by the state of liquidity preference. The other major component of aggregate demand, consumption, was also open to similar influences.

At any rate, the level of aggregate demand so generated determines the level of employment via the aggregate-supply function, $Z = \phi(N)$. This function, according to Keynes, is not a technological relation describing the causal relationship from the volume of employment N to the volume of output. Z is not the physical volume of output but the value of output, and the causation goes the other way round. In his own words, "Z is the proceeds the expectation of which will induce a level of employment N" (Keynes 1936, p. 44). These types of expectations were called "short-term" expectations (Keynes 1936, Chapter 5) as against the "long-term" expectations governing investment decisions (Keynes 1936, Chapter 12). Note also the effect of expectations through the "user cost" (Keynes 1936, Chapter 6).

We thus see that Keynes's model embraces all the parts of the economy as an inseparable whole, and hence the title of his book. The central policy question is, of course, how to control the level of expected proceeds or the level of effective demand.

It is plain that what we are given is a fairly complex general-equilibrium model – more complex than any of the stylized models of neoclassical origin. This complexity explains why so many "versions" of Keynes's theory have come into being. One of the oldest interpretations of Keynes's theory is the so-called neoclassical synthesis, which is latently still popular (e.g., Samuelson 1955). According to this view, Keynes's system is essentially the same as the neoclassical (static) system except that the former recognizes the possibility that the price system may not function well enough to absorb the shocks originating in the aggregate demand; that is, some prices may be "rigid" or "sticky." (We shall argue later that these concepts themselves are very neoclassical.) A special version of this class of models (i.e., the rigid-wage model) has long been the standard textbook Keynesian model. It implies that unemployment is due to money wages being "too high." But if the level of aggregate demand is controlled properly for a given level of money wages, we are back to the neoclassical world. The good old price system will take care of the allocation problem in the usual efficient manner. It follows, then, that Keynes had nothing really new to say and that his contribution consisted merely in an assertion that governmental intervention may be called on to stabilize the level of aggregate demand once in a while. However, we hardly need help from Arrow (1967) to question the validity of such a proposition. As a practical matter, neither the IS curve nor the LM curve is very stable. The positions of these curves depend on the levels of various stock and expectational variables, and consequently they are constantly shifting. Besides, there is little reason to believe that the temporary equilibrium of an economy stays at or near the intersection of the two curves. When one takes into account these dynamic forces and various lags inherent in any policy actions, it is evident that controlling the aggregate demand by policy means is easier said then done. One may further argue that an economy that must rely on constant and heavy doses of policy prescriptions is not a healthy economy, even though it is made operable by such policy prescriptions. For one thing, policies alter people's behavior itself, often in such a manner that an even larger scale of intervention will be needed to keep the economy going. Moreover, the preceding naive interpretation overlooks the fact that fiscal and monetary policy actions tend to create problems of their own by narrowing the policy choices available in the future.

Returning to the business at hand, the aim of this chapter and the two subsequent chapters is to attempt to determine if Keynes really had something new and important to say about the theory of an aggregative economy and, if so, what it was. We shall first survey the relevant literature and then offer a paradigm that we hope will capture the essence of Keynes's theory. For the purposes of the survey, the literature is divided into two parts. The first concerns the problem of market coordination in the presence of a given deficient effective demand. In this body of literature only the markets for goods and services are considered. The second part of the literature deals with asset markets. The two parts will be discussed in order in this chapter and the next chapters. One may well keep in mind that this kind of partitioning is invalid in view of the inseparability of Keynes's theory. Finally, in Chapter 7 we shall attempt to construct a unifying Keynesian paradigm.

5.2   The dual-decision hypothesis

Let us turn to the first part of the problem. Here the state of long-run expectations and the level of aggregate demand are assumed to be given at a level below what is consistent with full employment of the variable input, labor, at the prevailing prices and money wages in the usual neoclassical sense. Our concern is the working of the markets for products and labor services in such a situation. The following exposition relies on the work of Clower (1965), Barro and Grossman (1971), and Negishi (1974; 1979).

We begin by considering the behavior of the representative household whose choice problem is given by

$$\text{maximize } u(x,L) \quad \text{subject to} \quad px - wL \leq r \tag{5.1}$$

Where x is the amount (vector, if you like) of consumption goods purchased, p is the price (vector) of these consumption goods, w is the money-wage rate, L is the amount of labor services sold, and r is the amount of profits accruing to the household.

Let us first work out an individual experiment of the household under the assumption that it takes the price p and the money-wage rate w as given and independent of its choice. In this case, the problem is the usual one in which the choice variables are (x,L). This yields a solution (x^*,L^*) as a function of (p,w,r). If this representative household accounts for $1/H$th of all the households, L^*H is what is usually called the full-employment level of labor services. If $L^* > 0$ and the household has not reached a consumption satiation point, $r + wL^* - px^* = 0$.

Suppose, however, that the prevailing level of employment $\bar{L}$ is less than L^*, or, more precisely, $\bar{L}H < L^*H$. If the household brings L^* of supply to the market, it will not be able to find a buyer for the whole supply. Such an experience suggests that the household should change its strategy. But how? One possible way in which the household may modify its behavior was proposed by Clower in his dual-decision hypothesis: The household simply accepts $\bar{L}$ and offers this amount to the market. That is, the discrepancy $(L^* - \bar{L})H$ is rationed to the party on the long side of the market. Its choice now is, at most, between accepting this $\bar{L}$ and offering some L less than $\bar{L}$. But if its utility function is the usual quasi-concave type, and if $L^* > \bar{L} > 0$, it is easy to see that the household will choose $\bar{L}$ over any amount L less than $\bar{L}$ (Figure 5.1). Having accepted $\bar{L}$, its remaining choice is that of picking an optimal x, which may be denoted

$$\bar{x} = \bar{x}(r + w\bar{L}, p)$$

Clower called the pair (x^*,L^*) the *notional* magnitudes and the pair $(\bar{x},\bar{L})$ the *effective* magnitudes. Obviously what counts in the market is the latter. The basic idea behind this hypothesis is recognition of the manner in which tradings take place in a monetary economy. The owner of real resources must first exchange the resource services for money and then use the proceeds to acquire his desired goods. Because of this separation (both in space and in time) between the selling and buying activities, the second leg of transactions is generally conditioned by the outcome of the first leg. When the first leg fails, so does the second.

Let us turn to the behavior of the representative firm accounting for $1/F$th of the firm sector. According to Keynes's terminology, the preceding $\bar{L}$ was the level of employment induced by the firm's ex-

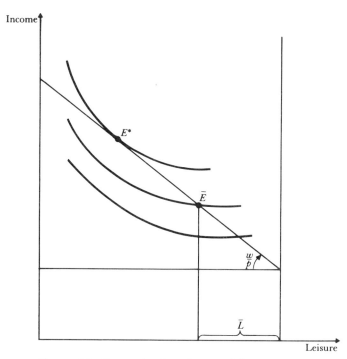

Figure 5.1. Constrained optimum of the household.

pected proceeds. How such an $\bar{L}$ came into being must now be explained. Let the firm's production function be $f(L)$, omitting the colla-
borating input K for simplicity. An individual experiment can be performed to produce the notional demand schedule for labor services
$L^{**}(W/p)$ under the assumption of given p and w and the corresponding notional supply of products $f(L^{**}) \equiv y^{**}$. But suppose,
again, that the quantity demanded of the products at given p and w is
less than y^{**}, say $\bar{y}$. This causes the firm to revise its hiring plan. Let us
postulate the same kind of behavior we assumed for the household.
That is, the firm accepts such $\bar{y}$ (which will indeed be true if the profit
function is quasi-concave). The remaining choice is the amount of
labor to hire. In the present single-output interpretation, this is given
simply as $\hat{L} = f^{-1}(\bar{y})$. It takes some imagination to figure out how the
two sets of decisions are to be brought into equilibrium (i.e., $\bar{L}H = \hat{L}F$,
$\bar{x}H = \bar{y}F$). But if an equilibrium is reached, it may be described as in
Figure 5.2. The downward-sloping curve is the notional demand
function for labor, and the upward-sloping curve is the notional
supply function of labor. These curves are cut off at $L = \bar{L}$, which lies

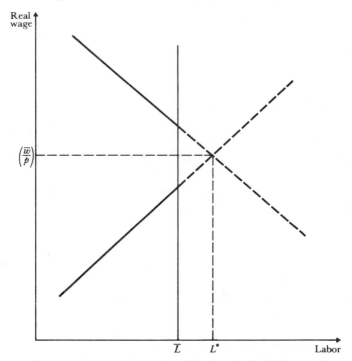

Figure 5.2. Constrained equilibrium in the labor market.

to the left of the full-employment level shown by the intersection of the two curves. The reason for the two notional curves being cut off at $L = \bar{L}$ is obvious. The interpretation of the quantity constraints by the household and the firm is such that the "marginal revenue" drops to zero past this level of L. Note that we do not need this kind of drastic fall in the marginal revenue to produce the desired result. All we need is that the perceived quantity constraints be translated into a difficulty in selling more and hence into a "slope" in the subjective-demand curves. Negishi (1974) adopted such general formulations of the subjective-demand functions. To put the preceding model formally, we have for households ($h = 1,2,...,H$):

$$\underset{\{x_h,L_h\}}{\text{maximize}} \; u_h(x_h,L_h) \quad \text{subject to} \quad \text{(a)} \; wL_h + r_h - px_h \geqq 0$$
$$\text{(b)} \; w - w_h(L_h) = 0$$
$$\text{(c)} \; x_h,L_h \geqq 0 \qquad \text{(H)}$$

and for firms ($f = 1,2,...,F$):

$$\underset{\{L_f\}}{\text{maximize}} \; pf_f(L_f) - wL_f \quad \text{subject to} \quad \text{(a')} \; y_f - f_f(L_f) = 0$$

$$\text{(b')} \; p - p_f(y_f) = 0$$

$$\text{(c')} \; L_f \gtreqqless 0 \qquad\qquad \text{(F)}$$

Here the functions in (b) and (b') represent general subjective-demand functions, of which the functions used by Clower and Barro and Grossman are special cases.

Given the fact that effective quantities rather than notional quantities govern the market, how do we write Walras's law? First, for the household,

$$w\bar{L} + \bar{r} - p\bar{x} = 0$$

and for the firm,

$$p\bar{y} - w\hat{L} - \hat{r} = 0$$

where $\bar{r}$ and $\hat{r}$ are the expected dividends on stocks. Adding the two equations, we get

$$w(\bar{L} - \hat{L}) + p(\bar{y} - \bar{x}) + (\bar{r} - \hat{r}) \equiv 0$$

Here the term $(\bar{r} - \hat{r})$ may be interpreted as an excess supply of firms (stocks). The preceding identity compares with the conventional Walras law:

$$w(L^* - L^{**}) + p(y^{**} - y^*) + (r^* - r^{**}) \equiv 0$$

In a world where effective quantities govern the economy, the conventional Walras law is irrelevant (Clower 1965).

5.3   An evaluation of the dual-decision hypothesis

The aim of the dual-decision hypothesis was to accommodate into the conventional Walrasian general-equilibrium framework such Keynesian difficulties as unemployment. Its key concept is the subjective-demand functions, which reflect the agents' concern about the realization of the first leg of transactions. Being subjective, these functions may vary from one agent to another; hence, at an "equilibrium" in which each agent has attained his (subjective) optimum, prices and wages need not, in general, be uniform (Arrow 1959).

Such differentials in prices and wages are a popular theme in labor economics and industrial organization, and this has produced a large body of literature called search theory and bargaining theory. From the macroeconomic point of view, however, we are more interested in some averages and in the common factors affecting such average behavior of many agents. Traditionally, certain macroeconomic indicators, such as the current employment rate and the current level of effective demand, have been employed. The dual-decision theory follows this tradition.

The implications of the dual-decision theoretical account of Keynes may be summed up as follows:

1. This theory explains unemployment as an imperfectly competitive equilibrium based on the agents' subjective assessments of their market opportunities.
2. Wages and prices are not postulated to be rigid or sticky. Rather, the stickiness is explained as part of the implications of the theory. In the situation described in Figure 5.2, changes in the employment level due to changes in the agents' market assessments need not accompany any changes in p or w.
3. When $\bar{L}$ is imposed on households, their demand functions for products become functions of p and incomes $w\bar{L} + \bar{r}$. This provides a rationale for the Keynesian notion of the consumption function.[1] Likewise, this theory, when applied to firms, leads to Keynes's notion of the aggregate-supply function (Keynes 1936, p. 44).
4. This theory predicts ambiguous effects of wage cuts on employment. In the situation described in Figure 5.2, the actual employment $\bar{L}$ lies to the left of L^*, but not because w is too high. Indeed, a cut in w may simply produce less wage income and less demand for products, which, in turn, may produce a further decline in employment (Keynes 1936, p. 269). To put it another way, unemployment can persist even at the Walrasian equilibrium prices.
5. Market adjustments, if any, will occur in response to effective excess demands (although such adjustment processes were never discussed in the previously cited literature). When $\hat{L} > \bar{L}$, for instance, money wages may rise even though $\bar{L} < L^*$. This does not, however, necessarily have a detrimental effect on employment. At any rate, the dynamics generated by the effective-excess-demand-induced market forces will generally be quite different from those generated by the notional magnitudes. Recall Keynes's multiplier process.

It thus appears that the dual-decision hypothesis does a better job of explaining Keynesian difficulties than its predecessors, which may be broadly described as the rigid-wage theory and the dynamic-disequilibrium theory. According to the rigid-wage theory, the behavioral properties of the model are the same as the neoclassical ones, except for the supply side of labor. Labor sets the money-wage rate at some level and acts as a quantity-taker at this wage rate. There are a number of difficulties with this theory. First, money wages have never been rigid. They fell substantially during the Great Depression. Second, Keynes never believed in such price administrations, despite his emphasis on the importance of money wages (as against real wages) in labor contracts. Third, even though we accept such controls of money wages by labor (on the basis of some rational behavior of labor choosing some optimal combinations of wage bill and employment), the factors affecting the choice of w may be extremely complex. The famous Phillips-curve hypothesis may be thought of as a sophisticated version of this brand of theory (to cope with the first two difficulties). But, as recent empirical studies have suggested, the factors responsible for determination of the location and the shape of the curve are indeed too complex and variable for such a partial relation (and seemingly a reduced-form relation of high order of derivation) to occupy a central place in macroeconomic theory. But the most crucial flaw of this theory seems to lie in the very concept of rigidity or stickiness. We admit that these concepts have always been used intuitively without any attempt at formalization. But if economists had to define it formally, they would do so by taking the ratio of the percentage change in money wages to the percentage rate of flow excess demand for labor services, for, after all, this conforms to the Walrasian tradition. If so, the validity of such a concept rests on the assumption that the labor market actually functions to coordinate between the daily flow of demand and supply of labor services. It is this implicit assumption about the labor market that is objectionable.

The other theory (the dynamic-disequilibrium theory) regards unemployment essentially as a friction. This theory (due to Marshall, Pigou, Patinkin, Leijonhufvud, and others) also accepts the behavioral properties of the neoclassical theory; that is, notional quantities prevail, and wages and prices are potentially flexible. But this theory asserts that attainment of (full-employment) equilibrium takes time because of lack of knowledge of equilibrium prices on the part of the market participants. Unless more can be said of the adjustment dynamics, however, this theory is rather void of content. It is also awkward to try to explain the prolonged high unemployment during the Great Depression as a friction. In this connection, the equilibrium account and the implied dynamic mechanism provided by the dual-decision hypothesis make a lot more sense, or so it seems.

But this is not to say that the dual-decision hypothesis is perfect. As we noted earlier, the hypothesis takes the level of aggregate demand as given and concerns itself entirely with the problems of market coordination. But it does not give us a clue as to how the level of aggregate demand is to be determined in the first place. Nor is it very clear about how the various agents form those subjective-demand functions.

This incompleteness aside, the hypothesis suffers from a serious logical flow. It should be stressed that the problem it addresses itself to is one of information. Within its framework, if every agent could communicate to others what his notional quantities are, the economy would be able to reach the classical full-employment equilibrium. The conventional Walras' law states exactly this. But in the situation envisaged by the hypothesis, whereas an unemployed worker might be able to communicate his L^* to others, he could not register his demand x^*, which is contingent on successful sale of L^*. So the type of "constrained" equilibrium described by the hypothesis must be due to informational barriers. In the Walrasian theory these informational barriers are removed by the fictitious market game called tâtonnement directed by an auctioneer. The dual-decision theorists must therefore have abandoned such a Walrasian device. The absence of an auctioneer was indeed emphasized repeatedly by Leijonhufvud. But once an auctioneer disappears, tradings will take place at "false" prices, markets will not clear, and errors are bound to happen. But where are these errors? Nowhere! Something has gone wrong, and that something is the treatment (or the lack thereof) of stocks.

It is useful at this point to ask why the Walrasian system of general equilibrium is of purely flow nature. The reason must be because there are no durable goods or because durable goods or stocks do not matter. Of these two reasons, the first one can be readily dismissed. This leaves the second. But why do stocks not matter? The answer is that errors, which take the form of unintended increases or decreases in stocks, are ruled out by tâtonnement. The Walrasian theory is the theory of an errorless economy. Unrealistic as it may be, it is logically consistent. Once we allow for errors, however, we must deal with stocks. Keynes's problem (1936, p. 294) was to understand how an economy, starting with some errors, will behave to correct them:

Money in its significant attributes is, above all, a subtle device for linking the present to the future, and we cannot even begin to discuss the effect of changing expectations on current activities except in monetary terms. We cannot get rid of money even by abolishing gold and silver and legal tender instruments. So long as there exists any durable asset, it is capable of possessing monetary attributes and, therefore, of giving rise to the characteristic problems of a monetary economy.

In order to handle this problem properly, one clearly needs a capital-theoretic formulation of individual behavior (e.g., of a firm starting with some "wrong" initial stocks and planning a sequence of corrective measures over time). The mistake of the dual-decision theorists was to try to fit the behavior of an error-stricken economy into the Walrasian tâtonnement framework. For a good explicit example of such an attempt, the reader is referred to an article by Benassy (1975). We shall pursue this point further in the next two chapters.

5.4 Was Keynes a Keynesian?

This question is borrowed from the title of an article by Grossman (1972*a*). The purpose of this section is to comment on a few things Keynes actually wrote in the *General Theory*. First, there is the famous passage in the concluding chapter (Keynes 1936, p. 378) that caused so much grievance to his followers:

Our criticism of the accepted classical theory of economics has consisted not so much in finding logical flaws in its analysis as in pointing out that its taut assumptions are seldom or never satisfied, with the result that it cannot solve the economic problems of the actual world. But if our central controls succeed in establishing an aggregate volume of output corresponding to full employment as nearly as practicable, the classical theory comes into its own again from this point onwards.

Here Keynes sounds as if he was advocating the simple "neoclassical synthesis" view.

Another point that created much confusion was his peculiar stress in Chapter 2 on the equality between the marginal product of labor and the real wage. In the language of the dual-decision theorists, this equality means that firms never perceive quantity constraints in the goods market. The previously mentioned article by Grossman used this fact to conclude that Keynes was not aware of the kind of unifying feature of his own theory as formalized by the dual-decision theorists. The previously mentioned equality goes counter to his notion of the aggregate-supply function and the general tone of the rest of the book. It should have described the state of equilibrium to which a sequence of stock adjustments was expected to converge. Keynes made it even worse by applying this equality to predict the countercyclical pattern of real wages over business fluctuations, which is not supported by the facts.[2]

However, despite these slips by Keynes, and despite Grossman's keen observation, the dual-decision theory is not a substitute for the *General Theory*. The dual-decision theory is an elegant formulation of the behavior of the individuals living in a troubled economy. It explains, fairly convincingly, why an economy, once it has fallen into de-

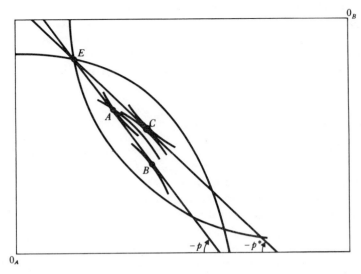

Figure 5.3. Exchange equilibrium at false prices.

pression, may be trapped in such a state. But it does not explain how the depression came into existence in the first place. Nor is it capable of explaining why some depressions are long and deep but others are not. We shall return to this point in Chapter 7.

Appendix

In this chapter we have registered our complaints about the dual-decision theory, especially about the following points: (1) how such a constrained equilibrium can be brought about; (2) what keeps the economy at such a constrained equilibrium other than a (somewhat unbelievable) persistent lack of communication among agents. In a recent article, Laroque (1978) offered an answer to the second question. He showed, in a multicommodity multiperson exchange model, that it is possible for some agents to be better off in such a constrained equilibrium than in a true Walrasian equilibrium. His point can be illustrated very simply by an Edgeworth-Bowley box diagram for the case of two goods and two traders. Let the width of the box in Figure 5.3 be the social total of good X and the height be the social total of good Y. We measure the quantities of agent 1 from the lower left corner and those of agent 2 from the upper right corner of the box. Point E is an arbitrary initial endowment point. Let p^* be the Walrasian equilibrium price and C be the corresponding equilibrium allocation. Now, in the spirit of this chapter, let $p \neq p^*$ be any false price at which tradings take place. Given p, point A is agent 1's optimum, and point B is agent 2's optimum. As Figure 5.3 has been drawn, agent 1 is on the "short side" and agent 2 is on the "long side" of the market. Applying the short-side principle, actually transactions will result in the allocation indicated by point A. At point A, agent 1 is clearly worse off than at C, but agent 2 may very well be better off than at C. Interestingly enough, it is agent 2, on the long side of the market, who is enjoying the constrained equilibrium.

Questions

5.1 Taking x (consumption) as a vector and using the definition of quasi-concave functions, prove that the household described in Section 5.2 will never choose an employment less than $\bar{L}$ when $\bar{L}$ is available.

5.2 It is possible to interpret the constrained-demand model of Clower and Barro and Grossman as a game of one agent against the rest.

(a) Using the notional and the constrained decisions as strategies, construct a plausible payoff matrix for the one agent. What will be his max-min choice?

(b) What is the nature of the full-employment equilibrium (i.e., the intersection of notional choices)? Is it stable?

(c) Interpret the role of a benevolent government in this context.

5.3 (a) Why should real wages move pro-cyclically at all?

(b) Suppose we combine a Phillips curve $[w = w_{-1}(1 - aU)]$ and a markup pricing rule $[p = bw + (1 - b)w_{-1}]$. Here U is the unemployment rate, and $a < 0$ and $1 > b > 0$ are constants. Given the two equations, how do real wages move over cycles of employment?

CHAPTER 6

Savings and investment in Keynesian temporary equilibrium

6.1 The investment function

Thus far we have taken the level of aggregate demand for goods and services as given and considered the problem of market coordination. In this chapter we turn our attention to the determinants of aggregate demand. Because investment demand is going to be our major concern, we must pay attention to asset markets and the state of long-run expectations. Asset markets capture the effects of speculative activities, of changes in the state of liquidity preferences, and of financial policies. The state of long-run expectations is embodied in the marginal efficiency of capital. In what follows we shall present a summary of Keynes's investment theory.

Although our exposition will focus on investment demand, this should not be interpreted to mean that aggregate consumption demand is a stable function of current income and wealth and is largely independent of psychological factors. Keynes made frequent mention of sudden changes in the marginal propensity to consume. Temin (1976) discovered that the fall in income and wealth could explain only 30 percent of the decline in consumption expenditures during the 1929–30 period. More recently, the energy crisis induced a similar sharp decline in consumption. It seems fair to say that our knowledge of consumption behavior needs some improvements.

6.2 The marginal efficiency of capital

The marginal efficiency of capital (MEC) was defined in the *General Theory* as "that rate of discount which would make the present value of the series of annuities given by the returns *expected* from the capital asset *during its life* just equal to its supply price" (Keynes 1936, p. 135). Having found such rates for various types of capital assets, "the greatest of these can then be regarded as the MEC in general" (Keynes 1936, pp. 135–6). Thus the MEC is not the same as the marginal return to be expected in the current period from an additional unit of capital equipment (i.e., the marginal product of capital).

94

Nor is it the same as the realized rate of return over the period on existing capital assets.

Although the notion of the MEC so defined was not novel (it is the same as Fisher's notion of the rate of return over cost, as Keynes himself recognized), Keynes's interpretation of it contained a few interesting features that are worthy of note. First, the returns in question are dollar values and not physical quantities of outputs. Fisher (1930) dealt with a one-commodity world, and hence there was no distinction between physical quantities and dollar values. But Keynes was quite explicit about this distinction. This means that the future conditions of both the product and the factor markets become highly relevant to the determination of the MEC (Keynes 1936, pp. 147–8). Future changes in tastes, technology, and even interest rates (to the extent that they are not incorporated in the current rates) will influence the MEC. Besides, decision-making firms may conceive of the possibility of demand deficiency in future periods (Grossman 1972b).

Second, the MEC is some average rate of return over the entire life of a capital asset. This may be interpreted to mean that the investing firm rules out the possibility of selling its equipments out in the interim (Arrow 1968), a representation of a type of capital-market imperfection, and it accounts for Keynes's clear distinction between speculation and investment (or "enterprise," as he called it on page 158), which would be immaterial if resale markets for capital goods were functioning well. By "speculation," Keynes meant "the activity of forecasting the psychology of the market" (in the next hour in the hope of making capital gains); by "enterprise," he meant "the activity of forecasting the prospective yield of assets over the whole life" (Keynes 1936, p. 158). The type of information speculators are interested in is different from the type of information investors are interested in. This suggests that the long-run expectations formed by investors and the short-term forecasts by speculators are largely independent of each other. If they were really independent in the sense that the short-term expectations had no influence on investment decisions, we would not need to be concerned so much about speculation, for it would amount to nothing more than a random redistribution of wealth among speculators. The truth, however, is that speculation influences investment decisions. For one thing, the management of a company cannot afford to ignore the performance of its share price, for the share price is often taken to reflect the owners' assessment of the competence of the management. In addition to this general psychological pressure, there is a more explicit route through which speculation affects investment. When a company's shares command a high price, the company can raise more capital by issuing additional shares on favorable terms, and this has the same effect as if the company could borrow at a low rate of interest (Keynes 1936, p. 151, footnote 1). (See Tobin's q in Section 6.6.)

6.3   A simple model of investment decisions

As usual, let us first work out a stylized neoclassical investment problem. Consider a firm in a competitive environment producing a certain commodity with a two-factor production function $F(K,L)$ that is assumed to be monotonically increasing, continuous, and concave in $(K,L) > 0$. The firm takes the product price p and money wage w as given. We assume, however, that the price of investment goods, denoted q, depends on how much the firm plans to invest. This last assumption may appear to be inconsistent with the assumption of competition, but it is not. Investment is a flow per unit time. Raising the rate of investment is like siphoning a larger volume of water off a pond per unit time, which will require a more powerful motor even if the surface of the pond is perfectly smooth and still. Similarly, even if materials can be purchased in any amounts at constant prices, the investor will incur an extra cost in order to have them shipped and set up faster. So we write $q = q(I)$ and assume that $C(I) \equiv q(I) \cdot I$ is convex in I. In general, p, w, and q are some prescribed functions of time, but we treat them as constant in our analysis. The problem of the firm is to maximize

$$\int_0^T [pF(K,L) - wL - C(I)]e^{-rt}dt \tag{6.1}$$

subject to

$$K(0) = K_0 > 0 \quad \text{given} \quad [K(T) \geqq 0]$$

$$I \geqq 0, \quad L \geqq 0$$

$$\dot{K} = I - \delta K \quad (\delta > 0)$$

From the Maximum Principle we get the following Kuhn-Tucker conditions:

$$pF_L(K,L) - w \leqq 0, \quad L \geqq 0, \quad [pF_L(K,L) - w]L = 0 \tag{6.2}$$

$$-C'(I) + \lambda \leqq 0, \quad I \geqq 0, \quad [-C'(I) + \lambda]I = 0 \tag{6.3}$$

We denote the solutions of (6.2) and (6.3) by $L(w/p,K)$ and $I(\lambda)$. Then the optimal solution of this problem is described by the continuous functions of time $K^*(t;K_0,r,p,w)$ and $\lambda^*(t;K_0,r,p,w)$ satisfying

$\dot{K}^* = I(\lambda^*) - \delta K^*$

$\dot{\lambda}^* = (r + \delta)\lambda^* - PF_K[K^*, L(w/p, K^*)]$

$K^*(0; K_0, r, p, w) = K_0$

$e^{-rt}\lambda^*(T; K_0, r, p, w) \cdot K^*(T; K_0, r, p, w) = 0 \qquad [\lambda^*(T; K_0, r, p, w) \geqq 0]$

$$[K^*(T; K_0, r, p, w) \geqq 0] \qquad (6.4)$$

Let the maximum value of the sum of discounted profits in (6.1) be $J^*(K_0; r, p, w)$. Then we know that

$$\partial J^*(K_0; r, p, w)/\partial K_0 = \lambda^*(0; K_0, r, p, w) \qquad (6.5)$$

that is, the optimal initial price is the marginal worth of the intial capital stock K_0. This $\lambda^*(0; K_0, r, p, w)$ is thus closely related to Keynes's notion of MEC. Indeed Keynes's MEC is defined as that rate of discount R for which the following equality holds:

$$C'(0) = \lambda^*(0; K_0, R, p, w) \qquad (6.6)$$

We can readily show that $\lambda^*(0; K_0, r, p, w)$ is a monotonically decreasing function of r. Hence, if the interest rate r is less than R,

$$C'(0) = \lambda^*(0; K_0, R, p, w) < \lambda^*(0; K_0, r, p, w) = C'(I^*) \qquad (6.7)$$

with $I^* > 0$, whereas if $R \leqq r$, the inequality is reversed, and $I^* = 0$.

Thus far we have simply given a mathematical expression to Keynes's MEC (1936, p. 135) and everything has looked clear. But Keynes's MEC notion has since met strong criticism, initiated by Lerner (1944, Chapter 25). The problem began when Keynes gave a dubious account of the MEC (1936, p. 136). There Keynes introduced two totally different "schedules" at once and gave the impression that he was confused between stocks and flows. One of the schedules comes from (6.6) or the left-hand equation of (6.7), relating R to the size of the initial stock K_0. Recall that $\lambda^*(0; K_0, R, p, w)$ is a decreasing function of R. Furthermore, it is a decreasing function of K_0. This comes from the concavity of the J^* function with respect to K_0. We differentiate (6.5) one more time with respect to K_0, holding r at R. The locus of (K_0, R) satisfying the preceding equation is therefore a negatively sloped curve in the (K_0, R) space. The other schedule comes from the right-hand equation of (6.7), relating the interest rate r to the rate of investment I^*, which is another downward-sloping curve in the (I^*, r) space. Keynes then said (1936, p. 136)

If there is an increased investment in any given type of capital during any period of time, the marginal efficiency of that type of capital will diminish as the investment in it is increased, partly because the prospective yield will fall

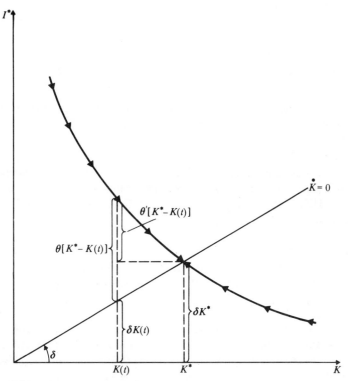

Figure 6.1. Optimal rate of investment.

as the supply of that type of capital is increased [our first schedule], and partly because, as a rule, pressure on the facilities for producing that type of capital will cause its supply price to increase [our second schedule, apart from the difference in the interpretation of the rising cost].

Keynes went on to call the latter schedule (the investment-demand schedule) the schedule of the marginal efficiency of capital (1936, pp. 142, 149). Lerner argued that the MEC schedule should refer to our first schedule and that our second schedule should properly have been called the marginal efficiency of investment (MEI) schedule. Although Lerner's point is well taken, the important fact is that the investment demand is determined by $\lambda^*(0;K_0,r,p,w)$, which measures the contribution of an additional unit of the initial capital stock to the profit sum.

Finally, let us take a brief look at the rationale for the accelerator-type investment theory. For this purpose we take T to be infinitely long in the preceding model. Using the relation $C'(I) = \lambda$ (ignoring corner solutions), we can describe the optimal investment program in the (K,I) space instead of the (K,λ) space (Figure 6.1). Consider any current position $K(t)$. The optimal rate of gross investment $I^*(t)$ corresponding to $K(t)$ consists of two parts. One is the replacement investment $\delta K(t)$, and the other part is net investment. This net-investment part clearly depends on the gap $K^* - K(t)$. Hence, we may write

$$I^*(t) = \delta K(t) + \theta[K^* - K(t)] \qquad (6.8)$$

or, alternatively,

$$I^*(t) = \delta K^* + \theta'[K^* - K(t)] \qquad (6.9)$$

Note, however, that the acceleration coefficients θ and θ' are generally variable.

6.4   Some Keynesian modifications of the investment theory

In this section we shall briefly consider two attempts at introducing some Keynesian features into the investment model. Grossman (1972*b*) introduced deficient demand in the product market. Suppose the product market can take less than what firms want to supply at going prices (or so they believe). Let the quantity constraint imposed on the representative firm be $\bar{y}$. Then its optimal employment of labor is the solution of

$$\bar{y} = F(K,L) \qquad (6.10)$$

Write it as

$$\bar{L} = \bar{L}(\bar{y},K) \qquad (6.11)$$

If we suppose that the firm expects the same constraint to continue forever, the optimal investment program is the solution of the following problem:

$$\text{maximize} \int_0^\infty [p\bar{y} - w\bar{L}(\bar{y},K) - C(I)]e^{-rt}dt \qquad (6.12)$$

subject to

$$K(0) = K_0 > 0 \quad \text{given}$$

$$I \geqq 0$$

$$\dot{K} = I - \delta K$$

Following the same procedure as before, we get

$$I^*(t) = \delta K^* + \theta''[K^* - K(t)] \qquad (6.13)$$

The only difference from the previous neoclassical case is the nature of the target stock K^*, which is now a function of $p\bar{y}$, r, and w. Thus the investment function has the general form

$$I^*(t) = I^*[p\bar{y}, r, w, K(t)] \qquad (6.14)$$

Arrow (1968), on the other hand, stressed the irreversible nature of investment decisions generated by the constraint $I \geqq 0$. In a fluctuating world, firms will expect variable profiles of prices, wages, and investment costs. In such an environment, a firm may find itself in a situation such that

$$-C_t'(0) + \lambda^*(t; K_t, r, \ldots) > 0 \qquad (6.15)$$

A time subscript has been attached to stress the fact that the C function is generally a variable function of time. When this happens, $I^*(t) = 0$. If all the parameters are continuous as functions of time, so will be λ, and (6.15) implies an interval $(t - t_1, t + t_2)$ $(t_1, t_2 > 0)$ in which $I^* = 0$. What (6.15) means is that the contribution of a marginal unit of investment to profits is negative. Hence, were it not for the nonnegativity constraint, the optimal I in such a case would be definitely negative; that is, the firm would like to dispose of a part of existing capital equipment. But, in fact, the firm is prevented from doing so because of the constraint. In this sense, the time interval $(t - t_1, t + t_2)$ is called a "blocked interval," in contrast to a "free interval," in which the nonnegativity constraint is not binding. By the assumed continuity of the time paths of K and λ, free and blocked intervals alternate in time, if they occur at all (Figure 6.2). Blocked intervals are typically experienced during depressed periods. Recognition of blocked intervals thus provided a justification for the so-called nonlinear accelerator models of business cycles of Goodwin and Hicks in the early fifties. This is an important idea. What is unsatisfactory about the conventional accelerator theory of business cycles is that it ignores prices and markets (i.e., ignores the general-equilibrium framework).

6.5   Keynes's theory of interest rates

As is well known, Keynes rejected the traditional theory that the rate of interest is the balancing factor that brings the demand for savings (in the form of new investment forthcoming at a given rate of interest) into equality with the supply of savings that results at that rate of

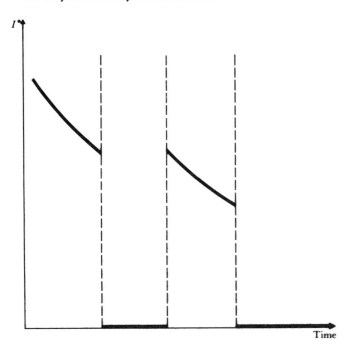

Figure 6.2. Blocked intervals in investment profile.

interest from the community's psychological propensity to save. The psychological time preference of an individual requires two distinct sets of decisions. The first is concerned with that aspect of time preference that Keynes called the propensity to consume, which determines how much of an individual's income he will consume and how much he will reserve in some form of command over future consumption. The second is concerned with the form in which he will hold the command over future consumption, in particular, whether in the form of immediate liquid command (i.e., in money or its equivalent) or in some other forms. If he chooses the latter alternative, he is prepared to part with immediate command for a specified or indefinite period, leaving it to future market conditions to determine on what terms he can, if necessary, convert deferred command over specific goods into immediate command over goods in general. Keynes called this kind of preference over asset forms the *liquidity preference*. More specifically, an individual's liquidity preference is "given by a schedule of the amounts of his resources, valued in terms of money or of wage units, which he will wish to retain in the form of money in different sets of circumstances" (Keynes 1936, p. 166). "The mistake in the accepted theories of the rate of interest," Keynes argued, "lies in their attempting to derive the rate of interest from the first of these two constituents of psychological time preference to the neglect of the second," whereas it is indeed "the reward for parting with liquidity." Thus, "the quantity of money is the other factor, which, in conjunction with liquidity preference, determines the actual rate of interest in given circumstances" (Keynes 1936, pp. 167–8).

Keynes then supplemented his theory of liquidity preference by an explanation of various motives for holding money: (1) the transactions motive; (2) the precautionary motive; (3) the speculative motive. The latter two motives are generated by uncertainty about future events. In the presence of highly organized markets for dealing in debts (i.e., financial markets), the precautionary motive loses much of its significance. (One major institutional change of late has been the popularization of credit cards.) In contrast, the speculative motive becomes more significant in such an environment. "The existence of an organized market gives an opportunity for wide fluctuations in liquidity preference due to the speculative motive" (Keynes 1936, pp. 170–1). Keynes continued on to his well-known remark on the possibility of a liquidity trap (1936, p. 172).

In search of the determinants of investment, Keynes thus introduced interest rates and money, the latter half of the title of his book. In order to complete his theory, we must therefore have a theory of asset choices or of portfolio selection. Although this is the logical place to review the theories of portfolio selection, we shall, because of its bulkiness, postpone the review to a later chapter. Instead, we shall consider a general-equilibrium model of asset markets as expounded by Tobin (1969).

6.6   Tobin's asset-market model

In his exposition, Tobin focused his attention on the capital accounts of economic units, or of sectors of the economy, regarding income variables as tentatively exogenous data for these portfolio decisions. The capital-account model thus has a menu of assets and debts and determines interest rates that clear the set of asset markets given the assumed values of outputs, incomes, and other flows. In other words, Tobin's asset-market model provides a general-equilibrium version of the LM schedule.

Let there be n types of assets, and let the private sector be composed of m sectors, the government being sector $m + 1$. For each type of asset, the sum across m private sectors provides the exogenous supply of the asset. If the asset embodies liabilities of a private sector, its exogenous supply is zero, whereas if the asset represents liabilities of the government sector, its sum across private sectors is what the government has issued. In any case, at any given time the exogenous supplies of the various assets are held or owned by various private sectors. It is assumed that each sector acts competitively in the sense that it is not perceived to have any influence on asset prices. Let i be the index of asset types ($i = 1,2,...,n$) and j be the index of sectors ($j = 1,2,...,m$). Denoting the amount of the ith asset held by the jth sector by f_{ij}, the adding-up property of this general-equilibrium system then implies

$$\sum_{i=1}^{n} \partial f_{ih}/\partial r_k = 0 \qquad (k = 1,...,n) \tag{6.16}$$

$$\sum_{i=1}^{n} \partial f_{ij}/\partial W_j = 1 \qquad (j = 1,...,m) \tag{6.17}$$

where r_k is the rate of return on the kth asset and W_j is the net wealth of the sector j. The same properties clearly hold for the aggregates $f_i \equiv \Sigma_{j=1}^{m} f_{ij}$. There are n such aggregate demands that, in equilibrium, are equal to the respective exogenous supplies. Of these n equations, only $n - 1$ equations can be independent.

As an application of this asset-market general-equilibrium model, consider a simple three-asset economy that has outside money, interest-bearing government debt, and real capital. Let W be the wealth of the entire private sector and Y be income, both measured in commodity units.

$$W = qK + (M + S)/p \tag{6.18}$$

where q is the ratio of the market price of existing capital goods (qp) to the price of currently produced capital goods (p), S is the total monetary value of the government debt, and M is the quantity of outside money. The two prices p and pq can be expected to equal each other in the long run. But in the short run they are allowed to diverge from each other because of the disturbances created by the speculative activities we alluded to earlier.

Assuming that the aggregate-asset-demand functions are functions of Y, W, and real rates of return (r_K,r_M,r_S), and also assuming that they are homogeneous of degree one in Y and W, the asset-market general equilibrium can be expressed as

$$f_K(r_K,r_M,r_S,Y/W)W = qK \tag{6.19}$$

$$f_M(r_K,r_M,r_S,Y/W)W = M/p \tag{6.20}$$

$$f_S(r_K,r_M,r_S,Y/W)W = S/p \tag{6.21}$$

Let R be the MEC, which Tobin interpreted as the average physical rate of return on real capital expected over its lifetime (this is not wrong, since $\int_0^T (pR)e^{-Rt}dt \doteq p$ for a large T). An investor buys a unit of capital (or a share) at a price qp for the return pR. Hence, his rate of return is $r_K = pR/qp = R/q$. We can therefore replace r_K by R/q in (6.19)–(6.21). Two further assumptions are made. One is that the partial derivatives of the f_i ($i = K,M,S$) functions with respect to their own rates of return are positive and all interest cross-effects are negative. The other is that $\partial f_K/\partial(Y/W) = 0$, $\partial f_M/\partial(Y/W) > 0$, and $\partial f_S/\partial(Y/W) < 0$. This latter assumption takes into account the fact that money is needed for transactions purposes, and whenever such a need arises, it is financed by selling bonds. The adding-up property, (6.16) and (6.17), also holds.

Needless to say, not all of the three equations (6.19)–(6.21) are independent; so we may drop equation (6.19). The reduced system is now

$$f_M(R/q, r_M, r_S, Y/W)W = M/p \tag{6.22}$$

$$f_S(R/q, r_M, r_S, Y/W)W = S/p \tag{6.23}$$

Finally, the real rates of return r_M and r_S are related to their nominal returns r'_M and r'_S by

$$r_M = r'_M - e \tag{6.24}$$

$$r_S = r'_S - e \tag{6.25}$$

where e is the expected rate of inflation. Substituting (6.18), (6.24), and (6.25) into (6.22) and (6.23), we get

$$f_M\{R/q, r'_M - e, r'_S - e, Y/[qK + (M + S)/p]\}[qK + (M + S)/p] = M/p \tag{6.26}$$

$$f_S\{R/q, r'_M - e, r'_S - e, Y[qK + (M + S)/p]\}[qK + (M + S)/p] = S/p \tag{6.27}$$

Against these two equations are the ten unknowns: M, S, p, K, q, Y, r'_M, r'_S, e, and R. Although there are many ways of solving this system, a reasonable "short-run" interpretation would be to fix M, S, p, K, Y, r'_M, e, and R and solve (6.26) and (6.27) for the pair (q, r'_S). Tobin reported the results of this comparative-statics exercise (Table 6.1). (He took r_S rather than r'_S as one of the endogenous variables.)

Now, what are the connections between the asset-market general equilibrium and the flow decisions? According to Tobin, the investment demand depends (if on anything) on q, the value of capital assets relative to their replacement cost. The higher is q, the greater will be the investment demand. So we may write $I = I(q)$ [$I'(q) > 0$].

Table 6.1. *Tobin's comparative-statics results*

			Change in					
Effect on	M	S	M (at expense of S)	r'_M	Y	R	p	e
q	+	?	+	−	−	+	−	+
r_S	−	+	−	+	+	?	?	−

It is tempting to identify this q with our previous $\lambda^*(0;K_0,r,...)$. Recalling that our investment decision was based on a comparison between $\lambda^*(0;K_0,R,...)$ and $\lambda^*(0;K_0,r,...)$, or between R and r, and also recalling that $q \equiv R/r_K$, it is clear that there is no essential difference between them, provided that our r be interpreted as r_K. Whether r should represent r_K or r_S is a matter to be decided by business practice. Keynes bundled the two rates into one and called it "the" interest rate. We shall have more to say on this point in Chapter 8.

Tobin concluded his article (1969, p. 29) with the following observation:

According to this approach, the principal way in which financial policies and events affect aggregate demand is by changing the valuations of physical assets relative to their replacement costs. Monetary policies can accomplish such changes, but other exogenous events can too. In addition to the exogenous variables explicitly listed in the illustrative models, changes can occur, and undoubtedly do, in the portfolio preferences – asset demand functions – of the public, the banks, and other sectors. These preferences are based on expectations, estimates of risk, attitudes towards risk, and a host of other factors. In this complex situation, it is not to be expected that the essential impact of monetary policies and other financial events will be easy to measure in the absence of direct observation of the relevant variables (q in the models). There is no reason to think that the impact will be captured in any single exogenous or intermediate variables, whether it is a monetary stock or a market interest rate.

This sums up the stand of Keynesians on monetary issues; one should also read the similar remark made by Keynes (1936, p. 173). These remarks should be read with the opposing monetarist view in mind.[1]

The reader may have noticed that we have made no mention of the IS relation (which would be required to close the model). We have carefully avoided making reference to the IS relation for the reason that such a relation, which represents a flow equilibrium in the goods and services market, is, in all likelihood, a wrong characterization of the error-stricken Keynesian temporary equilibrium. On this and other matters concerning a Keynesian temporary equilibrium, we shall have more to say in the next chapter.

6.7   Interactions between the goods market and asset markets

The preceding model by Tobin demonstrates how asset markets can influence investment and hence the goods market. As a model of temporary equilibrium, it is a fairly complete model. If we are justified in interpreting his assumption of fixed Y as reflecting the relatively slow adjustment of production rates, it is even a sensible causal model. But flow activities affect asset markets too, and some of these consequences are significant even in the very short run. In this section we shall take a brief look at the effect of the goods market on the asset markets.

The aggregate demand for goods in a closed economy is the sum of consumption, investment, and the government's purchase of goods. In symbols,

$$Y^d \equiv C + I + G \tag{6.28}$$

Consumption C and private savings SV, on the other hand, constitute private disposable income, which is total income minus taxes plus transfers from the government. Thus

$$C + SV \equiv Y - TX + TR \tag{6.29}$$

Substituting (6.29) into (6.28), we obtain the following identity:

$$(Y - Y^d) + (I - SV) + (G + TR - TX) \equiv 0 \tag{6.30}$$

In an arbitrary temporary equilibrium, none of these terms needs to be zero. It is these nonzero balances that influence the asset markets. First, the difference $Y - Y^d$ will result in an unintended increase or decrease in inventories. Although this term is zero in the static IS-LM model, the observed high variability in inventory investment suggests that this term is usually nonzero; that is, the goods market does not equilibrate very fast. Needless to say, not all observed inventory investments are due to this term. There may be an intended or planned component of inventory investment. To allow for that, we split total planned investment I into two components, inventory investment I_v and investment in fixed structures and equipments I_f. Denoting the size of the inventory stock by Z, we thus have

$$\dot{Z} = Y - Y^d + I_v \tag{6.31}$$

I_v is probably an increasing function of Y^d and a decreasing function of Z. The inventory stock Z is usually omitted from the list of assets or implicitly treated as part of "capital." But we single it out here for the reason that goods in inventory are, unlike fixed capital goods, relatively salable; i.e., there are fairly well organized regular markets for them. We shall say more on this point in Chapter 7.

Second, we obtain from I_f an equation for the accumulation of fixed capital:[2]

$$\dot{K} = I_f/q - \delta K \tag{6.32}$$

where q is the price of capital relative to goods, as in Tobin's model. Furthermore, the sum of the first two terms in (6.30) represents the ex-post "deficit" of the private sector in the sense that the sector's holdings of money and bonds are to be reduced by that amount. Multiplying by -1, we can write (6.30) as

$$SV - (Y - Y^d) - I = \frac{\dot{M}^d}{p} + \frac{\dot{S}^d}{p} \tag{6.33}$$

where M and S stand for (outside) money and government bonds, respectively.

Third, the term $(G + TR - TX)$ represents the government's budget deficit. Such a deficit must, of course, be financed by an increase in governmental liabilities. Thus

$$G + TR - TX = \frac{\dot{M}}{p} + \frac{\dot{S}}{p} \tag{6.34}$$

or, alternatively,

$$\frac{\dot{M}}{p} = \theta(G + TR - TX) \tag{6.35}$$

$$\frac{\dot{S}}{p} = (1 - \theta)(G + TR - TX) \tag{6.36}$$

where θ is a policy parameter representing the proportion of the deficit financed by increased money supply. When government debts S are already in existence, we must allow for the cost of servicing them by including interest payments in TR. We may express this as

$$TR = TR_0 + r_s S \tag{6.37}$$

The dynamic equations (6.31), (6.32), (6.33), (6.35), (6.36), and (6.37), along with the global constraint (6.30), show how flow activities make their effects felt in the asset markets. These equations remind us of the fact that a temporary equilibrium is in constant flux, with a certain definite direction of motion corresponding to it. By ignoring these dynamic aspects of the situation, static models tend to give us the misleading impression that the government and the monetary authority can act freely today to increase income without having to worry about the consequences of today's action on the future. Experience, of course, confirms that this happy world is unfortunately not real. For one thing, the behavior of the private sector (i.e., consumption and investment decisions) is subject to certain inherent lags, which means that current decisions are to some extent predetermined by past events. Hence, current government policies have only limited effects on current decisions. Second, current policies affect future policy choices by changing the size and composition of the government's liability.

The importance of such dynamic constraints was only recently recognized, but they have now become rather widely discussed in the literature (e.g., Blinder and Solow 1973; Turnovsky 1977). However, most authors tend to refocus their attention on the long-run equilibrium too soon. In the long-run equilibrium, they argue, the government's budget must be in balance. If so,

$$G + TR - TX = 0$$

If we write $TX = tY$, it follows immediately that the government-expenditure multiplier must equal $1/t$. But it must be recognized that such a long-run analysis cannot be of much interest, for the central problem in macroeconomics is to discover the laws of motion that generate the sequence of temporary equilibria over time, which is what we, for better or worse, experience and hence would like to understand.

Questions

6.1 Prove equation (6.5). Also show that $\lambda^*(0;K_0,r,p,w)$ is a monotonically decreasing function of r.

6.2 Referring to equation (6.9), compute an approximate value of θ' from the relevant differential system linearized around the long-run equilibrium point. What does the computed value of θ' depend on? What happens to it if the production function F is homogeneous of degree one in K and L?

6.3 What is Keynesian about Grossman's formulation of the investment function (6.14)?

6.4 Compute an approximate value of θ'' in equation (6.13) and study it.

6.5 Work out a simple investment model with blocked intervals due, for instance, to discontinuous price falls. Explain how expectations of imminent blocked intervals might affect current investment decisions.

6.6 Critically evaluate Jorgenson's model of investment (1963).

6.7 Critically evaluate Witte's model of aggregate investment (1963).

6.8 In the context of the longer-run model discussed in Section 6.7, what would be an appropriate definition of a balanced budget? Should it be $G - TX = 0$ or $G + TR - TX = 0$, where TR includes debt interest?

CHAPTER 7

Markets for stocks in Keynesian temporary equilibrium

7.1 The problem

Despite some slips and inconsistencies, Keynes's *General Theory* remains unsurpassed as a treatise on macroeconomics. No one has been able to produce a description and analysis of a "monetary economy" as vivid as that of Keynes. Although recent developments in temporary-equilibrium theory have improved our understanding of Keynes's theory significantly, there appear to be certain fundamental difficulties in wedding the static, flow-oriented Walrasian general-equilibrium mentality with the dynamic, capital-theoretic spirit of Keynes's theory.

From the standpoint stressing the role of durable goods or stocks, flow equilibrium of the Walrasian type represents, in fact, the very special state of the economy in which all stocks are at their optimal levels. Focusing on such a special state may be a useful strategy for an equilibrium analysis, whose aim it is to study the structure of prices or the relationships between prices that must be in a sustainable state of affairs. The equality between the price of a factor and the value of its marginal product is a typical example of such relationships. But during the process of dynamic adjustments, this equality need not hold. Indeed, a rational firm changing its labor stock in the presence of adjustment costs will find its "imputed" price of labor different from the going wage rate. It follows that such equilibrium relationships are applicable to only a very small subset of all the possible states an economy may occupy at a given point in time.

In order to handle the states that have thus been left out, the Walrasian strategy has been to postulate tâtonnement-type "dynamic" adjustments, the most popular version of which is the Samuelson (1941) rule:

$$\dot{p} = K[D(p) - S(p)] \tag{7.1}$$

where p is the vector of current market prices, $D(p)$ and $S(p)$ are the vectors of market demand and supply, and K is a positive diagonal matrix representing the adjustment speeds of the prices. Although the theory of tâtonnement was originally proposed as a fictitious market game in which participants engage themselves in a sequence of preliminary bids and offers under an auctioneer's direction, it has often been elaborated and used as a representation of realistic dynamics of markets out of equilibrium. The first such attempt was the Hahn-Negishi nontâtonnement model (1962). In a state of disequilibrium, a market participant will typically find himself simultaneously on the "short side" in some markets and on the "long side" in others. If prices do not adjust rapidly, such disequilibria impose additional restrictions on the individual's behavior. The result is the emergence of "actual" or "effective" demand and supply plans as against "target" or "notional" plans. The nontâtonnement model proposes to formulate the market dynamics in terms of actual or effective excess demands. The so-called neo-Keynesian models of disequilibrium can be thought of as refinements along this line. Thus the mechanical "short-side principle" of Hahn and Negishi has been replaced by more general subjective or perceived demand functions by Negishi (1974), by the monetary constraint by Arrow and Hahn (1971, Chapter 14), and by more detailed studies of quantity constraints under the assumption of fixed prices by Drèze (1973) and Benassy (1975).

Although these studies have contributed significantly to our understanding of the meaning and drawbacks of dynamic models like that of equation (7.1), they cannot be said to have improved our knowledge of how prices (and quantities) adjust in reality. What kind of realistic markets do these models claim to represent? In which markets and how often do we go out and come back empty-handed? What disequilibrium and what adjustment speeds? Even if we could find real-world examples of the market disequilibria described in these studies, the behavioral specifications would be arbitrary and might well conflict with the assumption of rationality. If the market participants know that disequilibrium is the fact of life, is it sensible for them to form plans on the basis of current prices only? The answer must be negative, since the gains from trade depend on the entire time paths of prices over the duration of the market period. More important, if the market participants anticipate difficulties in market transactions, they will almost certainly take some protective measures, the most natural being the carrying of inventories of goods. Even Walras (1900) was well aware of the "service d'approvisionnement" of various inventories as the source of demand for stocks, though not in the context of market transactions. Faced with the difficulty of correctly forecasting demand, actual firms typically produce to, and sell out of, inventories.[1] The same is true of firms engaged in various stages of marketing. Any developed economy constantly carries "business inventories" amounting to one-fourth to one-third of its annual gross national product. Even households carry several days' supplies in their cupboards and refrigerators. Whereas theorists in the Walrasian tradition are generally ambivalent about the holding of such stocks, they should recognize it as being caused, at least in part, by the uncertainty and costs related to market transactions. Indeed, market disequilibrium seldom takes the form described by the nontâtonnement-type models (namely, leaving some participants in the cold), thanks precisely to the existence of buffer stocks.

Ignoring stocks in dynamic modeling leads to a number of serious problems. First, it simply contradicts the facts. No developed economy lives from hand to mouth. It is hardly an exaggeration to say that the so-called material progress of modern times has, to a large extent, been a process of devising a variety of durable goods and storage facilities that provide greater flexibility in flow activities, both in time and in variety. In this sense, the economy modeled by the previously mentioned theorists is at least a few centuries behind our time. Second, whereas the availability of various stocks is conducive to better allocation of resources over time, the additional degrees of freedom these stocks provide for flow activities give rise to individual behavior that is qualitatively different from that described by tâtonnement-type models. Inertia and speculation, both of which are made possible by the existence of stocks, are among the main features of the dynamics of modern economies. Therefore, any model aimed at describing realistic dynamics cannot ignore stocks. Third, the dynamic properties of tâtonnement-type models depend crucially on the matrix of adjustment speeds, but flow models are totally incapable of explaining what the adjustment speeds really are. This inability becomes fatal when the list of variables is extended, as in macro models, to include expected variables. We believe, however, that we should be able to impose some a priori restrictions on these adjustment speeds by examining a proper stock-oriented model. Fourth, once stocks are recognized, producers' and consumers' flow decisions at any point in time depend not only on prices but also on their stock levels. In other words, the flow demand and supply functions depend parametrically on stocks. A firm carrying a high level of inventory of produced goods will wish to produce less than if it had a small inventory, ceteris paribus. Likewise, a household's decisions on consumption and factor supplies will depend on its wealth. Interpreting the Walrasian equilibrium as one corresponding to optimum stock levels assessed at static future expectations, and using it as a norm, one of the important determinants of the dynamics of the system must therefore be the actual levels of existing stocks. More specifically, the behavior of the system depends crucially on the "distance" between the existing and the optimal stock levels, namely, the magnitude of "errors" inherited from the past. Failure to recognize stock variables means that the model is applicable only to an "errorless" economy.

Turning now to macro models, we observe that most existing dynamic aggregative models have adhered to the Walrasian tâtonnement-type formulations; see, for example, the work of Lipsey (1960), Nagatani (1969), Solow and Stiglitz (1968), and Tobin (1975). Lipsey's article is on the Phillips curve, which is interpreted as money-wage rates reacting to a disequilibrium in the labor market measured by the rate of unemployment. The other three articles deal with an aggregative economy. Nagatani demonstrated that whether the neoclassical labor-market equilibrium or the Keynesian IS-LM intersection is a better approximation to the actual short-term equilibrium of the economy is a matter to be determined by the relative magnitudes of the money-wage flexibility and the price flexibility. The article by Solow and Stiglitz adds a few sophistications, but their model has essentially the same structure. Both these models postulate tâtonnement-type adjustments and hence are open to the criticisms enumerated earlier. Tobin's article is different from the others in that it aims explicitly at studying the dynamics of an economy in depression. In Tobin's view, Keynesian unemployment is strictly a dynamic disequilibrium phenomenon, in contrast to the equilibrium account popular in the literature. For this purpose he constructed a dynamic model that has the neoclassical full-employment position as the only equilibrium. The fundamental proposition of his article is that the dynamics of an economy far away from the equilibrium can be qualitatively different from that of the same economy operating at or near full employment. Tobin began his article with a tâtonnement-type model and a local stability analysis of it. But, recognizing the inadequacy of such analysis, he moved on to a global analysis, taking the "distance" between the current position and the full-employment position explicitly into account. His conclusion is that mainly because of the weakening of the Keynes effect[2] during depression, a depressed economy tends to move further away from full employment rather than returning to it.

This chapter is inspired by, and builds on, Tobin's article. We side with Tobin in the dynamic interpretation of Keynesian unemployment, but we find his graphic analysis somewhat short of his goal.

What his analysis amounts to is an ingenious extension of an IS-LM model to include the effects of the general price level and of its rate of change on aggregate demand along with adaptive expectations concerning the proportionate rate of price changes. Formally, his Walras-Keynes-Phillips model reads as follows:

$$\dot{Y} = A_y[E(p,x,Y) - Y] \qquad (7.2a)$$

$$\Pi = A_p(Y - Y^*) + x \qquad (7.2b)$$

$$\dot{x} = A_x(\Pi - x) \qquad (7.2c)$$

Equation (7.2a) states that output adjusts in proportion to the size of the excess demand for commodities. E is the aggregate demand in real terms, p is the price level, x is the expected rate of inflation or deflation, and Y is, of course, the aggregate output or real income. In equation (7.2b) Π is the actual proportionate rate of change in p, and Y^* is the given full-employment level of output. This equation states that the actual proportionate change in the price level depends partly on its expected change and partly on the gap between the actual output and the potential output. The gap $Y - Y^*$ is used as a proxy for the gap between the demand price of labor (the marginal product of labor) and the supply price of labor (real wage). Finally, equation (7.2c) is the usual adaptive-expectations formula. His graphic analysis consists in drawing a family of $E = Y$ loci in the (x,p) space for various levels of Y, using equations (7.2b) and (7.2c) to identify the direction of motion $(dp/dx = \dot{p}/\dot{x})^3$ and indicating the possibility that when the economy is far away from full employment, the direction of motion dp/dx may be toward an even lower Y.

Our doubts pertain chiefly to the first two equations of Tobin's model. Why should the flow rate of production adjust itself to the flow demand at all times, and especially when the economy is in serious depression? For a depression is typically a period in which the economy is burdened with stocks of both capital equipment and produced goods that are too large. As Figure 7.1 shows, the Great Depression during the 1930s was characterized by an unusually high level of inventories carried over from the 1920s.

In such a situation it seems quite reasonable that the production rate trails below demand until the inventories have been run down to a level deemed appropriate in light of the prevailing state of expectations. Also, during the Depression, prices and wages fell quite dramatically (Figure 7.2), and so did short-term interest rates (Figure 7.3).[4]

But this decrease in price variables did not seem to have any noti-

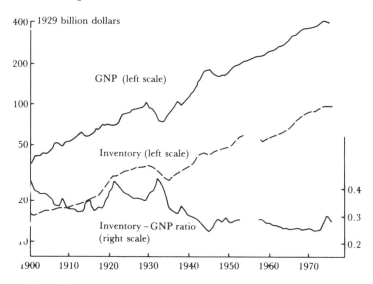

Figure 7.1. Behavior of inventories in the U.S. economy.

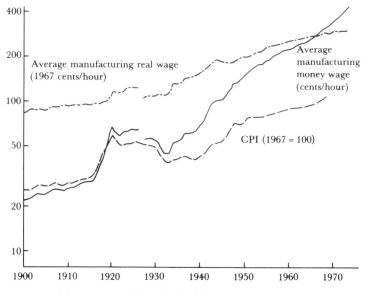

Figure 7.2. Wages and prices in the U.S. economy.

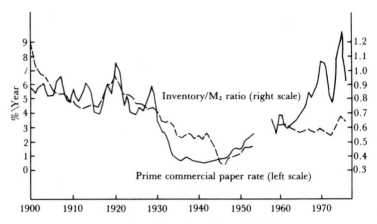

Figure 7.3. Inventories and interest rates in the U.S. economy.

ceable effect on the course of the economy. This type of inertia, apparently caused by the large inventories, seems to have been the most important reason for the extraordinary duration of the Depression. In the light of these considerations, equation (7.2a) cannot be accepted as an adequate representation of the dynamics of production. The second equation describing the dynamics of the general price level is no easier to defend. Tobin interpreted the use of $Y = Y^*$ as a proxy for the gap between the demand price and the supply price of labor, where these prices are measured along what the dual-decision theorists call notional demand and supply curves. But again, firms carrying large labor stocks are unlikely to respond to prices in this way. Furthermore, there is no reason that Π should always adjust by the full amount of changes in x.

The purpose of this chapter is to offer an alternative stock-oriented model suitable for global analysis of macrodynamics. The model has the following features: First, the economy carries a portfolio of stocks, financial and physical. These stocks are always willingly held by the agents in the economy. By use of the term "willingly" we do not mean that actual stocks are always equal to desired or planned stocks but merely that these stocks always command high enough (shadow) prices to make them worthwhile for the owners to keep. In this way, an arbitrary state of the economy is characterized by a stock equilibrium that we call a (Keynesian) temporary equilibrium. All firms produce to stocks, and as will be shown shortly, the inventory of produced goods plays a key role in determining the future level of flow activities. Physical stocks also include the usual physical capital goods and even labor. Treating labor as a stock is in the spirit of the implicit-contract theory of employment. A group of workers on the payroll of a firm have, from the point of view of the firm, the same status as its machines and other equipment. As the shadow price of the capital equipment determines the rate of investment, so the shadow price of the labor stock determines the immediate rate of net hiring or firing. These shadow prices depend on current stock levels and future prospects as well as current prices. Contrary to the implicit assumption in conventional tâtonnement-type models, which ignore the first two sets of factors and consequently place undue emphasis on current prices, it is precisely these ignored sets of factors that play the leading roles in macrodynamics. Because these shadow prices are decreasing functions of the corresponding stock levels, high stock levels (as in the 1930s) imply low shadow prices, which in turn imply a period of low scale of flow activities. Whereas it is true that an increase in the product price or a decrease in the interest rate or wage rate has a favorable effect on these shadow prices, the importance of such price effects is likely to be small when the economy is suffering from a major "error." In any event, in this chapter we shall first formulate and study such a stock-determined temporary-equilibrium model yielding a solution for the price level and interest rates. Some implications of the temporary-equilibrium solution will then be studied and compared with the existing theories of prices and interest rates.

Having fixed the temporary-equilibrium solution, the next stage is to "animate" it to trace out the time path of a sequence of temporary equilibria. The point of accumulation of such a sequence is simply the short-run flow equilibrium of the Walrasian or Keynesian type. The short-run equilibrium is characterized by equality between production and demand and equality between real wages and the marginal product of labor, among others. The stability question to which Keynes addressed himself in the *General Theory* and that Tobin (1975) discussed is now interpreted as the question whether or not the sequence of temporary equilibria will converge to a short-run equilibrium. This, I believe, is the fundamental problem in macroeconomics. But this is also a very complex problem, to which only a partial answer can be given.[5] One fundamental result is that the dynamics of stock models are quite different from those described by flow models. Equation (7.2a) states that the production rate responds to the size of the flow excess demand. If we call this a "proportional" adjustment rule, the dynamics of stock models, which aim at closing the gap between actual and desired stock levels, are described by an "integral" adjustment rule, since stocks are integrals of flow excess supplies. The actual adjustment process toward a short-run equilibrium depends also on the manner in which expectations are formed and policy variables behave. Although a full analysis of this adjustment process is not presented, an attempt will be made to identify what the so-called adjustment speeds really mean.

To summarize, the program of this chapter is as follows: In Section 7.2 we shall present a very simple model of a firm carrying a positive inventory of produced goods, in order to bring out the strategic role played by the inventory. In Section 7.3 we shall present our temporary-equilibrium model, followed by a discussion of the adjustment process toward a short-run equilibrium in Section 7.4. Section 7.5 concludes the chapter with a number of observations on the empirical relevance and other aspects of the present approach.

7.2   The role of stocks: a simple model of a firm

In order to highlight the strategic role played by inventories, we shall engage in a preliminary study of a simple model of a firm carrying an inventory of produced goods. This micro model forms the basis of a temporary-equilibrium analysis to be presented in Section 7.3.

We consider a firm that produces and markets a certain product. The flow rate of sales is denoted by $s(t)$ and the flow rate of production by $y(t)$. $R[s(t)]$ denotes the revenue function and $C[y(t)]$ the (production) cost function. Hereafter we omit the time variable and simply write $s(t) = s, y(t) = y$, etc. We assume that the revenue function is concave in s (i.e., the marginal revenue is nonincreasing) and that the production cost function is strictly convex in y (i.e., the marginal cost is rising). We further assume that the firm's marketing activities give rise to an additional cost that we denote by $D(s,z)$, where z stands for the inventory level. The idea is roughly as follows: The reasons for a firm to hold an inventory include uncertainty of demand, physical costs of marketing the products (e.g., shipping the products from the factory to the sales outlets), loss of goodwill if the firm fails to meet the demand, and high costs associated with accelerated production or the placing of rush orders. Besides these reasons, one central reason that actual firms carry inventories is the difficulty associated with adjustments in factors of production. This last reason is not explicitly recognized in this illustrative model, but it should never be forgotten in applications. Our $D(s,z)$ function is assumed to have the following properties: First, it is convex in the two arguments, with $D_{sz} < 0$. Second, it increases with s; that is, the marketing cost rises with sales for given levels of inventory. Third, for a given level of s, D first declines and then rises with an increase in z. This is because managing any given level of sales with a very low inventory means a high rush-order cost. As the inventory level increases, this component of cost will decline. But carrying an inventory is costly in itself (e.g., warehouse rents, insurance premiums, physical depreciation). This latter component of the cost will increase with z. When these two components are added, we expect a U-shaped curve describing D as a function of z for a given level of s.

The firm's objective is to maximize the discounted sum of profits over an infinitely long horizon:

$$\text{maximize } J \equiv \int_0^\infty [R(s) - C(y) - D(s,z)]e^{-it}dt \qquad (7.3)$$

where i denotes a given positive interest rate. The side constraints are as follows: First, product y must be nonnegative:

$$y \geqq 0 \qquad (7.4)$$

Second, sales s must also be nonnegative:[6]

$$s \geqq 0 \qquad (7.5)$$

Third, the stock level changes according to the difference between production and sales:

$$\dot{z} = y - s \qquad (7.6)$$

Fourth, the initial stock is given at an arbitrary positive level:

$$z(0) = z_0 > 0 \quad \text{given} \qquad (7.7)$$

To facilitate exposition, we assume sufficient smoothness (differentiability) in all the functions employed.

The problem is to find two functions of time y^* and s^* that maximize the J in (7.3). The Hamiltonian function for this problem is given by

$$H(t,z,q,s,y) \equiv e^{-it}[R(s) - C(y) - D(s,z) + q(y - s)] \qquad (7.8)$$

where q is interpreted as the shadow price of the inventory z. Applying the Maximum Principle, we first choose the controllers (y,s) so as to maximize H for given levels of (z,q) and at each t in the interval $[0,\infty)$. The resulting optimal controllers are given by (7.9) and (7.10):

$$y^* = \begin{cases} 0 & \text{if } q \leq C_y(0) \\ y(q) & \text{if } q > C_y(0) \end{cases} \qquad (7.9)$$

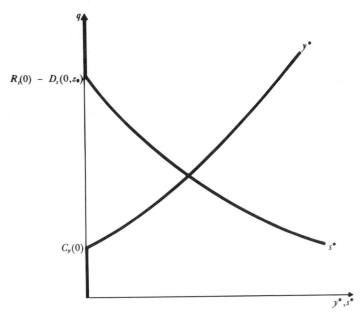

Figure 7.4. Optimal production and sales.

where subscripts denote derivatives and $y(q)$ is the solution of the equation $-C_y(y) + q = 0$, and hence $y_q(q) > 0$ by the convexity of $C(y)$.

$$s^* = \begin{cases} 0 & \text{if} \quad q \geqq \bar{q}(z) \\ s(z,q) & \text{if} \quad q < \bar{q}(z) \end{cases} \tag{7.10}$$

where $\bar{q}(z)$ is the value of q satisfying the equation $R_s(0) - D_s(0,z) = q$ and $s(z,q)$ is the solution of the equation $R_s(s) - D_s(s,z) = q$. By the assumed curvature of the R and D functions, $s(z,q)$ has the properties that $s_z > 0$ and $s_q < 0$. Figure 7.4 illustrates y^* and s^*.

The y^* schedule can be interpreted as the supply curve from the point of view of the production manager who faces the "selling price" q announced by the inventory manager. Likewise, the s^* schedule can be viewed as the demand curve determined by the sales manager and communicated to the inventory manager in response to the price q announced by the latter. In other words, the firm produces to, and sells out of, the inventory.

Although our analysis is not yet complete, the importance of inventories already manifests itself. When the controllers assume interior optima, we have, from (7.9) and (7.10),

$$C_y(y^*) = q = R_s(s^*) - D_s(s^*, z)$$

That is, the marginal revenue (net of marketing cost) and the marginal production cost are equated to each other through q. As is evident from Figure 7.4, an increase in q increases production but decreases sales. More generally, a change in q induces changes in y^* and s^* in opposite directions. The reason is the following: When the optimal program of the firm has been fully determined, the solution generates unique time profiles (z^*, q^*). Denoting the corresponding (maximized) value of the discounted sum of profits in (7.3) by J^*, it is easy to show that

$$\partial J^* / \partial z_0 = q^*(0)$$

Indeed, by the principle of optimality this relation holds at any t in $[0, \infty)$. It is in this sense that q is called the shadow price of z. An increase in q means that the given inventory has become more valuable to the firm, and hence the firm is induced to increase the inventory. How? By increasing production and reducing sales. In the usual flow model, on the other hand, the firm always seeks to equate y to s. This imposes an unduly severe restriction on the firm's choices. As we shall show later, whereas a once-and-for-all increase in the interest rate reduces both y and s in the long run, in accordance with the usual prediction on the basis of the flow-equilibrium model, the immediate effect of the higher interest rate is to lower q and hence to increase the rate of sales. Thus it seems that the predictions provided by flow models concern the long-run effect rather than the "impact effect" of a parametric change. If this is true, then the common practice of economists of using the long-run effect as a predictor of short-run changes is, strictly speaking, not a valid procedure. Such improper use of static- or flow-equilibrium models for short-run predictions constitutes, in our opinion, one of the basic drawbacks of conventional theorizing and especially of macroeconomics.[7] We now move on to the study of the optimal time paths of z and q, which is the task of the inventory manager. If a solution exists to the firm's problem, it is characterized by the following pair of differential equations (7.11) and (7.12) along with the transversality condition (7.13):

$$dz/dt = \partial H^* / \partial(qe^{-it}) \tag{7.11}$$

$$d(qe^{-it})/dt = -\partial H^* / \partial z \tag{7.12}$$

where H^* is the function obtained by replacing (y, s) in (7.8) by (y^*, s^*).

$$\lim_{t \to \infty} e^{-it} q(t) z(t) = 0 \tag{7.13}$$

Table 7.1. *Properties of the optimal solution*

q	y^*	s^*	$\dot{z}$	$\dot{q}$
$\bar{q}(z) \leqq q$	$y(q)$	0	$y(q)$	$iq + D_z(0,z)$
$C_y(0) < q < \bar{q}(z)$	$y(q)$	$s(z,q)$	$y(q) - s(z,q)$	$iq + D_z[s(z,q),z]$
$q \leqq C_y(0)$	0	$s(z,q)$	$-s(s,q)$	$iq + D_z[s(z,q),z]$

Table 7.1 summarizes the information contained in (7.9)–(7.12). The transversality condition (7.13) finally allows us to identify a unique optimal path (z^*,q^*) as the one that converges to the stationary point of the differential system (7.11) and (7.12). This optimal path is depicted by heavy arrows in Figure 7.5. For an arbitrary $z_0 > 0$, a profit-maximizing inventory manager will choose $q^*(0)$ such that the coordinate $[z_0,q^*(0)]$ is on the optimal path (shown by heavy arrows) and stick to it thereafter.[8]

The optimal program, as has just been described, depends on the various parameters of the system. In our model the interest rate is one such parameter. We can further introduce parameters affecting the revenue and cost functions, α and β, say. Doing so, the optimal solution can be written as $y^*(t;i,\alpha\beta)$, $s^*(t;i,\alpha,\beta)$, $z^*(t;i,\alpha,\beta)$, and $q^*(t;i,\alpha,\beta)$. Whenever any of these parameters takes on new values, the optimal path as depicted in Figure 7.5 shifts. In what follows we shall perform a comparative-dynamics analysis on this model of the firm, with special emphasis on the impact effect, because of its relevance to the subsequent analysis of temporary equilibrium. We begin with the effect of a change in the interest rate. Suppose the interest rate undergoes a small once-and-for-all increase from i_0 to i_1 at time 0. How will the optimal program of the firm be affected by it? In particular, what will be the firm's immediate reaction?

In order to study the effects of the interest change, let us first look at the relevant differential system, the middle row from Table 7.1:

$$\dot{z}(t;i) = y[q(t;i)] - s[z(t;i),q(t;i)] \tag{7.14}$$

$$\dot{q}(t;i) = iq(t;i) + D_z\{s[z(t;i),q(t;i)],z(t;i)\} \tag{7.15}$$

where the parameter in question, i, as well as time, has been written out fully for ease of exposition. The system (7.14) and (7.15) is interpreted as representing the optimal motion corresponding to a given value of i; that is, it represents the heavy arrows in Figure 7.5. Assuming that the solution $z(t;i), q(t;i)$ possesses continuous cross-derivatives,

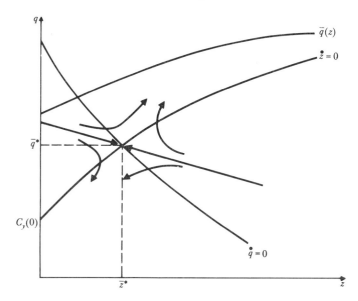

Figure 7.5. Optimal paths of (z,q).

we derive from (7.14) and (7.15) the following variational differential system:

$$\begin{bmatrix} \dot{z}_i \\ \dot{q}_i \end{bmatrix} = \begin{bmatrix} -s_z & y_q - s_q \\ D_{zz} + D_{sz}s_z & i + D_{sz}s_q \end{bmatrix} \begin{bmatrix} z_i \\ q_i \end{bmatrix} + \begin{bmatrix} 0 \\ q \end{bmatrix} \tag{7.16}$$

where $z_i \equiv \partial z(t;i_0)/\partial i$ and $q_i \equiv \partial q(t;i_0)/\partial i$ and all the derivatives in the coefficient matrix are evaluated along the optimal path at $i = i_0$. The sign pattern of the coefficient matrix in (7.16) is determined by the previously mentioned properties of the R and D functions and is given by[9]

$$\begin{bmatrix} - & + \\ + & + \end{bmatrix} \tag{7.17}$$

From (7.16) and (7.17) we first obtain the long-run effects by setting the left-hand side of (7.16) to zero. The results are

$$\bar{z}_i^* = q(y_q - s_q)/J < 0 \tag{7.18}$$

$$q_i^* = qs_z/J < 0 \tag{7.19}$$

where the values on the right-hand sides of (7.18) and (7.19) are all evaluated at $[\bar{z}^*(i_0), \bar{q}^*(i_0)]$ and J is the determinantal value of the coefficient matrix, which, according to (7.17), is negative. Thus the long-run effect of an increase in the interest rate is to reduce the inventory level as well as its shadow price. This means that both production $y(\bar{q}^*)$ and sales $s(\bar{z}^*,\bar{q}^*)$ will fall in the long run.

Next, in order to trace out the effect of the interest increase on the entire optimal path, we employ a graphic analysis similar to that in Chapter 3, taking $z_i = z_i(t;i_0)$ along the horizontal axis and $q_i = q_i(t;i_0)$ along the vertical axis. The pair (z_i,q_i) measures, for each t, the deviation of the optimal path at $i = i_1$ from that at $i = i_0$. We wish to see how such a deviation behaves over time, that is, what kind of a curve it traces out over time in the (z_i,q_i) space. We already know two things about such a curve. First, the results (7.18) and (7.19) show that the curve must terminate in the negative orthant (see the point E in Figure 7.6). Second, at time 0, the stock z_0 is given, and nothing can change it. This means that $z_i(0;i_0) = 0$; that is, the curve must start from a point on the vertical axis. With this much information we go back to the variational system (7.16). Suppose the curve starts from a point above the origin. Then the initial values will be $(0,+)$. Substituting these into (z_i,q_i) in (7.16), we see that $\dot{z} > 0$ and $\dot{q}_i > 0$ at that point. This means that the curve must move into the first orthant. On the other hand, suppose the curve starts from below the origin. Then the initial values will be $(0,-)$, and from (7.16) we have $\dot{z}_i < 0$ and $q_i \gtrless 0$ at that point. Hence the pair of arrows drawn from a point below the origin in Figure 7.6. Similarly, for an initial position $(+,0)$, we have $\dot{z}_i < 0$ and $\dot{q}_i > 0$; and for an initial position $(-,0)$, we have $\dot{z}_i > 0$ and $\dot{q}_i \gtrless 0$. Collecting all these, we conclude that $q_i(0;i_0) < 0$, with the curve as shown in Figure 7.6. One can easily see that if $q_i(0;i_0) > 0$ (i.e., if the curve starts from above the origin), it can never leave the positive orthant and hence can never reach the long-run equilibrium. The fact that the curve stays in the negative orthant means that the optimal path under $i_1(i_1 > i_0)$ has smaller z and q throughout the program than the optimal program under i_0. A smaller q means a lower rate of production for all $t \in [0,\infty)$. What about sales? At $t = 0$, the stock level is given. The impact of a higher interest rate is therefore felt only through q. Because q falls immediately, and because $s_q < 0$, it follows that the rate of sales increases immediately. Such an increase in the rate of sales cannot, of course, be maintained forever. The opposing force coming from smaller stocks will eventually dominate. This is the type of gap that may exist between the long-run effects and the impact effects, and it has, we believe, some important implications for the behavior of prices in the short run.

For the sake of completeness, we report on the comparative dynam-

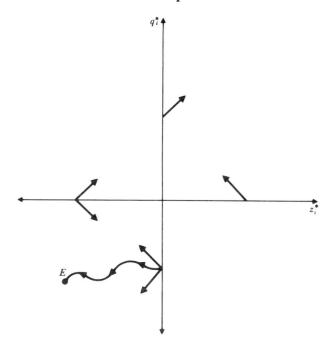

Figure 7.6. Effect of interest rate on $[z^*(t), q^*(t)]$.

ics of the other two parameters. To fix ideas, we assume that an increase in α shifts the entire marginal-revenue curve upward. Because
$R_s(s,\alpha) = D_s(s,z) = q$, we write $s^* = s(z,q,\alpha)$ with $s_\alpha > 0$. Similarly, we
assume that an increase in β shifts the entire marginal-cost curve upward. Because y^* is now the solution of the equation $-_y(y,\beta) + q = 0$,
we write $y^* = y(q,\beta)$, with $y_\beta < 0$. The results are summarized in Figures 7.7 and 7.8. As for the increase in revenue (Figure 7.7), the impact effect on q is unambiguously to raise it. Hence the production
rate rises immediately. Also, because q is higher in the long run, the
production rate will stay higher. In the long run, therefore, the rate
of sales must also increase. But the impact effect on sales is more intri-
cate, because although the increase in α induces the firm to sell more
immediately, the increase in q due to the increase in α works in the opposite direction. The competition between the two, along with the significance of the term D_{sz} (which measures the importance of inventories on the marketing cost), determines the immediate direction of
change in the stock. The long-run effect on the stock also depends on

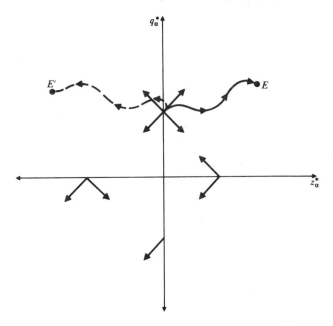

Figure 7.7. The effect of a shift in marginal revenue on $[z^*(t), q^*(t)]$.

the magnitude of D_{sz}. As for the effect of an increase in β (Figure 7.8), we see that the long-run effect is to reduce z and raise q. Indeed, q must rise immediately and stay higher. This means that the impact effect of such a cost increase is to reduce sales. The immediate effect on production again depends on the two opposing forces, one pushing y up (the increase in q) and the other discouraging y (the increase in β).

Finally, a word on the effect of the size of the initial stock, z_0. Such initial values, too, are parameters of the firm's optimization problem, but they are simple ones to deal with. First of all, the value z_0 has no permanent effect; that is, $(\bar{z}^*, \bar{q}^*)$ is unaffected by it. As for the impact effect, we note that under the given curvature of the R, C, and D functions, J^* is concave in z_0. Hence

$$\frac{\partial^2 J^*}{\partial z_0^2} = \frac{\partial q^*(0)}{\partial z_0} < 0$$

This means that an increase in the initial stock level reduces q^* immediately, which in turn implies an increased rate of sales and a reduced rate of production. For a given market demand, this means a fall

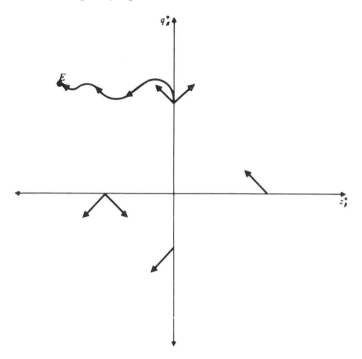

Figure 7.8. The effect of a shift in marginal cost on $[z^*(t),q^*(t)]$.

in the product price. If we denote this relation by $p = p(z)$, with $p_z(z) < 0$, we see that $\dot{p} = -k\dot{z}$, where $k = -p_z(z) > 0$. But because $\dot{z} = y - s$, we have $\dot{p} = k(s - y)$. This relation is formally identical with equation (7.1). But this is only a partial relation. In the macroeconomic context, the determinants of the price level are multiple, as will be shown in Section 7.3.

7.3   The temporary-equilibrium model

The object of this section is to construct a stock-oriented temporary-equilibrium macro model in the spirit of the model presented in Section 7.2 and in combination with the conventional asset-market general-equilibrium theory. We begin with the stocks of physical goods.

We suppose, in accordance with reality, that all the firms in the economy carry inventories of relevant inputs and outputs. In the real world there are, of course, many different outputs and inputs, and

firms are distributed over different stages of commercial activities
from producers to retailers. But we assume, for simplicity, that all the
products are one, and we consider a representative firm that produces and markets this composite commodity to serve $1/N$th of the
economy-wide final demand for the commodity. Besides the commodity inventory, the firm carries two types of inputs, called capital
and labor. Capital is firm-specific so long as investment goods fetch a
positive price, and existing capital goods cannot be resold. The firm's
labor stock can, on the other hand, be altered by hiring and firing.
But because of the nature of typical labor contracts, skills maintenance, and training, these activities are costly. Hence the labor stock is
also, to some extent, firm-specific. In the very short run under investigation, we assume that these input stocks cannot be traded. What
about the commodity stock? This stock has a fairly well organized
market in which producers, wholesalers, retailers, and pure speculators trade among themselves regularly. Commodity exchanges are
examples of such markets. As a first approximation, we postulate that
there is a very well organized market for the commodity stock, so that
the market, through arbitrage, establishes a single price at any given
time. From the point of view of individual firms, this means that they
can choose, through trade and on the basis of a given price and interest rate, those levels of commodity inventories at which the following
equation holds:

$$\dot{q} = iq + D_z[s(z,q),z] \tag{7.20}$$

Equation (7.20) is identical with the one shown in Table 7.1, but its
meaning is considerably different. One major difference is in the interpretation of the price variable q. In the model of Section 7.2, q was
purely an imputed price, but in the present context it is nearer to a
market price. It is indeed the price at which various firms trade stocks
among themselves. If we assume a perfect market in stock trades, q
becomes a market price. If we do not (i.e., if the stocks are not freely
tradable), there remains some imputation problem. Our strategy here
is to take the easier route and identify q with a (wholesale) market
price. Another difference is in the matter of causation. Whereas individual firms take q as given and choose optimal stock levels, it is the
total stock that is given at any point in time. Hence, from the macro
point of view, it is the existing stock that determines the price level.
Also, it is more appropriate in this connection to spell out the final demand to suit a macroanalysis. We propose to replace $s(z,q)$ with an
aggregate-demand function (or $1/N$th thereof), which we assume to

depend on the price level, the real interest rate, the current real income, the current real wealth, and, of course, all the fiscal-policy parameters. Rewriting q more conventionally as p, and capitalizing aggregate quantities, we express equation (7.20) as

$$p(i - x) + D_Z(E,Z) = 0 \qquad (7.21)$$

where x is the expected proportionate rate of change in the price level and E is the real aggregate demand. The function E can be taken to possess the general form

$$E = E(\overset{-}{p},\overset{-}{r},\overset{+}{Y},\overset{+}{W}) \qquad (7.22)$$

where $r \equiv i - x$, Y is the current real income or output, and W is the real private wealth, defined by

$$W = \frac{R}{r} K + \frac{M}{P} + Z \qquad (7.23)$$

In equation (7.23), R/r is "Tobin's q" (Tobin 1969), K is the capital stock, M is the money stock, and Z is, of course, the existing inventory level. Equation (7.21) is an aggregative expression for aggregative equilibrium in the market for stock trades. For a given r and E (at least subjectively by firms), p adjusts to clear this market so that any given existing stocks will be held willingly by the set of firms. We shall have more to say about this market later.

The temporary equilibrium is defined as the pair (p^*,i^*) that satisfies equations (7.21) and (7.24):

$$m\left(\overset{-}{r},\overset{-}{x},\frac{\overset{+}{Y}}{W}\right) W = \frac{M}{P} \qquad (7.24)$$

Equation (7.24) is the simplest form of the demand-for-money function familiar from the work of Tobin (1969). Figure 7.9 depicts the temporary-equilibrium pair (p^*,i^*).

The comparative statics on this temporary-equilibrium model are somewhat tedious but routine. The Jacobian matrix for this problem has the form

$$\begin{bmatrix} r + D_{ZE}(E_p + E_W W_p) & P + D_{ZE}(E_r + E_W W_r) \\ -W_p[1 - m(1 - e)] & m_r W + m(1 - e)W_r \end{bmatrix} \qquad (7.25)$$

where e is the income elasticity of demand for money and is assumed to be between 0 and 1. Its sign pattern is therefore

$$\begin{bmatrix} + & + \\ + & - \end{bmatrix}$$

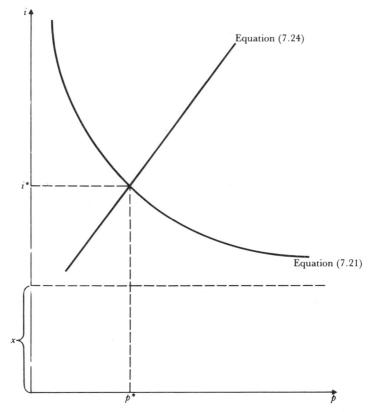

Figure 7.9. Temporary-equilibrium pair (p^*,i^*) relative to given stocks and expectations.

and its determinantal value J' is negative. We then have

$$[J'] \begin{bmatrix} dp \\ di \end{bmatrix} = \begin{bmatrix} -D_{ZZ} - D_{ZE}E_w \\ -m(1-e) \end{bmatrix} dZ + \begin{bmatrix} -D_{ZE}E_Y \\ -me \end{bmatrix} dY$$

$$+ \begin{bmatrix} P + D_{ZE}(E_r + E_wW_r) \\ m_rW - m_xW + m(1-e)W_r \end{bmatrix} dx + \begin{bmatrix} -D_{ZE}E_wW_R \\ -m(1-e)W_R \end{bmatrix} dR$$

$$+ \begin{bmatrix} -D_{ZE}E_w \\ 1 - m(1-e) \end{bmatrix} \frac{dM}{P} + \begin{bmatrix} -D_{ZE}E_G \\ 0 \end{bmatrix} dG \qquad (7.26)$$

where the last parameter G is some factor that stimulates the aggregate demand (e.g., government expenditure). Given the assumptions made earlier, every term except three can be signed offhand. One of the ambiguous terms is the first element appearing in front of

Table 7.2. *Temporary-equilibrium comparative statics*

	Change in					
Effect on	Z	Y	x	R	M	G
p	$-$	?	$+$	?	$+$	$+$
i	?	$+$	$+$	$+$	$-$	$+$

dZ (i.e., $-D_{ZZ} - D_{ZE}E_W$). We take this term to be negative, the justification for which was provided in footnote 9. The other ambiguous term is the second element in front of dx [i.e., $(m_r - m_x)W + m(1 - e)W_r$]. This coefficient, as a whole, measures the effect of an accelerated inflation on the demand for real balances (multiplied by -1). Because the wealth effect and the substitution effect work in opposite directions, no a priori knowledge can be claimed. We tentatively assume this coefficient to be positive.[10] The comparative-statics results are shown in Table 7.2. Each of the three question marks in Table 7.2 reflects a compound effect of two opposing forces and therefore cannot be determined on prior grounds. When Y is allowed to deviate from E and when it is costly to adjust inputs, Y is a measure not of the demand pressure but of the productive capacity.[11] p_Y can therefore be negative. An increase in R means improved future prospects for business (e.g., an expected increase in demand, an expected decrease in production costs). Depending on the source of the expected change and the exact time pattern of the change, firms' evaluations of their inventories may go up or down. Similarly, an increase in Z tightens the money market through the wealth effect. But the collateral fall in p works in the opposite direction. An educated guess would be that $i_Z > 0$. Z is the least liquid of all the marketable assets, an increase in Z at given M is expected to exert some pressure in the money market. Figure 7.3 supports this theory.

Summarizing the preceding results, we arrive at the temporary-equilibrium solution:

$$p^* = p(\overset{-}{Z}, \overset{?}{Y}, \overset{+}{x}, \overset{?}{R}, \overset{+}{M}, \overset{+}{G}) \tag{7.27}$$

$$i^* = i(\overset{?}{Z}, \overset{+}{Y}, \overset{+}{x}, \overset{+}{R}, \overset{-}{M}, \overset{+}{G}) \tag{7.28}$$

As we noted earlier, our notion of temporary equilibrium is quite broad and covers virtually all possible states of the economy at any given time, including those states that have conventionally been treated as "disequilibrium." Apart from various simplifying assumptions employed in our exposition, the pair (p^*, i^*) in equations (7.27) and (7.28) is what we observe at all times. Moreover, despite its extreme generality, our temporary equilibrium is based on a firm choice-theoretic foundation. Finally, our approach stands in sharp contrast to the conventional approach in macroeconomics, according to which one first specifies a flow equilibrium of one's liking and then covers all other disequilibrium states with some intuitive but ad hoc dynamic-adjustment equations. Not surprisingly, these conventional models have generally fared badly. Take, for example, the past studies of prices. There have been proposed versions of the excess-demand hypothesis, Phillips curves, and, of course, the monetarist theory. The excess-demand hypothesis can be interpreted as the $Z \rightarrow p^*$ relation in our model, as we remarked briefly at the end of Section 7.2. The Phillips-curve theory of prices can be identified with an element of the $R \rightarrow p^*$ relation, and the monetarist theory with the $M \rightarrow p^*$ relation. A logarithmic differentiation of equation (7.27) with respect to time will produce all these theories, but only as partial relations. However, the advantages of our approach do not stop at mere generality. It also enables us to relate the "adjustment coefficients" to the forms of the asset-demand functions. But, above all, its merit lies in the recognition of inventories and their effects on the position of the temporary equilibrium. The downward pressure on prices and the (probably) upward pressure on interest rates that the commodity inventories exert represent, no doubt, one of the fundamental relations of macrodynamics.

7.4   From temporary equilibrium to short-run equilibrium[12]

The temporary equilibrium presented in Section 7.3 is a snapshot of an economy with given levels of stocks, a given state of expectations, and even a given level of production. What equations (7.27) and (7.28) determine is the pair (p^*, i^*) that clears the markets for stock trades. The partial derivatives indicated in these equations predict the directions in which the pair (p^*, i^*) is to move in response to changes in the data. In this sense, our temporary-equilibrium analysis corresponds to the "Fundamental Equations" of Keynes's *Treatise* (1930, Volume 1, Chapter 10). One should also see the work of Hicks (1969, Chapter 11) on this point. In other words, the main theme of the temporary-equilibrium analysis is the dynamics of flexible prices to clear the given levels of existing stocks. This does not mean that all prices are assumed flexible. Many prices, and especially factor prices, are constrained by the existing contracts in the very short run under consideration. Wages, rents, and the prices of some intermediate goods must be regarded as rigid. In the model in Section 7.3 we implicitly assumed this to be the case. Thus the cost function $D(E,Z)$, which includes such prices as warehouse rents, insurance premiums, and ordering costs, was assumed to be given. Our $(p*,i*)$ was an equilibrium pair relative to these fixed costs as well as stocks.

In the *General Theory*, Keynes shifted his emphasis from temporary equilibrium to the short-run equilibrium and emphasized the adjustments of flow quantities. The fact that Keynes stressed quantity adjustments has given rise to the interpretation that Keynes assumed rigid prices. But this is not a correct interpretation. The process toward a short-run equilibrium can be thought of as a sequence of temporary equilibria. Writing the set of flexible prices (including interest rates) as P, the set of fixed prices as Q, and the collection of stocks (including fixed capital goods, employment stock, and financial assets in this context) as Z, the economy proceeds as follows: At time 0, a temporary-equilibrium price P_0 is established in the manner described in the previous section. We write this solution as $P_0 = P(Q_0,Z_0)$. At the price P_0, $E(P_0;Q_0,Z_0) \neq Y(P_0;Q_0,Z_0)$ in general; that is, the commodity market does not clear in the usual sense of the term. This results in a change in the commodity inventory and also in changes in the input stocks (although gradual, because of adjustment costs). The sense in which Keynes treated prices as given was that these quantity adjustments are to be made on the basis of the temporary-equilibrium price established a moment ago. But by the time a round of quantity adjustments has been completed, agents observe another temporary-equilibrium price, $P_1 = P(Q_0,Z_1)$, say. Agents then plan another round of quantity adjustments on the basis of the new prices (P_1,Q_0), which leads to yet another temporary-equilibrium price $P_2 = P(Q_0,Z_2)$, and so on. Of course, it is possible that the commodity market will clear at the initial temporary-equilibrium price, so that $E(P_0;Q_0,Z_0') = Y(P_0;Q_0,Z_0')$ at some $Z_0' \neq Z^0$. Although there may be some theoretical interest in studying such a possibility, there is absolutely no justification for it. Prices do change in reality. Even the set of "rigid" prices Q need not remain absolutely rigid, especially when the economy stays long and far out of short-run equilibrium. At any rate, the reasons Keynes deemphasized prices in his short-run analysis seem to have been the following: (1) the previously mentioned fact that quantity adjustments are planned on the basis of temporary-equilibrium prices; (2) the fact that the sequence $\{P_0, P_1, \ldots\}$ does not behave so as simply to close the gap between E and Y but is subject to a complex set of forces; (3) the possibility that the sequence of temporary equilibria may not converge (i.e., the possible instability of the short-run equilibrium).

It may be useful to reflect for a moment on the notion of short-run equilibrium. We have said that a short-run equilibrium is a state in which all the flow demands and supplies are equal. This is not wrong, but it is not sufficient. We may recall Arrow's critical remark (1967) on Samuelson's notion (1955) of the "Neoclassical Synthesis." For the purpose of defining the short-run equilibrium, a good starting point is Keynes's discussion (1930, p. 125) of the society's money income. Adapting his statement slightly, we may define a short-run equilibrium as the level of aggregate demand (which equals production) that, if agents were to open to make new bargains with all the factors of production at the currently prevailing rates of earnings (P, Q), would leave them with no motive either to increase or to decrease their scale of operations. What this means is that the state $E(P_0; Q_0, Z_0') = Y(P_0; Q_0, Z_0')$ at some arbitrary prices (P_0, Q_0) is generally not a short-run equilibrium, even if such a Z_0' exists and is realized. For, in spite of the flow equilibrium, there might be a tendency for some elements of Z to change in one direction or another. In order for such a state to be a short-run equilibrium, we must have $\dot{Z} = 0$ not only for the commodity inventory (which is satisfied automatically by the equality between E and Y) but also for all other stocks such as capital and employment. Fiscal policy, for example, could realize the $E = Y$ equality at an arbitrary price-stock combination, but the result would not generally be a short-run equilibrium. The remaining dynamic forces would destroy the equality at the next instant.

The quantity adjustments as planned by our representative firm can be described by the solution of the following problem:

$$\text{maximize } V \equiv \int_0^\infty e^{-rt}[pE - pvL - A(I) - B(H) - D(E,Z)]dt \quad (7.29)$$

subject to

$$\dot{Z} = Y(K,L) - E \quad (7.30)$$

$$\dot{K} = I - \delta K, \quad I \geqq 0 \quad (7.31)$$

$$\dot{L} = H, \quad H \gtreqless 0 \quad (7.32)$$

$$A(I), A(0) = \bar{A} \geqq 0, \quad A_I(I) > 0, \quad A_{II}(I) > 0 \quad (7.33)$$

$$B(H), B(0) = \bar{B} \geqq 0, \qquad B_H(H) \gtreqless 0 \quad \text{as} \quad H \gtreqless 0, \qquad B_{HH}(H) > 0 \qquad (7.34)$$

$$Z(0) = Z_0 > 0, \qquad K(0) = K_0 > 0, \qquad L(0) = L_0 > 0 \qquad \text{all given} \qquad (7.35)$$

In (7.29), p and i (which appears implicitly in r) are understood to be the current temporary-equilibrium pair. The term pv is the real wage rate evaluated at the current price p. In view of the observed stability of real wages (see Figure 7.2), we assume that the real wage rate v is expected to remain constant. The functions A and B are the adjustment cost functions associated with capital investment I and net hiring and firing H of the labor stock L, respectively. Both functions are assumed convex. We have written them as separate functions, but this is, of course, just a simplifying assumption. The controllers of this problem are (E, I, H). The application of the Maximum Principle to E yields equation (7.21). When the same principle is applied to I and H, it yields functions $I^* = I(q_K)$ and $H^* = H(q_L)$, where q_K and q_L are the co-state variables associated with K and L and are again interpreted as the shadow prices of these stocks. The convexity of the A and B functions implies that I^* and H^* are increasing functions of q_K and q_L, respectively. This fact, though obvious, is quite important. The prices q_K and q_L, being shadow prices, depend on the size of realized "errors" (the current stock levels) and on the expected future conditions of the economy. In order to stimulate investment and employment, these prices must be sufficiently high. In a depressed economy, knowing how to raise the values of these prices is the key to recovery; because these prices are inversely related to the current stocks K and L, the existence of idle capacities works against a smooth recovery from depression. True, a reduction in real wages or interest rates would have some favorable effect on these prices, other things being equal; but when the stock levels are too high and expectations are depressed, such an effect is very unlikely to be strong.

The dynamics of the firm's optimal plans are given by the following system of differential equations:

$$\dot{Z} = Y(K, L) - E(p, x, Y, W) \qquad (7.36)$$

$$\dot{K} = I^* - \delta K \qquad (7.37)$$

$$\dot{L} = H^* \qquad (7.38)$$

$$\dot{I}^* = A_{II}^{-1}[(r + \delta)A_I(I^*) - pY_K] \qquad (7.39)$$

$$\dot{H}^* = B_{HH}^{-1}[rB_H(H^*) + pv - pY_L] \qquad (7.40)$$

along with the temporary-equilibrium solution (7.27) and (7.28), the initial conditions (7.35), and appropriate transversality conditions.

From this system, the short-run equilibrium of the economy can be seen to satisfy

$$Y = E \tag{7.41}$$

$$A_I(\delta K) = \dot{q}_K = \frac{PY_K}{r + \delta} \tag{7.42}$$

$$v = Y_L \tag{7.43}$$

and

$$\dot{p}/p = x \tag{7.44}$$

These are all familiar expressions in macroeconomics. In particular, the equality between Y and E (the IS relation) and the equality between the real wage and the marginal product of labor (the labor-market balance relation) have been established as part of the short-run equilibrium conditions. To these we have added the condition of consistent price expectations.

In order to derive a plausible dynamic aggregative model from the preceding model of an individual firm, a few loose ends must be fixed. These loose ends concern mainly expectational matters. We have thus far assumed that the representative firm knows the exact form of the aggregate-demand function. This is obviously unrealistic. Ideally, we should work with some subjective estimate of the true aggregate-demand function. This means that the firm will be constantly reestimating such a function throughout the adjustment process. Some specification of such a reestimation procedure is called for.[13] Second, the preceding optimal program of the firm has been based on the given values of i and x, where i is the current temporary-equilibrium value. Because there is no reason to beleive that i is going to stay constant or that the price path is going to be given by $p_0 e^{xt}$, constant revisions in the program are again necessary. How to fix these revision rules remains a problem. Besides, one must make some assumptions concerning the behavior of the policy variables. Tangential as they may sound, how one chooses to fix these loose ends is very crucial. It has been well known, for example, that the adjustment equation for the x variable almost completely determines the stability property of the model by itself. It may be that the model is misspecified[14] or that people in the real world react to changes only very slowly.

7.5 Some concluding remarks

The idea expressed in this chapter has grown out of a dissatisfaction with the existing macroeconomic models. The essential problem is not that these models are wrong or yield poor results. On the contrary. There are dozens of macro models, and they are capable of producing practically any result one may wish to hear. Furthermore, macro models have become more and more sophisticated in analytical content. And yet, when it comes to answering the fundamental questions, such as what determines the price level, interest rates, employment, and wages, the existing models have generally been unsuccessful. Too many ad hockeries and too little theorizing may be the reason. Many theorists believe that macroeconomics can be improved by laying better micro foundations. But, in some fundamental sense, macroeconomics is different from microeconomics. Besides, the central questions in macroeconomics are broad questions. It may very well be that such broad questions are best handled by broad methods. What we have stressed in this chapter is one such broad approach.

From an empirical viewpoint, macroeconomic investigations have had a tendency to become a treasure hunt, that is, a search for some stable relationships among aggregates in the fluctuating world. The search has sometimes appeared to be successful. The Phillips curve, the monetary velocity, and the Gibson paradox are examples of such discoveries. But these empirical laws cannot really satisfy us. We do not understand why they should be true. Worse still, they are not robust enough. These relationships tend to shift up and down with the fluctuations of the economy. For them to be useful, it is therefore necessary to identify the factors that cause such shifts. In terms of our temporary-equilibrium solution, the behavior of the price level and the monetary velocity depends on a host of factors. Also, whether the price level and the (nominal) interest rate are to show a positive or a negative correlation depends on the initiating parametric change.

Our basic idea has been to develop a sufficiently weak concept of (temporary) equilibrium that embraces all possible states of the economy, using stocks (especially commodity inventories) as a measure of the "distance" from the conventional flow equilibrium. Once these stocks are properly taken into account, there remains little wonder why, for instance, the U.S. economy in the thirties should have taken the course it actually did.[15]

On the other hand, even if our model were accepted as valid, it would not be very useful for predicting the future course of the economy. There are simply too many unknowns. Perhaps the best we can do is to gain a good empirical knowledge of the equations such as (7.27) and (7.28).[16]

This chapter has been concerned with temporary equilibrium. Taking the IS-LM model of short-run equilibrium as a point of departure, what we have attempted is its extension toward an even shorter run. This is based on our belief that the main feature of developed capitalist economies is the abundance of durable goods, both financial and physical, that important information concerning prices and interest rates can be gained by studying the market for those durable goods, and that through such attempts one can gain better understanding of the models of the short-run equilibrium.

The preceding discussion also has a bearing on the famous debate between Keynes and Hawtrey (1879–1975) over the effects of monetary policy. Whereas Keynes emphasized the monetary effect on long-term investment through something like Tobin's q, Hawtrey focused on a more immediate effect through inventory and production decisions (1950, pp. 427–8). In this sense, our analysis in this chapter should perhaps be called Hawtreyan rather than Keynesian. The Hawtreyan mechanism has the advantage of being more directly measurable and testable than the Keynesian mechanism, which takes a long time and which must go through a complex sequence of events (such as changes in the term structure of interest rates) before a given monetary change makes itself felt in long-term investment.

Another direction in which the IS-LM model may be extended is toward a longer run. This extension should follow the line of argument presented in Section 6.7, where the relevant dynamics are the paths generated by a sequence of short-run equilibria. We shall return to long-run problems in Chapter 13.

Questions

7.1 Indeed, a rational firm changing its labor stock in the presence of adjustment costs will find its "imputed" price of labor different from the going wage rate. Explain this statement. [Hint: equation (7.40).]

7.2 An alternative and more conventional way of capturing the dynamic nature of temporary equilibrium is to introduce various lags into the IS-LM framework, as in the following model:

$$Y = C + I + \bar{G} \tag{7.Q1}$$

$$C = \bar{C} + c(1 - t)Y^* \qquad (1 > c > 0, \quad 1 > t > 0) \tag{7.Q2}$$

$$Y^* = aY + (1 - a)Y_{-1} \qquad (1 > a > 0) \tag{7.Q3}$$

Table 7.3. State of the U.S. economy (1927–34)

Year	Real GNP[a]	Labor input[b]	Prices[c]	Money wages[d]	Commercial paper rate[e]	Baa bond rate[f]	Real government expenditures[g]	Real business inventory[a]	High-powered money[i]	Bank reserves[j]	Deposit/reserve[k]	Deposit/currency[l]	Money supply[m]
1911–13 av.	60,948	71.4	56	0.27	5.45		4,550	19,033	3,350	1,524	8.27	7.13	14,788
1927	97,337	97.2	102	0.54	4.11	5.48	7,890	35,507	7,238	3,287	12.30	10.23	44,384
1928	98,503	97.8	100	0.56	4.85	5.48	8,230	35,509	7,150	3,225	13.00	10.68	45,861
1929	104,436	100.0	100	0.56	5.85	5.90	8,482	35,745	7,102	3,191	13.16	10.74	45,918
1930	95,130	92.7	98	0.55	3.59	5.89	9,435	36,356	6,908	3,227	12.90	11.31	45,303
1931	89,454	83.7	90	0.51	2.64	8.62	9,965	35,626	7,302	3,307	11.67	9.66	42,598
1932	76,403	73.7	80	0.44	2.73	9.30	9,483	33,600	7,788	2,829	10.44	5.95	34,480
1933	74,178	73.5	76	0.44	1.73	7.76	9,415	30,935	7,944	2,995	8.39	5.08	30,087
1934	80,718	75.2	78	0.53	1.02	6.32	10,924	29,153	9,260	4,676	6.09	7.08	33,073

Notes: [a] In 1929 million U.S. dollars. [b] Index: 1929 = 100. [c] CPI: 1929 = 100. [d] Average hourly wages, all manufacturing. [e] Prime commercial paper rate (%/year). [f] Average class corporate bonds by Moody's ratings (%/year). [g] In 1929 million U.S. dollars. [h] Private domestic inventories in 1929 million U.S. dollars. [i] End of June. [j] End of June. [k] Total bank deposits/currency, end of June. [l] Total bank deposits/currency in circulation, end of June. [m] M2, end of June.

$$I = \bar{I} - bi^* + dY^* \qquad (b > 0, \quad d > 0) \tag{7.Q4}$$

$$i^* = fi + (1 - f)i_{-1} \qquad (1 > f > 0) \tag{7.Q5}$$

$$\bar{M}/p = kY - hi \qquad (k > 0, \quad h > 0) \tag{7.Q6}$$

$$p = m[nw + (1 - n)w_{-1}] \qquad (m > 1, \quad 1 > n > 0) \tag{7.Q7}$$

$$w = w_{-1}(1 - rU) \qquad (r > 0) \tag{7.Q8}$$

$$U = (\bar{L} - L)/\bar{L} \tag{7.Q9}$$

$$L = sY^* \qquad (s > 0) \tag{7.Q10}$$

where Y is income, C is consumption, I is investment, and G is government expenditure, all in real terms; i is the interest rate, w is money wages, p is the general price level, and L is employment; the asterisks denote expected magnitudes.

(a) Explain each equation in words.

(b) Show how the model determines the values of Y, i, and p in the short run.

(c) Work out the effects of once-and-for-all changes in $\bar{G}$ and $\bar{M}$ in the short run and in the long run.

(d) How does this model compare with the model presented in this chapter?

7.3 The model used by Feldstein and Auerbach (1978) is as follows in continuous time:

$$\dot{Y} = a(Y^* - Y) \tag{7.Q11}$$

$$Y^* = S + Z^* - Z \tag{7.Q12}$$

$$Z^* = bS + cS^e \tag{7.Q13}$$

$$\dot{S}^e = d(S - S^e) \tag{7.Q14}$$

$$\dot{Z} = Y - S \tag{7.Q15}$$

where Y is actual output, Y^* is desired output, S is actual sales, S^e is expected sales, Z is actual inventory of produced goods, Z^* is desired inventory of produced goods, and a, b, c, and d are positive constants. The model is closed by specifying S. Assuming the simplest demand function $S = sY$, study the dynamics of the model. Write out the stability conditions and interpret them in words.

7.4 Table 7.3 presents a summary of the state of the U.S. economy during the period 1927–34. Critically evaluate the past attempts at modeling and prescribing for this economy.

CHAPTER 8

Capital markets and money

8.1 Capital markets in macroeconomics

Following Keynes's emphasis on the importance of asset markets as the determinants of flow variables, asset-market studies came to constitute an integral part of macroeconomics. Keynes's theory is a dynamic theory, and thus it shares certain basic features with classical dynamics. But there is an important difference between them: Whereas classical theory was a "real" theory revolving around the dynamics of resource supplies and technology, Keynes's aim was the study of a "monetary economy." In so doing, Keynes stressed the following two points: First, advanced economies carry a stock of financial assets much larger than the stock of reproducible physical capital. From the realist point of view, financial assets are of no consequence because they net out to zero in the aggregate. In contrast, Keynes argued that economies with large stocks of financial assets are fundamentally different in behavior from those without them, for it is in these financial-asset markets that savings are converted into investment. Second, the "price" of loans by savers to investors, namely, the money rate of interest, consists mainly of liquidity premium in a monetary economy. By combining these facts, Keynes transformed the realist dynamic theory of the classical school into a monetary dynamic theory. As a consequence, the prospective rate of return on capital, which holds the key to the performance of the economy in both theories, became more dependent on market psychology and future market conditions than on technology and resource constraints. Financial policies are also expected to make their effects felt in the real side of the economy through these asset markets. Monetary policy, for example, is a swapping of one form of government debt for another, and its effect on the economy depends on the manner in which the altered composition of government debt affects various interest rates.

The purpose of this chapter is to study some basic models of financial behavior of households (wealth owners) and investing firms using a well-known theory called the mean-variance (MV) theory of port-

141

folio selection. The MV theory was originally proposed as a theory of demand for money. As such, its significance and limitations and some alternatives are then discussed. The chapter closes with a broad observation on the status of monetary theory in macroeconomics.

8.2   The MV theory: personal equilibrium

Consider a wealth owner who owns a vector $\bar{x} = (\bar{x}_1,...,\bar{x}_n)$ of n assets. Let $p = (p_1,...,p_n)$ be the vector of their current prices. Throughout this chapter, all vectors are defined as column vectors. Transpositions are indicated by primes. Our wealth owner's initial wealth in dollar terms is therefore $A \equiv p'\bar{x}$. We assume that A is positive. The individual can reshuffle his initial wealth and obtain any vector x provided that

$$p'(\bar{x} - x) = 0 \quad \text{or} \quad A - p'x = 0 \tag{8.1}$$

The investor attempts to choose his portfolio x so as to obtain the best result in terms of future (end-of-period) wealth $Q'x$, where $Q = (Q_1,...,Q_n)$ is the vector of the future asset prices. But at the time of his portfolio decision, he does not know Q with certainty. Hence the future value of his portfolio, $W \equiv Q'x$, is a random variable. Given a subjective distribution of Q, W is a function of x. This means that the investor faces the problem of ordering among a set of random variables $W(x)$. The MV theory postulates that the set of random variables is ranked by means of two characteristics: the mean and the variance. This postulate ensures that the ordering is complete, provided, of course, that for the subjective distribution of Q these two moments exist.

Letting $E(Q) = q$ and $E(Q - q)(Q - q)' = S$, the mean of $W(x)$ for a given x becomes

$$M = M(x) = q'x \tag{8.2}$$

and the variance of $W(x)$ becomes

$$V = V(x) = x'Sx \tag{8.3}$$

where S is taken to be a positive definite matrix. The investor's preferences are represented by a utility function of the form

$$u(M,V) \quad (u_M > 0, \quad u_V < 0) \tag{8.4}$$

The negative u_V means that the investor is a risk-averter. Formally, his problem is to maximize $u[M(x),V(x)] \equiv U(x)$ subject to $A - p'x = 0$, which is a familiar problem. In order to bring out some important features of the MV model, however, we proceed in steps.

First, we solve the following subsidiary problem:

For a given level of M, find x that minimizes V (8.5)

The Lagrangian function of this problem may be written as

$$L(x,y_1,y_2) \equiv \tfrac{1}{2}x'Sx + y_1(A - p'x) + y_2(M - q'x) \tag{8.6}$$

Assuming that x is otherwise unconstrained, the necessary conditions for a V-minimizing solution are

$$Sx - y_1p - y_2q = 0 \tag{8.7}$$

$$A - p'x = 0 \tag{8.8}$$

$$M - q'x = 0 \tag{8.9}$$

Premultiplying x' on (8.7) and using (8.8) and (8.9) yields

$$V = y_1A - y_2M = 0 \tag{8.10}$$

On the other hand, solving (8.7) for x,

$$x = S^{-1}(y_1p + y_2q) \tag{8.11}$$

Substituting (8.11) into (8.8) and (8.9) yields

$$A - (p'S^{-1}p)y_1 - (p'X^{-1}q)y_2 = 0 \tag{8.12}$$

$$M - (p'S^{-1}q)y_1 - (q'S^{-1}q)\bar{y}_2 = 0 \tag{8.13}$$

Because the Jacobian determinant associated with (8.12) and (8.13),

$$J \equiv (p'S^{-1}p)(\bar{q}'S^{-1}q) - (p'S^{-1}q)^2 \tag{8.13'}$$

is positive by the Cauchy-Schwartz inequality, these two equations can be solved for y_1 and y_2. Substituting these solutions into (8.10) and rearranging, we get the quadratic function

$$V = \frac{p'S^{-1}p}{J} \left(M - \frac{p'S^{-1}q}{p'S^{-1}p} A \right)^2 + \frac{1}{p'S^{-1}p} A^2 \tag{8.14}$$

which yields the market-opportunity curve between M and V called an "efficient frontier." Alternatively, if we use the standard deviation σ instead of variance as the measure of risk, the efficient frontier becomes a hyperbola with asymptotes

$$M = \frac{p'S^{-1}q}{p'S^{-1}p} A \pm \left(\frac{J}{p'S^{-1}p} \right)^{1/2} \sigma \tag{8.15}$$

Of particular interest is the case in which one of the assets is riskless. Let the nth asset be this riskless asset. Then S becomes singular. So we assume the first $(n - 1) \times (n - 1)$ submatrix S of S is positive definite. We shall use underbars to denote the corresponding $(n - 1)$ subvectors. In this case we have the Lagrangian function

$$L'(x, y_1, y_2) \equiv \tfrac{1}{2}\underline{x}'\underline{S}\underline{x} + y_1(A - \underline{p}'x) + y_2(M - \underline{q}'x) \tag{8.6'}$$

and the following parallel results:

$$\underline{S}\underline{x} - y_1\underline{p} - y_2\underline{q} = 0 \tag{8.7'}$$

$$y_1 p_n + y_2 q_n = 0 \tag{8.7''}$$

$$A \quad - p'x = A - \underline{p}'\underline{x} - p_n x_n = 0 \tag{8.8'}$$

$$M - q'x = M - \underline{q}'\underline{x} - q_n x_n = 0 \tag{8.9'}$$

$$V \quad - y_2(\underline{q} - r_n\underline{p})'x = 0 \qquad r_n \equiv q_n/p_n \tag{8.10'}$$

$$\underline{x} \quad = \underline{S}^{-1}y_2(\underline{q} - \underline{p}r_n) \tag{8.11'}$$

Eliminating x_n from (8.8') and (8.9'), we get

$$M - r_n A = (\underline{q}' - \underline{p}'r_n)\underline{x} \tag{8.16}$$

which, on substitution from (8.11'), yields

$$y_2 = (M - r_n A)/(m'\underline{S}^{-1}m) \tag{8.17}$$

where $m \equiv (\underline{q} - \underline{p}r_n)$. Substituting the last two expressions into (8.10') finally gives the expression for the efficient frontier as

$$V = (M - r_n A)^2/(m'\underline{S}^{-1}m) \tag{8.14'}$$

or

$$M = r_n A + \Pi\sigma \tag{8.15'}$$

where $\Pi = (m'\underline{S}^{-1}m)^{1/2}$. Equation (8.15') is a straight line in the $\sigma - M$ space.

Thus far we have ignored possible nonnegativity constraints on x. If x is constrained to be nonnegative (no short sales), the efficient frontier (8.15') cannot extend indefinitely. In order to raise M beyond a certain level, the safe asset must be given up. Beyond such a point, the portfolio consists only of the $n - 1$ risky assets. It can also be shown that in order for the total investment in the risky assets to be positive, M must exceed $r_n A$, the sure rate of return the investor can earn on his investment.

A typical efficient frontier is shown by the curve BCD in Figure 8.1. The portion BC is linear, meaning that it represents portfolios with positive amounts of the riskless asset. The curve portion CD represents portfolios with only risky assets.

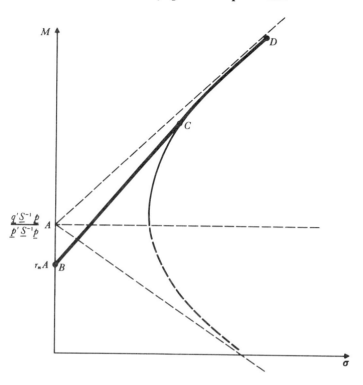

Figure 8.1. Efficient frontier for portfolio selection.

Having obtained the efficient frontier, the second step is to pick a point on it so that $u(M,\sigma)$ becomes maximal. If the investor is a "diversifier," that is, if his indifference curves are convex below, his optimal solution tends to be characterized by a mixture of different types of assets.

The chief reason the MV model has been so popular as an asset market model in both theoretical and empirical studies is its operationality. As can be seen, the model yields an explicit solution for x along an efficient frontier. Moreover, when a riskless asset exists and is held in positive amounts (i.e., along the linear section of the efficient frontier), it can be shown (and left for the reader's exercise) that the relative quantities of the risky assets held in the portfolio are constant (depending only on m and $\underline{S}$, but independent of the investor's tastes u). In this sense the risky assets are aggregatable into one along the linear section of the efficient frontier. This fact is known as the separation theorem in the portfolio literature.

8.3   The MV theory: market equilibrium

In this section[1] we shall study an asset-market general equilibrium in which a set of investors engage themselves in competitive trading of assets. In order to facilitate the analysis, a number of simplifying assumptions are made. First, all investors are single-period MV maximizers. Second, they are all assumed to be diversifiers. Third, there exists a riskless asset (we continue to take the nth asset as the riskless asset). Fourth, all investors have identical subjective probabilities concerning future asset prices. Fifth, short sales are freely allowed. The last three assumptions ensure that all the investors face linear frontiers and that the slopes of these frontiers are all the same. Sixth, each investor has a given endowment of assets, and the social endowment of each asset is fixed. That is, the model is a pure exchange model. Finally, we assume that an equilibrium exists in this competitive exchange economy.

The individual h ($h = 1,...,H$) maximizes $u^h(M_h,\sigma_h)$ subject to his budget constraint $p'(\bar{x}_h - x_h) = 0$. Writing the Lagrangian function as

$$L^h \equiv u^h[q'x_h,(\underline{x}_h'S\underline{x}_h)^{1/2}] + y_h p'(\bar{x}_h - x_h)$$

and carrying out the maximization, we get the following first-order conditions:

$$p'(\bar{x}_h - x_h) = 0 \tag{8.18}$$

$$u_1^h \underline{q} + u_2^h \underline{S}\underline{x}_h/\sigma_h - y_h \underline{p} = 0 \tag{8.19}$$

$$u_1^h q_n - y_h p_n = 0 \quad \text{or} \quad u_1^h r_n - y_h = 0 \tag{8.20}$$

Substituting (8.20) into (8.19) and rearranging, we find

$$R_h(\underline{q} - r_n \underline{p}) + \underline{S}\underline{x}_h = 0 \tag{8.21}$$

where $R_h \equiv u_1^h \sigma_h/u_2^h < 0$. Summing over h and using the equilibrium conditions $\Sigma_h x_h = \bar{X}$, we obtain

$$\underline{S}\bar{\underline{X}} = R \cdot (r_n \underline{p} - \underline{q}), \qquad R \equiv \sum_h R_h \tag{8.22}$$

Thus, if we can determine the value of R, we will have solved for an equilibrium-price vector as

$$m^* = \underline{q} - r_n \underline{p}^* = -(1/R^*)\underline{S}\bar{\underline{X}} \tag{8.23}$$

In order to get some mileage, let us assume that all the investors have identical utility functions, and this common utility function has the property that

$$-u_2/u_1 = k(\sigma) \tag{8.24}$$

where $k(\sigma)$ is a continuous and increasing function of σ with $\lim_{\sigma \to 0} k(\sigma) = 0$.[2] The power of these assumptions is as follows: From the assumption of identical probabilities, each individual equates his MRS, $-u_2^h/u_1^h$, to Π. What (8.24) does is ensure that all the investors purchase the same amount of σ regardless of wealth sizes. Letting σ be this common value, R can be written as

$$R = -H\sigma/k(\sigma) \tag{8.25}$$

Alternatively, using the relation $\Pi = k(\sigma)$,

$$R = -Hk^{-1}(\Pi)/\Pi \tag{8.25'}$$

In equilibrium, therefore, we have, from (8.23),

$$m^* = \frac{\Pi^*}{k^{-1}(\Pi^*)} \cdot \frac{S\bar{X}}{H} \tag{8.26}$$

where, of course,

$$\Pi^* = (m^{*\prime} \underline{S}^{-1} m^*)^{1/2} \tag{8.27}$$

The last two equations implicitly determine an equilibrium-price vector m^*.

In order to study the properties of the equilibrium, we substitute (8.26) into (8.27) and obtain

$$\Pi^* = k\left(\frac{(\bar{X}'\underline{S}\bar{X})^{1/2}}{H}\right) = k[(\bar{x}'\underline{S}\bar{x})^{1/2}] = k(\bar{\sigma}) \tag{8.28}$$

where $\bar{x} = \bar{X}/H$ is the vector of average per-capita assets and $\bar{\sigma} \equiv (\bar{x}'\underline{S}\bar{x})^{1/2}$. Equation (8.28) states that the cost (price) of risk aversion Π^*, which is the common slope of individual efficient frontiers, depends positively on the per-capita asset variance $\bar{x}'\underline{S}\bar{x}$. We say that the risky assets are "positively risky" if $\underline{S}\bar{x}$ is a positive vector. Under the assumption of this positive riskiness, it follows from (8.28) that

$$\partial \Pi^*/\partial \bar{X}_i > 0 \quad \text{and} \quad \partial \Pi^*/\partial r_i = 0 \quad \text{for all } i \quad (\partial \Pi^*/\partial H < 0)$$

$$\partial \Pi^*/\partial \sigma_{ij} > 0 \quad \text{for all } i,j \tag{8.29}$$

On the other hand, substituting (8.28) into (8.26), we obtain

$$m^* = \frac{k(\bar{\sigma})}{\bar{\sigma}} \underline{S}\bar{x} \tag{8.30}$$

the ith component of which is

$$m_i^* = \frac{k(\bar{\sigma})}{\bar{\sigma}} \left(\sum_j \sigma_{ij}\bar{x}_j\right) \tag{8.30'}$$

It turns out that the curvature of the k function matters for determinate comparative-statics results on m^*. If it is convex, the effects of changes in the endowments ($\bar{X}_j$ values) and in σ_{ij} values on m^* are determinate when combined with the assumption of positive riskiness. Under the two assumptions, we obtain

$$\partial m_i^*/\partial H < 0 \quad \text{for all } i, \quad \partial m_i^*/\partial \bar{x}_j > 0 \quad \text{if } \sigma_{ij} \geq 0 \quad \text{for all } i,j$$
$$\partial m_i^*/\partial \sigma_{jk} > 0 \quad \text{for all } i,j,k \tag{8.31}$$

We shall conclude this section with a few remarks. First, equation (8.26) shows that if the risky assets are positively risky, then $m^* > 0$; that is, $r_j^* \equiv q_j/p_j^* > r_n$ for all $j = 1,2,\ldots,(n-1)$. The converse statement is also true, at least in the special model considered here, in the sense that if any element of $\underline{S}\bar{x}$ is negative, this implies the negativity of the corresponding element of m^*. To the extent that we observe a positive m^* in the real world, the assumption of positive riskiness is thus justified. Second, m^* declines with an increase in the number of investors H and approaches zero (as a vector) as H goes to infinity. An increase in H for given social totals of risky assets means a decline in the average size of investors. This result indicates that the importance of risk diminishes as more of smaller investors participate in the market. Third, under the assumption of identical probabilities and utilities, everyone holds a certain given percentage of the social totals of all the risky assets. If one individual holds h percent of every risky asset, another individual holds h' percent of every risky asset, and so on. This is a direct consequence of the separation theorem. Hence, given positive social totals of risky assets and given positive individual wealths, no one will go short. Fourth, the special utility function we assumed earlier [equation (8.24)] is not a very interesting one from the point of view of monetary theory. If we interpret the riskless asset as money, a pure increase in its supply does not have any impact on the prices of the risky assets, provided r_n remains unchanged. A more interesting class of utility functions is one in which the MRS, $-u^2/u^1$, depends on both M and σ. But it is quite difficult to find a general and yet operational class of utility functions in this context. Even Cobb-Douglas functions present some difficulties.

8.4   The cost of capital and the optimal capital structure of the firm

In the model of the investing firm in Chapter 6, we treated the discount rate r as given. This was perfectly legitimate in a world of certainty. But in a world of uncertainty, where wealth owners have aversion to risk, the question arises what the appropriate discount rate should be for an investing firm. There is a related question: Given that the firm has several alternative ways of financing a given investment project (e.g., issuing of bonds and new shares), can the firm minimize the cost of capital by choosing a proper combination of debt and equity? In this section we shall apply the MV model presented earlier to answer these questions. This study also extends the analysis of Section 8.3 to accommodate the supply behavior of financial assets.

For ease of illustration, we shall employ a very simple utility function of the form

$$U(M,\sigma) = aM - \frac{b}{2} \sigma^2 \qquad (8.32)$$

for all wealth owners. Given this special utility function and the assumption of common probabilistic beliefs, the equilibrium-price vector p^* can easily be shown to be

$$\underline{P}^* = \frac{1}{r_n} (\underline{q} - h\underline{S}\underline{\bar{X}}) \qquad (8.33)$$

where $h \equiv H(a/b)$. Define the market return on risky assets as

$$R_m \equiv \underline{Q}'\underline{\bar{X}}/\underline{P}^{*\prime}\underline{\bar{X}} \qquad (8.34)$$

Using (8.33), (8.34) can be rewritten as

$$E(R_m) - r_n = \frac{hE(R_m)}{\underline{q}'\underline{\bar{X}}} \underline{\bar{X}}'\underline{S}\underline{\bar{X}}$$

$$= \frac{h}{\underline{P}^{*\prime}\underline{\bar{X}}} \mathrm{var}(\underline{Q}'\underline{\bar{X}})$$

$$= h(\underline{P}^{*\prime}\underline{\bar{X}})\mathrm{var}(R_m) \qquad (8.35)$$

Next we choose an arbitrary risky asset, denote its gross return $R_j \equiv Q_j/P_j^*$, and perform a similar operation. The end result is

$$E(R_j) - r_n = h(\underline{P}^{*\prime}\underline{\bar{X}})\mathrm{cov}(R_j,R_m) \qquad (8.36)$$

Combining (8.35) and (8.36), we arrive at the fundamental capital-asset pricing model (CAPM) formula:

$$E(R_j) - r_n = \mu \, \mathrm{cov}(R_j,R_m) \qquad (8.37)$$

where μ is a positive number given by $\mu = [E(R_m) - r_n]/\mathrm{var}(R_m)$, which is a constant parameter to a competitive firm. This CAPM formula can be depicted as in Figure 8.2. This line will be referred to as the *market line*.

With this preparation, let us return to the problem faced by an in-

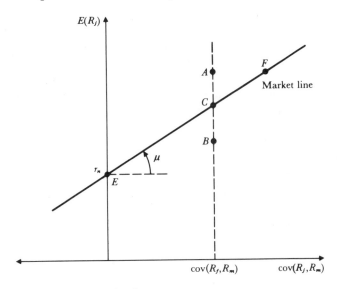

Figure 8.2. The market line.

vesting firm. Equation (8.37) holds for an arbitrary risky asset and, in particular, for the shares of the firm under consideration. We shall call them asset f. Given the nature of the industry to which it belongs and other individual characteristics of the firm, $\text{cov}(R_f,R_m)$ will be determined. Its intersection with the market line, point C in Figure 8.2, then determines the expected rate of return on the firm's shares. In other words, the firm's shares must command a price P_f^* such that its expected rate of return must lie on the market line at C in asset-market general equilibrium. Indeed, the market line shows the equilibrium expected rate of return on each risky asset in the market.

Let us now suppose that the firm's shares were at point C before it undertook the investment project in question. Such an investment project is itself a risky asset and therefore can be depicted by a point in Figure 8.2. If the investment project causes a marginal increase in the scale of the firm's activities, the project can be thought of as having the same $\text{cov}(R_f,R_m)$ as before. This does not mean, however, that the expected rate of return from the investment project is that shown by point C; it will generally be either above or below point C. If the expected rate of return on the investment is higher than that of the existing shares, such as that shown by point A, the firm should go ahead with the project, for the share price will rise with the investment in the process of pulling point A down to point C. If, on the other hand, the expected rate of return on the investment is below that shown by point C, the carrying out of the project will result in a fall in the firm's share price. To sum up: The firm should proceed with an investment project only if its expected rate of return exceeds that of point C. In this sense, point C tells us what the appropriate discount rate or the cost of capital should be in a world of uncertainty. As Figure 8.2 shows, this rate is generally different from the risk-free rate r_n, with the difference depending crucially on $\text{cov}(R_f, R_m)$.

Let us now turn to the financial side of the firm's investment decision. Suppose the firm has decided, in the manner described earlier, that a given investment project is worth carrying out. The question we ask is how the project should be financed, that is, whether or not the firm can increase the share price or reduce the cost of capital by choosing an appropriate composition of D and S. If the firm can, this implies that there exists an optimal capital structure for the firm in that it maximizes the share price and that the firm can manipulate both the asset and liability sides to achieve its goal. Indeed, such is the belief that has long been held by many business managers. However, in a well-known article, Modigliani and Miller (1958) showed that under the assumptions of competitive capital markets there is no such thing as an optimal capital structure for the firm; that is, the firm cannot affect the cost of capital by choosing between debts and shares. This is the result known as the Modigliani-Miller (MM) theorem. Their argument may be summarized as follows: Consider two firms with identical probabilistic streams of operating profits (i.e., profits before deducting interest costs). One firm relies entirely on S for its funds, whereas the other firm relies partly on D. Call the former firm U and the latter firm L, and denote their firm values by V_U and V_L, respectively. Let the common operating profits be X. Now take an investor who owns a fraction α of firm U's shares S_U. The sum he has invested in these shares is αV_U, and the return on this investment is αX. On the other hand, an investor who owns a fraction α of firm L's shares S_L and the same fraction α of firm L's debts D_L has invested the sum $\alpha(S_L + D_L) \equiv \alpha V_L$ and is entitled to a return $\alpha(X - rD_L) + \alpha rD_L = \alpha X$. In other words, these two investments promise the same return. By the assumptions of competitive capital markets, investors can substitute freely among different assets. As a result of arbitrage operations by investors, the values V_U and V_L will quickly be brought into equality in the asset markets. This is the first part of the MM theorem.

The second half of the MM theorem states that whether the carrying out of a given investment project raises or lowers the current value of the shares of the firm depends solely on the value of the firm after investment and not on how it is financed. Let the value of the firm before investment be $V_0 = P_0 S_0 + D_0$, and suppose that the cost of investment $C(I)$ is financed by a combination of S and D such that

$$C(I) = P_0 \Delta S + \Delta D$$

Now the value of the firm after investment may be written as

$$V_1 = (P_0 + \Delta P)(S_0 + \Delta S) + (D_0 + \Delta D)$$

From these three equations, one has

$$\Delta P(S_0 + \Delta S) = V_1 - V_0 - C(I) \tag{8.38}$$

Equation (8.38) shows that whether or not the present shareholders gain from investment (i.e., $\Delta P \gtreqless 0$) depends only on whether or not the postinvestment value V_1 exceeds the preinvestment value V_0 plus the cost of investment. But the latter condition is completely determined by the characteristics of the investment project under consideration. In terms of Figure 8.2, what this means is the following: Levering action by the firm partitions the total net revenue from investment into two parts; that is, it produces two different financial assets. If point C indicates the expected rate of return on the shares of the initially unlevered firm, a levering operation by the firm produces two assets, one yielding r and the other yielding $(X - rD)/S$. If we ignore default risks on bonds for the moment, $r = r_n$, and the bonds will be represented by point E. The firm's shares with such leverage are now more risky, which calls for an increase in its expected rate of return. The firm's shares after the leverage are shown by point F. The cost of capital relevant to the investment project is an appropriate weighted average of the bonds and shares. The thrust of the MM theorem is that the weighted average remains at point C.

The MM theorem has since met a few criticisms. One of these asserts that in the presence of corporate income taxes, the theorem is invalid. According to the existing tax laws, interests paid on borrowed funds are allowed to be costed, whereas dividends are not. Such a differential in treatment between interest and dividend payments should destroy the firm's indifference between the two methods of financing. This argument, however, lacks a proper general-equilibrium consideration. If D were indeed preferable to S for the firm, all firms would wish to switch to D. The consequence of that would be a sharp drop in bond prices and a sharp increase in share prices, as indicated by equation (8.33). These price changes should be such that the bias caused by the tax system is completely eliminated. Another criticism has stressed the possibility of bankruptcies of the firm. As the firm increases leverage, the proportion of fixed costs to be paid out of random net revenue rises, and this increases the probability that rD will exceed X. The firm will then become insolvent. It is the concern over such a danger that weighs against the apparent advantage of debt financing. In other words, this criticism asserts that there exists an optimal capital structure, the MM theorem notwithstanding. But this criticism suffers from the difficulty raised earlier, and, moreover, it invites doubts whether or not the product of bankruptcy costs and the probability of bankruptcy (which normally is a fraction of 1 percent) can outweigh the relative benefit of debt financing under a 50 percent corporate income tax rate. Even if an interior optimum exists, it will be very close to all-debt financing, which leaves the existence of virtually unlevered firms in the real world (such as Kodak and IBM) unexplained. Yet another criticism has been directed to the assumption of perfectly competitive capital markets and, in particular, to the assumption that firms and individuals can borrow any amount of money at the same interest rate. This assumption is indeed unrealistic. In reality, the terms of borrowing vary on the basis of who the borrower is, what the collaterals are, and many more characteristics. Financial assets are, in this sense, fundamentally "named goods."

One of the drawbacks of the conventional MV model formulation is the lack of time elements. But the term of a loan is of crucial importance to both borrower and lender. The static MV model assumes, in effect, that long-term (multiperiod) bonds are riskier than short-term (one-period) bonds. This is consistent with the theory of term structure of interest rates proposed by Hicks in *Value and Capital* (1946, p. 147). Indeed, if all investors are one-period MV maximizers, this must be the case. Once we allow for multiperiod horizons for investors, however, the conclusion is no longer obvious. In order to stabilize the wealth value at a distant future date, an investor may find long-term bonds less risky than (a sequence of) short-term bonds. Thus the Hicksian "risk premium" on long-term bonds may indeed to negative. Modigliani and Sutch (1966) proposed a "preferred (maturity) habitat" theory of term structure of interest rates to accommodate such possibilities. Empirically, the relationship between the term-to-maturity yield of bonds and the term to maturity, called the yield curve, normally shows a systematic "crescendo," but there are times, such as at present, when short-term rates (e.g., treasury-bill rate and six-month prime commercial paper rate) exceed long-term bond yields (e.g., yields on twenty-five-year federal bonds and Aaa corporate bonds).

The point is that markets do seem to attach significance to the term
of bonds, with the result that bonds with different maturities consti
tute different assets and that the yield curve is influenced by the
market forces of demand and supply for each of these assets. In orde
to study these phenomena fully, one needs a synthesis of dynami
(multiperiod) models of portfolio selection and capital appropriation
Such a model, though nonexistent at the moment, would be useful in
studying the effects of financial policies in general.

8.5   Theories of demand for money

Why do people want to hold money? What does the amount of mone
held depend on? The history of researches into these questions i
long, but their output had remained meager until the late nineteent
century, when the choice-theoretic foundation of economic theor
was built. Jevons (1875), Menger (1892), Walras (1900), an
Edgeworth (1881; 1888) each made a significant contribution to th
theory of exchange and, in particular, to the theory of the use and hold
ing of money. Jevons and Menger focused on the mechanism (i.e., th
use side) of monetary exchange, whereas Walras and Edgewort
stressed the holding of money. The MV theory discussed earlier is a
example of theories that attempt to explain people's holding c
money. In this section we shall continue to focus on the latter, that i
on the holding of money.

One of the great difficulties Walras faced in writing his theory c
general economic equilibrium concerned the treatment of money. I
the first three editions of his *Elements* (first edition 1874), he borrowe
the simple quantity-theory formula and appended it to the rest of th
equilibrium equations that had been rationally deduced from mode
of optimal behavior. It was in his fourth edition (1900) that Walr
first succeeded in integrating money into his general-equilibriu
system, which he recorded in the preface to the fourth edition wit
gratification. Walras's idea was to regard money as a capital good an
base its demand on the "service d'approvisionnement" (the service c
availability), just like the demand for any other form of capital good
Although Walras's analysis of the demand for and supply of capit
goods was not quite satisfactory, it should be remembered that he re
ognized inventories of durable goods and that his idea of services
availability was a correct one to generate demands for such invent
ries, including, among others, the demand for money. The proble
with his formulation, however, was that the speculative and preca
tionary motives, which supposedly induced demands for inventorie
were largely irrelevant in his tâtonnement world.

Edgeworth (1888) proposed what might be called a liquidity theory of demand for money in his discussion of the appropriateness of the reserves of the Bank of England. To put his discussion in a general context, the point of his argument was that an individual's demand for money is primarily caused by the uncertainty about his future cash needs. Think of an individual who has a certain subjective-probability distribution of his cash needs. If he keeps enough cash balances, these needs may be met without trouble. But if he does not, and if cash needs should turn out to be high, he will be compelled to liquidate his other assets, which will be more or less costly. This theory leads to a stochastic model of transactions demands for cash. This model does not require risk aversion as an essential ingredient to rationalize people's demands for cash, although risk aversion can certainly be superimposed. The asset-demand functions derived from this model exhibit considerably different properties than those derived from the MV model.

To illustrate the working of this model in the simple case of risk neutrality, consider an investor (e.g., a commercial bank) facing a prospect of random cash needs at a certain future date (e.g., the net deposit withdrawal for a bank). Let N be the random cash needs, and let $f(N)$ ($N \in [\underline{N}, \bar{N}]$, $\underline{N} < \bar{N}$) be the probability density function of N. Let there be four assets in which to hold wealth. If we denote the initial wealth by A and the dollar values of the four assets held by M, X_1, X_2, and X_3, where these assets are numbered in an ascending order of yields and transactions costs, the expected profit $E(\Pi)$ of the investor corresponding to a given portfolio $X = (M, X_1, X_2, X_3)$ can be written as

$$
\begin{aligned}
E(\Pi) = & \int_{\underline{N}}^{M} [r_1 X_1 + r_2 X_2 + r_3 X_3 - K] dF \\
& + \int_{M}^{M+X_1} [r_1(M + X_1 - N) + r_2 X_2 + r_3 X_3 - c_1 - K] dF \\
& + \int_{M+X_1}^{M+X_1+X_2} [r_2(M + X_1 + X_2 - N) + r_3 X_3 - c_1 - c_2 - K] dF \\
& + \int_{M+X_1+X_2}^{M+X_1+X_2+X_3} [r_3(M + X_1 + X_2 + X_3 - N) - c_1 - c_2 - c_3 - K] dt
\end{aligned}
$$

(8.39)

where r_1, r_2, and r_3 are the net yields of the three income-earning assets, c_1, c_2, and c_3 are the transactions costs per transaction of the nonmoney assets, K is all costs of the investor other than the transaction costs, and $dF \equiv f(N)dN$. It is assumed here that $r_1 < r_2 < r_3$ and $c_1 < c_2 < c_3$. It is also assumed that money M has a zero net yield and that should the investor sell any of the income-earning assets, he not

Table 8.1. *Comparative-statics results*

| | | Effect on | | |
Change in	M	X_1	X_2	X_3
A	0	0	0	1
r_1	−	+	−	0
r_2	0	−	+	−
r_3	0	0	−	+
c_1	+	−	+	0
c_2	0	+	−	+
c_3	0	0	+	−

only incurs a positive transactions cost but also gives up the accrued interest. Now the investor maximizes $E(\Pi)$ subject to a budget constraint

$$A - M - X_1 - X_2 - X_3 = 0 \qquad (8.40)$$

Assuming an interior maximum, we get the comparative-statics results shown in Table 8.1 (besides the obvious adding-up properties, certain symmetry conditions hold). The most interesting property of this solution is that the effects of a change in any r and c are confined to the asset in which the change originated and the two adjacent assets. A slight adaptation of this model seems particularly fit for the portfolio behavior of commercial banks.

The idea of random cash needs can also be applied to households, in which case $E(N)$ may be thought of as the planned spending, and the randomness may be interpreted as cash needs arising from all sorts of "accidents," such as sudden illnesses and unexpected guests. For a discussion of this class of models, the reader is referred to the work of Nagatani (1978, Chapter 4).

In the meantime, the validity of the MV model as a theory of demand for money has often been questioned. Although the MV model (and the more general expected-utility theory, for that matter) asserts that an asset is held for its high expected yield or for its safety, there are, in reality, a number of near monies that are as safe and liquid as cash and yet have much higher yields than cash. Tsiang (1972) argued that the slope of the efficient frontier in a typical condition of the financial markets is much greater than the MRS of indifference curves obtained from a reasonable class of utility functions and that it would therefore be difficult to explain a positive demand for money in terms of the MV theory. This suggests that the MV theory is perhaps not a very good theory of demand for money, even though it may be a good theory of demand for other assets. It also suggests that perhaps we should pursue alternative theories more seriously.

One of the serious defects of the conventional formulation of a model of portfolio selection lies in its assumption of once-and-for-all fixed probabilities. Once the probabilities are given, assets are chosen on the basis of two criteria: risk and return. This formulation presents a difficulty in justifying people's holdings of barren cash. In reality, however, an important reason that people should hold cash is to retain flexibility in anticipation of sudden changes in probabilities. Suppose there are two assets other than cash, both of which are certain to yield higher returns than cash under the probabilities prevailing at the moment. The conventional theory predicts that the demand for cash is zero in such a case. But suppose now that the wealth owner anticipates a substantial change in probabilities in the near future, but the nature of the anticipated change is vague, so that he does not know which one of the two assets will do better than the other under the new probabilities. In such a case, he may very well choose to hold on to his cash for the time being, despite the fact that the two assets dominate cash at the moment. What we really mean by speculative demand for cash is the cash held in such an interim, and this sort of demand for cash has very little to do with the profitability of cash under the currently prevailing probabilities. An attempt to reformulate the theory along this line was made by Jones and Ostroy (1979).

Finally, whereas the conventional theory of portfolio selection has confined itself to choices among a set of financial assets, there is no compelling reason that the scope of portfolio selection should be confined to financial assets. In the spirit of Chapter 7, our economy carries a variety of stocks of physical assets. To most agents, there is no intrinsic difference between the financial and physical assets. When speculative activities soared and the call rate rose past 10 percent per annum during the 1920s, many manufacturing firms turned themselves into suppliers of these funds. The devaluation of the U.S. dollar in 1971 caused many financial institutions abroad to buy up real estate with their excess liquidity. These examples show that there is no meaningful distinction between the two types of assets.

8.6   Money in macroeconomics

Oscar Wilde once said, "When I was young, I used to think that money was the most important thing in life; now that I am old, I know it is." Such is the view held toward money by the average man on the street. But whether or not money is the most important thing in economics is a moot question. The past life of monetary theory in economics has been a rather unhappy one, as indicated by the following remarks by Schumpeter (1954):

The history of economic analysis *begins* with Real Analysis in possession of the field. Aristotle and the scholastic doctors all adhered to it. This is perfectly understandable, since there was nothing to face them except the preanalytic sentiments of the public. . . . The history of economic analysis in this period *ends* with a victory of Real Analysis that was so complete as to put Monetary Analysis practically out of court for well over a century, though one or two efforts were made on its behalf in the court of scientific economics, and though it continued to lead a lingering life outside of that court, in an "underworld" of its own. [Beginnings to about 1790, p. 282.]

Wicksell, in the preface to his *Geldzins and Güterpreise* (1898) was able to say that "a closer study of the writings of Tooke and his followers" had convinced him "that there really was no theory of money other than the quantity theory and that if the latter was wrong, we actually have no theory of money at all." This means that one of the men who were most competent to judge refused to consider Tooke's approach as an acceptable alternative to Ricardo's. I confess that I cannot understand such overstatement in a writer of Wicksell's competence and fairness. But he did no more than overstate a truth. [From 1790 to 1870, p. 710.]

Once more the bulk of the vast literature on money and related subjects which the period under survey produced, grew out of the discussions of current problems. It contained, as the literature on money always did and does, a large quantity of completely worthless publications and a still larger quantity of publications which, though more or less meritorious within their range, are uninteresting from the standpoint of a history of analysis. [From 1870 to 1914 and later, p. 1074.]

After the 1930s, the extreme realist view disappeared from the profession; economists all became fundists and even monetarists to the extent that they believed that money mattered. Since the publication of the *General Theory*, a great deal of theorizing has aimed at integrating money into the realist general-equilibrium framework. Hicks (1946), Pigou (1941; 1949), Lange (1944), Metzler (1951), and Patinkin (1965) are the best-known authors along this line of research. The works of Hicks and Lange attempted to reformulate Keynes's theory in a neoclassical setting, whereas the works of Pigou, Patinkin, and Metzler repudiated Keynes's central proposition by establishing what might be called the wealth doctrine. Pigou used his famous "wealth effect" to reject the possibility of underemployment equilibrium in an economy with flexible prices. In his argument, the nominal money stock was held fixed and hence became a major source of the wealth effect. Patinkin applied the same idea to a dynamic implementation of the money-stock – price-level causation of the classical quantity theory. Metzler further analyzed the effect of wealth on savings decisions. From the point of view of monetary theory, the Pigou-Patinkin-Metzler wealth effect soon came to be recognized as one of the important channels through which money influences the economy. According to this wealth doctrine, money matters only insofar as it constitutes part of net private wealth. The conjecture was, in other words, that the aggregate value of the various private assets, money being one of them, significantly influenced spending decisions.

An alternative view of money may be termed the liquidity doctrine. According to this view, existing assets can be ordered according to degree of liquidity, money being the most liquid one. A monetary change exerts its influence on the economy primarily by changing the total amount of liquidity in the system and, given the state of liquidity preference, by changing the interest-rate structure. Needless to say, the liquidity doctrine is an integral part of Keynes's theory, whereas the wealth doctrine can be associated with monetarist theory.

Granted that financial-asset markets play an important role in determining both production and spending decisions, just how to model these markets in an aggregate setting has remained an unsettled issue. The monetarist approach, which follows the tradition of the quantity theory of money, adopts a strategy of singling out a certain subset of financial assets called money, suppressing the rest of financial assets, and postulating a direct, albeit implicit, causation from money to income. With the alleged (but largely unproven) stability of the demand-for-money function, money becomes the key determinant of nominal income. In contrast, the Keynesian approach insists on retaining the general-equilibrium nature of the asset markets. It stresses the substitutability among assets in people's portfolios, and because of this, it denies the kind of stable relationship from money to income posited by monetarists. A number of issues are involved in the debate between the two schools. The first one is the definition of money. To the monetarists, who take a partial approach to financial assets, the existence of a certain homogeneous entity to be called money is essential. Strangely enough, however, the monetarists have largely avoided this issue and have adopted the rather astute position that whichever aggregate explains income variation best is money (Friedman and Schwartz 1970). To the Keynesians, who adopt a multiple-asset general-equilibrium approach, how one defines money is not essential

(Keynes 1936, footnote p. 167). The second issue is the stability of the demand-for-money function. Since Friedman's famous 1959 study, the monetarists have tried to empirically establish the stability of the demand-for-money function or, more specifically, the income velocity of money. Interest inelasticity, exogeneity of real rates of return on assets, and finally rational expectations have been employed to justify the stability of the monetary velocity. But the experience during the seventies was rather unfavorable; the demand-for-money function became much less stable during this decade. Keynes himself started as a quantity theorist, but after observing the wild fluctuations in the demand for money for financial transactions in the twenties, he parted with it in his *Treatise* (1930, Volume I, p. 229). Our experience during the seventies seems to be somewhat similar to what Keynes saw then. Between 1968 and 1978 in Canada, for example, the assets (and deposits) of chartered banks and near banks expanded sixfold in the face of a threefold increase in nominal GNP. Roughly speaking, the money stock expanded twice as fast as income. A principal reason for the rapid increase in the money stock seems to be increased demand by the public for financial transactions, including the purchase of real estate, gold, and other assets that were thought to be a good hedge against inflation. This is certainly not a case of a very stable demand function for money. The third issue concerns the question of policy. Given the stability of the monetary velocity, the autonomy of the money supply, the monetarist's prescription is a simple one of stabilizing the time path of the money stock. Keynesians are skeptical of the efficacy of such monetary policy, mainly because of the instability of the demand-for-money function. They advocate, instead, a close check on interest rates and the general credit condition. They take the view that the nominal income and the price level are determined largely by factors other than the money stock, especially in the short run, and that the effects of money-supply policy on these crucial variables are unpredictable and possibly undesirable. These differences in policy prescription are particularly important at present. Annoyed by persistent inflation, some American monetarists are recommending, on the basis of a crude rational-expectations hypothesis, a very sharp (announced) decline in the growth rate of the money stock instead of the gradualist policy adopted in the past. The idea is that such a policy will produce a correspondingly quick decline in the inflation rate, with minimum disturbance to the real part of the system. Keynesians would argue that the Federal Reserve System might not have enough control over the money stock in the first place and that in a situation where credit has been expanding mainly because of growing demand for financial purposes, such a sharp change in the monetary growth rate might choke up the current economic activities (Keynes 1930, Volume I, pp. 254–5). One also must not forget that the ongoing massive transfers of ready purchasing power from the PIC to the OPEC have aggravated the present situation by creating the need for greater financial intermediation and thereby contributing to the increase in (short-term) interest rates. The fourth and final point is the time span over which monetary effects are evaluated. Patinkin's main conclusion was that an increase in the money stock would temporarily lower interest rates and possibly increase real income, but eventually produce an equiproportionate increase in the general price level, leaving all the real variables intact ("the final neutrality"), as was asserted by the classical quantity theory. Patinkin used his real-balance effect to explain such an adjustment process. The increase in the money stock creates additional demand for commodities through the real-balance effect and drives up the commodity prices. The general increase in commodity prices reduces the amount of real balances, and hence the real-balance effect becomes increasingly weaker and eventually disappears as commodity prices catch up with the initial increase in the money stock. Money thus has only a transient effect. See also the work of Archibald and Lipsey (1958).

The preceding describes the general result one obtains from any static monetary model with wealth effects. But in a more dynamic setting, we may consider a continuous monetary change rather than the once-and-for-all type of change Patinkin dealt with. The result is a continuous change in the general price level, and as the change affects the agents' expectations, the so-called Wicksell effect arises. This is the effect the changing real rate of return on money has on portfolio choices. When the Wicksell effect is superimposed on the previous Pigou effect, money can be nonneutral even in the long run. Furthermore, the dynamics of the model become more complex, because whereas the Pigou effect is stabilizing, the Wicksell effect is not. On these points, see the work of Tobin (1965).

An additional matter to be mentioned in this context is the treatment of the money supply. In most of the theoretical literature the nominal money stock has traditionally been treated as an exogenous quantity. This seems a natural thing to do in a static model, but it is highly questionable in dynamic models. First of all, the monetary authority does not have direct control over the monetary stock (which conventionally consists of currency in circulation and certain categories of bank deposits). All the central bank can control directly is the amount of high-powered money or the money base. The money stock is some multiple of the money base, and the value of the multiplying factor depends on the commercial banks' decisions on cash reserves and the public's choices between cash and bank deposits. The actual money stock will not be exogenous but will depend on variables endogenous to the system, such as interest rates. Second, even if it were feasible to treat the money stock as a policy variable, what kind of policy rule should we employ in positive and normative analyses? At the positive level, some attempts have recently been made to estimate the money-supply equation empirically. At the normative level, attempts have also been made to identify an optimal rule of monetary management. But these exercises are severely limited by lack of knowledge about the underlying structure of the economy and the operationality of the model.

As this brief survey indicates, our knowledge about money is severely limited. From its definition down to policy prescriptions, there is little consensus. Although we all feel that money somehow matters, we don't exactly know how. The problem looks very complex. One might perhaps argue that it is nevertheless better to do something rather than nothing. That, indeed, seems to be Friedman's idea, and we all should be sympathetic to his view. But the value of his contribution is subject to a rather wide margin of uncertainty. We shall have more to say on this issue in Chapter 12.

Questions

8.1 Show that $S = E(Q - q)(Q - q)'$ is a nonnegative definite matrix. What may cause it to be singular? Why is it important that S be positive definite?

8.2 Show that when S is positive definite, the function $V(x) = x'Sx$ is convex in x, where x is drawn from some nonempty convex subset of R^n.

8.3 Use the Cauchy-Schwartz inequality to prove that J in equation (8.13′) is generally positive (but see Question 8.4).

8.4 Show that if q is proportional to Sp, J in (8.13′) can be zero. What conditions on S make it zero?

8.5 Show in the one-safe-asset MV model that M must be greater than r_nA for positive holdings of the risky assets.

8.6 Prove the separation theorem.

8.7 Explain in what sense Π^* is the cost (price) of risk aversion.

8.8 Explain how the expected-utility theory of portfolio selection is more general than the MV model. When are the two equivalent? [Hint:

$$EU(W) = U(M) + \sum_{k=2}^{\infty} \frac{U^{(k)}(M)}{k} M_k$$

where $M = E(W)$, and M_k is the kth central moment.]

8.9 Writing $U[q'x,(x'Sx)^{1/2}]$ as $u(x)$ and maximizing $u(x)$ subject to $A - p'x = 0$, derive the Slutsky equation and study it.

8.10 What is the real-balance effect? Using a simple aggregative model, explain how it works.

8.11 Using Tobin's model (1965), analyze the role played by the Wicksell effect.

CHAPTER 9

Stabilization policies

9.1 Phillips's three stabilization policies

Stabilizing the economy has long been one of the widely accepted goals of economic policy, but on the other hand, the analytics of stabilization policies have a relatively short history. This brief history can be attributed to the lack of appropriate dynamic tools that prevailed until recently. We can safely start our survey with the classic work by Phillips (1954). In that article Phillips defined three types of stabilization policies and examined their effects in a simple dynamic income-expenditure model. The recent introduction of optimal-control techniques in the field has resulted in an enormous amount of sophistication and precision in the concepts and forms of optimal-stabilization policies. In this chapter we shall briefly trace these developments.

Let us begin by describing the three types of stabilization policies defined by Phillips. Take real income Y as the index of performance of the economy and government spending G as the policy controller. The class of feedback controls can be defined as a set of policy rules that relate G to the observed path of Y. Suppose, for the purpose of illustration, that the path of Y is given as in Figure 9.1. It is assumed that $Y = Y^*$ up to $t = t_0$, where Y^* is some desirable equilibrium level of real income. This equilibrium level of Y^* has been maintained at some constant level of government spending G^*. Starting at $t = t_0$, however, errors begin to emerge, as shown by the sine curve in Figure 9.1. Suppose we stand at $t = t_1$.

The first of Phillips's three policies is called a *derivative policy*. This is the policy in which G is activated in response to the direction of change in Y (i.e., the derivative of the time path of Y). If we assume linearity in policy functions, this policy may be written as

$$G(t) = G^* - g_a \dot{Y}(t) \qquad (g_a > 0) \tag{9.1}$$

Referring to Figure 9.1, $\dot{Y}(t_1) < 0$. Hence the derivative policy calls for a $G(t_1)$ greater than G^*. The second policy is called a *proportional policy*. As the name suggests, G reacts to the size of the error $Y - Y^*$.

164

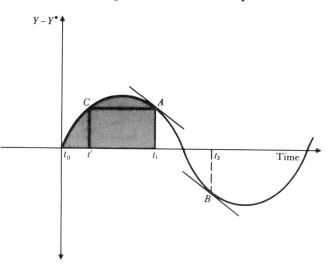

Figure 9.1. Derivative, proportional, and integral policies.

The proportional policy can therefore be written as

$$G(t) = G^* - g_p[Y(t) - Y^*] \qquad (g_p > 0) \tag{9.2}$$

At $t = t_1$ the error is measured by the ordinate of the point A, which is positive. Hence the proportional policy calls for a smaller G at $t = t_1$. Finally, the third policy is called an *integral policy*. According to this policy, G reacts to the cumulative or integral errors committed in the past. Formally, this policy can be expressed as

$$G(t) = G^* - g_i \int_{t_0}^{t} [Y(\tau) - Y^*] d\tau \qquad (g_i > 0) \tag{9.3}$$

Phillips then studied the effects of these policies on the time path of Y, which was generated by a production lag. A few more complex models were also studied in an appendix to his article.

To illustrate the effects of these policies, let us consider a very simple production-lag model

$$Y(t + 1) = cY(t) + A + G \tag{9.3'}$$

or, in continuous time, and ignoring the term A,

$$\dot{Y} = -(1 - c)Y + G = -sY + G \qquad [Y(0) = Y_0] \tag{9.4}$$

The absence of policy may be interpreted as $G \equiv G^*$. In this case, the solution of (9.4) is

$$Y(t) = Y^* + [Y_0 - Y^*]e^{-st} \qquad (0 < s < 1, \quad Y^* \equiv G^*/s) \qquad (9.5)$$

When the derivative policy (9.1) is used, we have

$$\dot{Y} = -\frac{s}{1 + g_d} Y + \frac{G^*}{1 + g_d} \qquad (9.6)$$

whose solution is

$$Y(t) = Y^* + [Y_0 - Y^*] \exp\left(-\frac{s}{1 + g_d} t\right) \qquad (9.7)$$

With the proportional policy (9.2), the differential equation becomes

$$\dot{Y} = -(s + g_p)Y + G^* + g_p Y^* \qquad (9.8)$$

which yields the solution

$$Y(t) = Y^* + [Y_0 - Y^*]e^{-(s+g_p)t} \qquad (9.9)$$

Finally, with the integral policy (9.3), the differential equation becomes

$$\ddot{Y} + s\dot{Y} + g_i Y = g_i Y^* \qquad (9.10)$$

whose solution is given by

$$Y(t) = Y^* + c_1 e^{\lambda_1 t} + c_2 e^{\lambda_2 t} \qquad (9.11)$$

where

$$\lambda_1, \lambda_2 = \frac{-s \pm \sqrt{s^2 - 4g_i}}{2} \qquad (9.12)$$

and the coefficients c_1 and c_2 are the solutions of

$$\begin{bmatrix} 1 & 1 \\ \lambda_1 & \lambda_2 \end{bmatrix} \begin{bmatrix} c_1 \\ c_2 \end{bmatrix} = \begin{bmatrix} Y_0 - Y^* \\ \dot{Y}_0 \end{bmatrix} \qquad (9.13)$$

In the simple model (9.4), all the paths (9.5), (9.7), (9.9), and (9.11) converge asymptotically to Y^*. But suppose we measure the welfare loss by the sum $\int_0^\infty [Y(t) - Y^*]^2 dt$. Then the losses corresponding to the three policies become

$$L_d = (Y_0 - Y^*)^2 \frac{1 + g_d}{2s} \qquad (9.14)$$

$$L_p = (Y_0 - Y^*)^2 \frac{1}{2(s + g_p)} \qquad (9.15)$$

$$L_i = (Y_0 - Y^*)^2 \frac{1}{2s} - \left[\frac{\dot{Y}_0}{g_i(Y_0 - Y^*)} + \frac{\dot{Y}_0^2}{2sg_i(Y_0 - Y^*)^2} \right] \qquad (9.16)$$

which compare with the loss under a policy of no stabilization:

$$\bar{L} = (Y_0 - Y^*)^2 \frac{1}{2s} \tag{9.17}$$

It is readily apparent that $L_p < \bar{L} < L_d$, namely, that the proportional policy is better than "no policy," whereas the derivative policy is worse than no policy, in terms of the preceding criterion. The evaluation of the integral policy is more complex. The first term in the square brackets in (9.16) produces $\bar{L}$. The remaining terms depending on $\dot{Y}_0$ are not likely to be zero and can be either positive or negative, depending on the history up to time zero. If we ignore the history up to time zero, then $\dot{Y}_0 = -sY_0 + G^* = -s(Y_0 - Y^*)$, and the two terms in brackets can be combined to yield $(3s/2g_i)(Y_0 - Y^*)^2$, implying that $\bar{L} < L_i$.

In any case, the effects of these policies depend crucially on the specification of the underlying dynamics of the structural model, and thus the preceding specific results should not be taken too seriously. Generally speaking, each of the three policies has some merits as well as demerits. The derivative policy captures the direction of motion of the economy but fails to pay attention to the position of the economy. It cannot distinguish between points A and B in Figure 9.1. The proportional policy recognizes the position of the economy correctly but fails to make distinctions regarding the direction of motion. It treats points A and C equally. The integral policy seems to partake of a certain fanatic perfectionist mentality in that it insists on eliminating the cumulative errors completely. But it applies more deflationary pressure at A, where the economy is already on the decline, than at C, where the economy is still on the rise. We may predict that if the problem is cast in an explicit optimal-control theoretical framework, the solution, if it exists, is likely to be some combination of these policies.

Intuitively, the integral policy appears to be the least rational of the three stabilization policies. Nevertheless, that type of adjustment policy seems relevant in some realistic situations. Think of X as the level of foreign reserves and Y as the balance of payments. The current level of reserves can then be written as

$$X(t) = X(0) + \int_0^t Y(\tau)d\tau$$

where $X(0)$ is the initial level of foreign reserves, which for simplicity we assume to be equal to the desired or target level of reserves. Now, $Y(t)$ can be influenced by traditional fiscal and monetary instruments. In order to restore the reserves level $X(0)$, the government must set the whole time integral of Y to zero. That then requires an integral policy. Another example is a firm with "wrong" levels of stocks. Such a firm also tends to follow an integral policy in an attempt to eliminate the errors. The dynamics of the adjustment processes following an integral policy tend to be quite different from those following other (e.g., proportional) policies, which are probably the right types of policies in the absence of stocks.

9.2   Optimal-stabilization policies: deterministic case

Let us begin by reformulating the problem of stabilizing the simple economy of the previous section in an optimal-control theoretical framework. For this purpose we postulate a T-period problem with the following loss functional:

$$J\{G\} = \tfrac{1}{2}f[Y(T) - Y^*]^2 + \tfrac{1}{2} \int_0^T [m_1\{Y(t) - Y^*\}^2$$
$$+ m_2\{G(t) - G^*\}^2]dt \quad (f, m_1, m_2 > 0) \quad (9.18)$$

The first term represents the evaluation of the terminal state, and the terms following the integral sign measure the loss incurred along the way. The criterion chosen in (9.18), though crude, is a fairly common one in the literature. The state variable Y follows the law

$$\dot{Y} = -sY + G, \qquad Y(0) = Y_0 \quad \text{given} \quad (9.4)$$

The Hamiltonian function can be written as

$$H(Y,q,G,t) \equiv m_1(Y - Y^*)^2 + m_2(G - G^*)^2 + q(-sY + G) \quad (9.19)$$

from which the optimal controller is obtained as

$$G_{opt}(t) = G^* - q(t)/m_2 \quad (9.20)$$

assuming an interior optimum. The dynamics of the variables (Y,q) are given by

$$\dot{Y} = -sY + G^* - \frac{q}{m_2} \quad (9.21)$$

$$\dot{q} = sq - m_1(Y - Y^*) \quad (9.22)$$

which are a pair of first-order, linear, constant-coefficient, nonhomogeneous differential equations that can be easily solved explicitly for $[Y(t), q(t)]$.

For T finite, we first solve a fixed-end-point problem with $Y(T) = Y_T$ given, and then we substitute the solution in (9.18) and choose Y_T so as

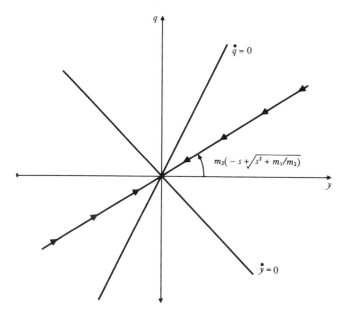

Figure 9.2. Optimal-stabilization policy.

to minimize J^* as a function of Y_T. Note that the optimal Y_T so determined need not equal Y^* in a finite-horizon problem. The solution of this problem, especially its "synthesis," turns out to be quite complex and is not reported here. Instead, we consider the case of $T = +\infty$, for which the answer is quite simple.

When $T = +\infty$, the terminal value of Y must equal Y^*, with q converging to zero. Defining $Y(t) - Y^* \equiv y(t)$, the phase diagram of the system (9.21) and (9.22) can be easily derived as in Figure 9.2. Clearly, the optimal trajectory is the one indicated by the multiple arrowheads. The slope of this curve is constant and is equal to $m_2[-s + (s^2 + m_1/m_2)^{1/2}]$. Thus the synthesis solution is

$$q_{\text{opt}}(t) = m_2(-s + \sqrt{s^2 + m_1/m_2})y(t) \tag{9.23}$$

Substituting (9.23) into (9.20) and recalling the definition of $Y(t)$, we finally obtain

$$G_{\text{opt}}(t) = G^* + (s - \sqrt{s^2 + m_1/m_2})\,[Y(t) - Y^*] \tag{9.24}$$

which is a proportional policy with $g_p = -s + (s^2 + m_1/m_2)^{1/2}$.

How "robust" is this result? That is, how general are the conditions under which the proportional policy is optimal? The answer seems to be rather negative. To illustrate this point, consider a model similar to the preceding one, but in which "errors" in the form of stocks influence flow decisions. Denoting the stock of produced goods by Z, such a model may be specified as

$$\dot{Y} = -sY + G - k(Z - Z^*) \qquad (k > 0) \tag{9.25}$$

where Z^* is some desired or normal stock level. The law of motion of Z is simply

$$\dot{Z} = Y - (C + G) = sY - G \tag{9.26}$$

Combining (9.25) and (9.26), we get

$$\dddot{Y} + s\ddot{Y} + ksY - kG - \dot{G} = 0 \tag{9.27}$$

The problem is now a third-order problem. Again taking T to be infinity, the optimal policy can be shown to be a certain combination of proportional and integral policies; that is, it takes the form

$$G_{\text{opt}}(t) = G^* + \theta_1[Y(t) - Y^*] + (\theta_1\theta_3 + \theta_2)e^{\theta_3 t}$$
$$\times \int_0^t [Y(\tau) - Y^*]e^{-\theta_3\tau}d\tau + [G(0) - G^* - \theta_1(Y_0 - Y^*)]e^{\theta_3 t} \tag{9.28}$$

where θ_1, θ_2, and θ_3 are constant parameters determined by the structural parameters of the model. For details, the reader is referred to the work of Turnovsky (1973, pp. 80–3), although Turnovsky did not rely on stocks for his results. It is obvious that there is no saying, a priori, which type of policy should be optimal. This depends on the underlying structure of the economy. But categorically speaking some elements of proportional and integral policies seem essential. The significance of the latter looms large as the capital-theoretic nature of decision making is stressed. To these policies the derivative policy may be appended for the purpose of fine tuning.

Two obvious difficulties are faced when it comes to implementing such stabilization policies. The first involves the informational requirements concerning the structure of the economy combined with the technical problem of arriving at a synthesis that is simple enough to be adopted as the policy rule by administrators. But here we face a dilemma. Simple policy rules are likely to come from simple (which often means partial) specification of the model, which will then expose us to the danger of policy misbehavior. If we want to minimize such danger, optimal policy rules may not be identifiable.

The other difficulty concerns the possible reactions of the private sector to policy rules. As is evident from our earlier discussion, we have been assuming that the behavior of the private sector is totally insensitive to the choice of policy rules. This is typically untrue. But once we allow for such sensitivity, once we allow for the dependence of C and I on the policy rule G, even the notion of an optimal policy becomes obscure, as has been argued by Sargent and Wallace. It may well be that the government is better off if its policy rule is kept from the public. For a useful discussion of various issues concerning policy optimization, the reader is referred to the work of Helliwell (1977). Shupp (1976) had an interesting application for wage-price controls. For more complete coverage of optimal-stabilization policies, the reader is referred to the work of Turnovsky (1977, Chapters 13 and 14).

9.3   Optimal-stabilization policies: stochastic case

In the seventies we have witnessed a flourishing of stabilization-policy models cast explicitly in stochastic terms. Those of Poole (1970), Sargent and Wallace (1975), and Turnovsky (1975; 1977, Chapter 14) are some examples. All these models summarize the structure of the system in terms of a simple linear stochastic IS-LM model and a quadratic loss function. The combination of linear structural equations and a quadratic loss function is not an accident. Earlier, Simon (1956) and Theil (1954) had shown that, for such models, the first-period optimal decision of a T-period dynamic programming problem in which expected loss is minimized is identical with that of the strategy that neglects uncertainty by minimizing loss, setting all stochastic variables equal to their expected values (the first-period certainty-equivalence theorem). Hence, where this theorem is applicable, the stabilization problem becomes much simpler, although the price paid for such simplicity is certainly not negligible. For an exposition of optimal stochastic stabilization theory, we follow the work of Poole (1970).

Let the structure of the economy be represented by the following simple IS-LM model:

$$Y = a_0 + a_1 r + u \qquad (9.29)$$

$$M = b_0 + b_1 Y + b_2 r + v \qquad (9.30)$$

where Y is (real) output, r is the interest rate, M is the money stock, a and b are (nonstochastic) constants, and u and v are disturbance terms with the properties that $E[u] = E[v] = 0, E[u^2] = \sigma_u^2, E[v^2] = \sigma_v^2$, and $E[uv] = \sigma_{uv} = \rho_{uv}\sigma_u\sigma_v$. Suppose further that the performance criterion is given by the loss function

$$L = E[(Y - Y^*)^2] \qquad (9.31)$$

where Y^* is a certain desired level of Y. Poole's main concern in his article was to determine the relative effectivenesses of two kinds of monetary policy: an interest policy and a money-supply policy.

First, consider an interest policy. Denoting the interest rate that makes $E[Y] = Y^*$ in (9.29) by r^*, it is obvious that the loss function assumes the value

$$L_r = \sigma_u^2 \tag{9.32}$$

when r is set equal to r^*. Next, consider a money-supply policy. With M controlled, equations (9.29) and (9.30) may be solved for Y and r. Again denoting the money stock for which the expected value of the solution for Y equals Y^* by M^*, the loss associated with the policy $M = M^*$ becomes

$$L_M = (a_1 b_1 + b_2)^{-2}(a_1^2 \sigma_u^2 - 2\rho_{uv} a_1 b_2 \sigma_u \sigma_v + b_2^2 \sigma_2^2) \tag{9.33}$$

The relative effectivenesses of the two policies are determined by comparing the values of the loss functions in (9.32) and (9.33). Taking the ratio of the latter to the former, we obtain

$$L_M/L_r = (a_1 b_1 + b_2)^{-2}(a_1 X^2 - 2\rho_{uv} a_1 b_2 X + b_2^2) \tag{9.34}$$

where $X \equiv \sigma_v/\sigma_u$. Now one can show that $L_M < L_r$ if $X < b_1$. The terms in the second set of parentheses may be rewritten as

$$a_1 X^2 - 2\rho_{uv} a_1 b_2 X + b_2^2 = (a_1 X + b_2)^2 - 2a_1 b_2 X(1 + \rho_{uv})$$
$$\leq (a_1 X + b_2)^2 \tag{9.35}$$

since $a_1 < 0$ and $b_2 < 0$ by convention. Thus,

$$L_M/L_r \leq (a_1 X + b_2)^2/(a_1 b_1 + b_2)^2$$

The right-hand side is clearly less than unity if $b_1 > X$, that is, if the LM relation is sufficiently less volatile than the IS relation. On the other hand, because

$$a_1 X^2 - 2\rho_{uv} a_1 b_2 X + b_2^2 = (a_1 X - \rho_{uv} b_2)^2 + b_2^2(1 - \rho_{uv}^2)$$

the L_M/L_r ratio rises without bound as X increases past $\rho_{uv} b_2/a_1$. For X sufficiently large, therefore, the L_M/L_r ratio certainly exceeds unity. It thus follows that "in a stochastic world one policy may be superior to the other depending on the values of the structural parameters and the variances of the disturbances" (Poole 1970, p. 206). Poole went on to investigate the effectiveness of a "combination policy" in which the money supply was dependent on the interest rate: $c_0 M = c_1 + c_2 r$. The conclusion was that whereas "the expected losses under the combination policy may be substantially less than the expected losses under either of the pure policies," the complex expressions for the optimal values of c suggest that "a combination policy based on intuition may be worse than either of the pure policies" (Poole 1970, p. 209). One remark should be made about Poole's statement to the effect that such a policy-choice question is irrelevant in a deterministic model (1970, pp. 199–200). This statement is not quite right. Whether or not such a choice question is meaningful depends not so much on the deterministic or stochastic nature of the model as on whether or not the loss function includes adjustment costs of policy controls, as we saw in the previous section.

9.4   Stabilization policies: an assessment

As the preceding simple models illustrate, the determination of which policy is likely to be effective depends crucially on the structure of the underlying system. The lesson we learn from these exercises is essentially negative in nature: There does not seem to exist an intuitively appealing policy rule that always works. A policy rule will depend crucially on what the model builder believes to be the central dynamic force driving the economy. In this sense the difficulty is one of information. If our knowledge of the structure were more complete and the model were specified in much greater detail (as in some large-scale econometric models), it might be possible to identify a correct optimal policy. But in practice the dynamic properties of large-scale models are virtually unknowable, and it is extremely unlikely that an optimal policy rule, if it can be identified, will appeal to one's intuition. Finally, we must be concerned with various sources of policy lags in actual policy implementations. When these lags are allowed for, what appeared to be a very effective stabilizing policy in their absence may prove to do more harm than good.

Faced with this situation, one must consider more modest alternatives. One such alternative may be the following: We list the dynamic mechanisms that appear to be important (or are known to have been important in previous instances) and include them formally in a few operational models. Each of these models contains policy variables as parameters. It is realistic to assume that we do not know, in the absence of policy (in the sense defined in Section 9.2), whether or not any of these models are stable. Next we consider a general class of feedback controls and tabulate a collection of feedback policies that are intuitively appealing (i.e., that sound "sensible"). Then we try to work out whether or not one of these policies meets the qualitative requirements that it stabilizes all the models relative to "no policy" at all times (i.e., irrespective of the magnitudes of the structural parameters) and that it can never be too strong (i.e., it stabilizes the economy for all possible values of the feedback coefficients). If such a policy is found, it will be worthy of more careful study.

Questions

9.1 Work out the differential-equation solutions (9.5), (9.7), (9.9), and (9.11), as well as the loss functions, under different policies, that is, (9.14), (9.16), and (9.17).

9.2 Explain why Y_T in the finite-time-horizon problem in Section 9.2 is, in general, not equal to Y^*. Also comment on the case in which Y_T is fixed (and not equal to Y^*) but the time horizon T is free to be chosen. Why is $T < \infty$ in this case?

9.3 Identify an optimal policy for either the open-economy model or the firm model discussed at the end of Section 9.1.

9.4 The simplest way of introducing a policy lag is to let $\dot{G} = v(G^* - G)$, where G^* is the (already identified) optimal policy without a policy lag and v is some finite positive parameter representing the policy lag. Using this formulation, assess the effect of the policy lag in the context of the simple production-lag model presented in equation (9.3′).

CHAPTER 10

Inflation

10.1 Inflation and welfare

We may characterize inflation broadly as a general sustained upward trend in the prices of goods and services. The potential causes of inflation are many. In some cases the actual causes are readily identifiable, but in other cases they are not. The potential effects of inflation are also numerous. There may, for instance, be significant distributional effects, and inflation probably also affects the growth rate of the economy. However, economists have yet to develop a comprehensive framework in terms of which to assess the welfare implications of inflation. It is customary, in the literature, to distinguish between the short-term and long-term effects of inflation, and this corresponds roughly to the distinction between unanticipated inflation and anticipated inflation.

The purpose of this chapter is twofold. First, we shall consider a simple economy in a steady state and examine how, in this economy, the steady-state social welfare of the economy depends on the prevailing rate of inflation. This is a study of the long-run effects of a fully anticipated inflation. The pioneering work along this line was performed by Bailey (1956), but it was Friedman (1969) who made it a popular subject. But, as usual, Friedman's analysis suffers from the limitations of a partial-equilibrium model. We shall therefore reexamine the issue in a general-equilibrium framework. This analysis will also serve as an exercise in optimal taxation. The remainder of the chapter will deal with the short-run aspects of unanticipated inflation from the point of view of risk allocation and effectiveness of macroeconomic policy. The chapter will conclude with speculation on the behavioral theory of price formation and inflation.

10.2 Friedman's concept of monetary optimum

Before examining Friedman's analysis, let us briefly describe the idea of the optimum quantity of money. A complete characterization of a monetary optimum inevitably brings up fundamental questions such as what money is and what money does. Here, however, we follow the convention of simply assuming that money renders some amenity yields in the form of liquidity services.

Consider a wealth owner in a steady-state economy. He has several alternative forms in which to hold his wealth. Suppose, for simplicity, that there are only two types of assets, which we call capital and money. In a steady state, the own rate of return on capital is equal to the rate of time preference in some average sense. We denote this rate of return on capital by r_K. Let the (real) rate of return on money, denoted r_m, be equal to the rate of deflation prevailing in the steady state. So we have $r_m = -(\dot{p}/p)$. In order for money to coexist with capital, the difference between r_k and r_m must be made up for by money's extra attraction, namely, its liquidity services. In other words, individuals value the nonpecuniary services of money as measured by the difference $r_K - r_m$. In an inflationary state the opportunity cost of holding money is high. Hence, individuals will hold small amounts of cash balances. However, if the cost (to the society) of creating additional cash is low, individuals' cash holdings are needlessly restricted, resulting in a socially suboptimal state.

Friedman's analysis is simply the following: First, the personal optimality condition, as discussed earlier, can be written as

$$r_K = r_m + \text{MNPS}_m \tag{10.1}$$

where MNPS_m means marginal nonpecuniary services of money (measured in dollar terms). In a steady state, this condition becomes

$$\text{IRD}(0) = -(\dot{p}/p) + \text{MNPS}_m \tag{10.2}$$

where $\text{IRD}(0)$ stands for an internal rate of discount at zero rate of saving. The social-optimality condition, on the other hand, is

$$\text{MNPS}_m = \text{MSC}_m \tag{10.3}$$

where MSC_m means the marginal social cost of creating additional cash. Friedman then assumed that the creation of additional cash is virtually costless (i.e., $\text{MSC}_m = 0$). Under this additional assumption, it is plain that the personal and social optima will coincide if and only if

$$\text{IRD}(0) = -(\dot{p}/p) \tag{10.4}$$

Thus monetary optimum calls for deflation at a rate equaling the internal rate of discount prevailing in the steady state.

Friedman then estimated the order of magnitude of the welfare loss due to inflation as follows: Using data for the U.S. economy in early 1968, he first estimated the quantity of high-powered money to be about six weeks' personal disposable income. This he regarded as a "minimum" estimate of the quantity of money. Then, allowing for other non-interest-bearing financial assets, he estimated the quantity of money to be about ten weeks' personal disposable income (he included one-half of demand deposits). This figure he used as a "maximum" estimate of the quantity of money. Next he assumed that the rate of anticipated inflation at that time was 2 percent per annum. Finally, he specified a demand-for-money function of the Cagan-Bailey type:

$$\log M = a - 10(\dot{p}/p) \tag{10.5}$$

Suppose IRD(0) was 5 percent. Then the optimal rate of deflation was also 5 percent. A movement from a 2 percent inflation to a 5 percent deflation means a fall of 7 percent in the cost of holding non-interest-bearing cash balances. According to the money-demand function (10.5), a 7 percent fall in $(\dot{p}/p)$ raises $\log M$ by 0.7. The antilog of 0.7 is about 2, meaning that money balances would slightly more than double. Using the "minimum" estimate, the money balance would increase from six weeks' to twelve weeks' personal disposable income. Assuming that the $MNPS_m$ had initially been 7 percent but would be zero in optimum, and adopting a simple linear averaging device, Friedman calculated the welfare gain per week's personal disposable income as

$$\frac{(0.07 - 0.00)}{2} \times (12 - 6) = 0.21$$

Multiplying this by the weekly personal disposable income, the welfare gain corresponding to the assumption of 5 percent IRD(0) and the "minimum" estimate of the quantity of money was calculated to be $2.3 billion per year. Because the U.S. GNP in 1968 was $880 billion, a $2.3 billion welfare gain amounted to less than 0.3 percent of the GNP. Needless to say, the welfare gain would be greater, the wider the gap between the initial rate of inflation and the optimal rate of deflation, and the larger the quantity of money. Using the "maximum" quantity of money and assuming rather high IRD(0) values, Friedman indicated that the welfare gain might be as high as 10 percent of the GNP.

10.3   A reexamination in a general-equilibrium framework

What is wrong with Friedman's analysis? Many things. It is one thing to describe a long-run optimum. It is quite another to characterize the optimal path toward it. How can we be sure that a long-run equilibrium with a constant rate of monetary contraction is stable? To these dynamic questions, one can add questions concerning measurement of the IRD(0), the effects of uncertainty, etc. The most obvious defect of Friedman's analysis, however, is the absence of a proper general-equilibrium framework, without which the implications of such pervasive economic variables as money can hardly be correctly understood. In what follows we shall study a minimal general-equilibrium model à la Sidrauski (1967) from the point of view of the theory of optimal taxation.

Consider an economy made up of households that have infinitely long lives. There are two assets in the economy, called capital and money. Money is valued by the households for its liquidity services. We recognize this fact by writing their utility functions as $u(c,m)$, where c is the rate of physical consumption per member of the household and m is the real balances per member, but interpreted as the (flow) liquidity services real balances render to each member. At any given point in time, the representative household owns capital k, also measured in per-member units, which produces a homogeneous output $f(k)$, where $f(k)$ is the usual increasing concave production function. Throughout the analysis, this homogeneous output is used as a "numeraire." The household's income is the sum of the output it produces and a per-capita lump-sum transfer payment (of money) v from the government. So we can express income as

$$y = f(k) + v \tag{10.6}$$

This income is allocated among (1) consumption, (2) investment in physical capital, and (3) addition to real balances, or

$$y = p_c c + p_k i + x \tag{10.7}$$

where i is per-capita gross investment in physical capital and x is per-capita gross addition to real balances. We assume that the government levies two specific commodity taxes on c and i so that the price at which the household purchases these goods is not unity but somewhat greater than unity. Note that the single output is distinguished according to use. This fact is represented by the pair of after-tax prices p_c and p_k. Note also that x is exempt from taxes. We assume that the membership of the household grows at a constant rate n. We can then write

$$i = \dot{k} + nk \tag{10.8}$$

$$x = \dot{m} + (n + e)m \tag{10.9}$$

where e is the expected rate of inflation. Combining these four equations, we arrive at the household's flow constraint:

$$\dot{a} = f(k) - p_c c + \dot{p}_k k - n p_k k - (n + e)m + v \tag{10.10}$$

where, of course,

$$a \equiv p_k k + m \tag{10.11}$$

Finally, we assume that the household acts so as to maximize

$$J\{c,m,k\} \equiv \int_0^\infty e^{-\delta t}\, u(c,m)dt \tag{10.12}$$

The side constraints are, of course, (10.10), (10.11), and appropriate initial conditions. The Hamiltonian function can be written as

$$H(a,q,c,m,k,\mu,t) \equiv e^{-\delta t}\,[u(c,m) + q\{f(k) - p_c c + \dot{p}_k k - p_k n k \\ + v - (n + e)m\} + \mu\{a - p_k k - m\}] \tag{10.13}$$

Routine calculations yield the following set of first-order conditions, which with proper curvature assumptions will also be sufficient:

$$u_c - q p_c = 0 \tag{10.14}$$

$$u_m - q(n + e + r) = 0 \tag{10.15}$$

$$f'(k) - p_k(n + r - \dot{p}_k/p_k) = 0 \tag{10.16}$$

$$\dot{q}/q = \delta - r \tag{10.17}$$

$$\lim_{t \to \infty} e^{-\delta t}\, q(t)a(t) = 0 \tag{10.18}$$

where $r \equiv \mu/q$.

Let us now move to a steady state. In such a state, $\dot{a} = \dot{k} = \dot{m} = \dot{p}_k = 0$, $r = \delta$, and $(n + e)$ may be equated to the rate of monetary expansion θ. The system of equations relevant to the steady state is as follows:

$$u_c - q p_c = 0 \tag{10.19}$$

$$u_m - q(\theta + \delta) = 0 \tag{10.20}$$

$$f'(k) - p_k(n + \delta) = 0 \tag{10.21}$$

$$f(k) + v - p_c c - p_k n k - \theta m = 0 \tag{10.22}$$

These four equations may be solved for (c,m,k,q) as functions of the policy parameters (θ, p_c, p_k, v).

So much for households. Now the government is interested in choosing its policy parameters so as to maximize the welfare of the households. We assume that the government uses the steady-state utility of a representative household as the social-welfare function:

$$W(\theta,p_c,p_k,v) \equiv u[c(\theta,p_c,p_k,v),m(\theta,p_c,p_k,v)] \tag{10.23}$$

In doing so, the government faces a budget constraint

$$\bar{g} + v = (p_c - 1)c + (p_k - 1)nk + \theta m \tag{10.24}$$

where $\bar{g}$ is a prescribed level of the government's expenditure on goods. We assume further that the transfer payment v arises exclusively from the government's monetary operation, so that for a representative household

$$v = \theta m \tag{10.25}$$

This means that all the revenues from commodity taxes are directed toward the purchase of goods $\bar{g}$. Thus the constraint (10.24) is broken down to (10.25) and

$$\begin{aligned} \bar{g} &= (p_c - 1)c + (p_k - 1)nk \\ &= f(k) - c - nk \end{aligned} \tag{10.26}$$

where c, m, and k are regarded as the solution of (10.19)–(10.22). Letting the Lagrangian function of the government's maximization problem be

$$W(\theta,p_c,p_k,v) + \lambda[f(k) - c\,nk - \bar{g}] + \mu(\theta m - v)$$

and using (10.19) and (10.20), the first-order conditions become the following:

$$\begin{aligned} p_c c_v &+ (\theta + \delta)m_v &= \mu' \\ p_c c_\theta &+ (\theta + \delta)m &= \lambda'c - \mu'(m + \theta m_\theta) \\ p_c c_{p_c} &+ (\theta + \delta)m_{p_c} &= \lambda'c_{p_c} - \mu'\theta m_{p_c} \\ p_c c_{p_k} &+ (\theta + \delta)m_{p_k} &= \lambda'[c_{p_k} + (n - f')k_{p_k}] - \mu'\theta m_{p_k} \end{aligned} \tag{10.27}$$

where $\lambda' \equiv \lambda/q$ and $\mu' \equiv \mu/q$. Note that k depends only on p_k from (10.21). Note also that (10.22) imposes various restrictions on the partial derivatives of the demand functions.

The question is whether or not (10.27) implies, in general, a solution of the form $\theta_{\text{opt}} = -\delta$. Using the elasticity notion E_{xy} for the elasticity of x with respect to y, (10.22) implies the following restriction:

$$E_{c\theta}E_{mp_c} = (1 + E_{m\theta})(1 + E_{cp_c})$$

The second and third equations of (10.27), on setting $\theta + \delta = 0$, imply, on the other hand, the following restriction:

$$E_{c\theta}E_{mp_c} = (1 + E_{m\theta})E_{cp_c}$$

Clearly, the two conditions are not compatible unless $1 + E_{m\theta} = 0$ and $E_{c\theta}E_{mp_c} = 0$. We must therefore conclude that in a general-equilibrium framework no such simple optimality rule is expected to hold.

10.4 Allocation of inflationary shocks

Let us now turn to the shorter-run aspects of inflation. When we shift to the short run, inflation becomes more or less unanticipated, and this creates some interesting problems. First, the presence of uncertainty about the future course of prices frequently introduces a provision of risk allocation or risk sharing into contracts. A popular example is wage indexation during inflationary periods. An article by Shavell (1976) considered this problem from the point of view of a Pareto optimum, and an article by Gray (1976) examined its effects on macroeconomic stability. The same uncertainty also poses an interesting question about the short-run effects of various policy measures. As is well known, it has been Friedman's basic view that monetary policy has only temporary effects on real variables such as employment and (real) interest rates; for example, his presidential address (1968). Even these temporary effects have recently been questioned by promoters of the rational-expectations hypothesis, notably by Sargent and Wallace (1975). In what follows, we shall look at these two issues in turn.

10.5 Wage indexation

In his article, Shavell considered a simple two-party risk-sharing rule that is Pareto-optimal. Let the two transactors be U and V, and let $x(s)$ be the payment to be made by V to U if state s occurs. Also, let $u(s)$ and $v(s)$ be the expected wealths, given s, of the two transactors U and V, respectively, exclusive of the payment mentioned earlier. Then, denoting the transactors' subjective probabilities by $d_u(s)$ and $d_v(s)$, the expected utilities of the two transactors, inclusive of the payment, may be written as

$$E_u = \int_S U[u(s) + x(s)]d_u(s)ds \tag{10.28}$$

$$E_v = \int_S V[v(s) - x(s)]d_v(s)ds \tag{10.29}$$

where S is the domain of s (i.e., the set of all possible states of nature).

It is assumed that all the functions appearing in (10.28) and (10.29) are differentiable and that $d_u(s) = 0$ if and only if $d_v(s) = 0$.

A Pareto-optimal risk-sharing rule is defined as the $x(s)$ that maximizes E_u for a given level of E_v. The necessary condition for Pareto optimality is given by

$$d_u(s)U'[u(s) + x(s)] = \lambda d_v(s)V'[v(s) - x(s)] \tag{10.30}$$

where λ is a positive constant (Lagrangian multiplier). If neither transactor is a risk lover, (10.30) is also sufficient. In order to see what a Pareto-optimal risk-sharing rule looks like, we differentiate (10.30) with respect to s and solve the expression for $x'(s)$, which yields

$$x'(s) = \frac{v'(s)[-V''(s)/V'(s)] \; - \; u'(s)[-U''(s)/U'(s)] \; + \; \{[d_u'(s)/d_u(s)] \; - \; [d_v'(s)/d_v(s)]\}}{[-U''(s)/U'(s)] + [-V''(s)/V'(s)]}$$

$$\tag{10.31}$$

where $U'(s) = U'[u(s) + x(s)]$, and similarly for $U''(s)$, $V'(s)$, and $V''(s)$. This expression shows how a Pareto-optimal risk sharing depends on the states of nature. There are essentially three factors involved: (1) the degree of absolute risk aversion of the transactors involved, (2) the difference in the probabilistic beliefs between the transactors, and (3) the nature of the expected wealths as functions of s.

Let us consider some interesting special cases under the assumption of identical probabilities. When probabilities are identical, (10.31) may be written

$$x'(s) = v'(s)k(s) - u'(s)[1 - k(s)],$$

$$k(s) \equiv \frac{V''(s)/V'(s)}{[U''(s)/U'(s)] + [V''(s)/V'(s)]} \tag{10.32}$$

Clearly, $0 \leq k(s) \leq 1$, with $k(s) = 0$ (or 1) occurring when transactor V (or U) is risk-neutral. When $k(s) = 0$, $x'(s) = -u'(s)$, meaning that transactor U's wealth gross of payment becomes constant. When $k(s) = 1$, on the other hand, it is V's wealth that becomes constant. In both cases, risk is borne entirely by the risk-neutral transactor. Equation (10.32) shows also that the derivatives $u'(s)$ and $v'(s)$ are crucial in determining the function $x'(s)$. If $u'(x) = v'(s) = 0$, $x'(s) = 0$ irrespective of the value of $k(s)$. If $u'(s)$ and $v'(s)$ are of opposite signs, $\text{sign}[x'(s)] = \text{sign}[v'(s)]$. This is the clear case when risk-sharing payments can be readily instituted. When $u'(s)$ and $v'(s)$ are of the same sign, the room for mutually beneficial payments may be quite limited.

Now, in order to apply formula (10.32) to wage indexing under inflation, let us interpret U as households and V as firms, s as the rate of inflation, $x(s)$ as the wage contract in real terms, $u(s)$ as the household's nonlabor income in real terms, and $v(s)$ as the firms' profits before wage payments, also in real terms. Because everything, especially $x(s)$, is measured in real terms, a full indexation of nominal wages corresponds to $x(s) = $ constant, or $x'(s) = 0$. But as we found earlier, $x'(s) = 0$ is Pareto-optimal only if $u'(s) = v'(s) = 0$. But we have reason to believe that $u'(s) < 0 < v'(s)$ is the likely situation under inflation. If so, a Pareto-optimal indexing would call for $x'(s) > 0$. In any case, the most crucial information needed for a qualitative determination of sign$[x'(s)]$ is that on $u'(s)$ and $v'(s)$ and on the relative degrees of risk aversion between households and firms.

Gray's article examined the effect of wage indexation on the stability of a macroeconomy, and its conclusion is that an optimal indexation from the point of view of stability is likely to be a partial indexation, depending on the sources of disturbances. In order to demonstrate this result, Gray formulated a very simple macro model, as follows:

$$Y = \alpha G(L), \quad \alpha = 1 + \mu \quad \text{(production function)} \quad (10.33)$$

$$M^s = \beta \overline{M}, \quad \beta = 1 + \xi, \quad \overline{M} = \text{constant}$$
$$\text{(money-supply function)} \quad (10.34)$$

$$M^d = kpY \quad \text{(demand-for-money function)} \quad (10.35)$$

$$M^s = M^d \quad \text{(money-market balance equation)} \quad (10.36)$$

Thus far, the novelty is the pair of stochastic terms α and β (or μ and ξ). Both μ and ξ are assumed to be symmetrically distributed, with mean zero. They are called real shocks and monetary shocks, respectively. It is against these shocks that money wages are to be indexed.

Next, production is assumed to be a discrete process taking place once in each "period." All wage contracts are assumed to have a duration of one period and to be written at the end of the last period (before the realization of shocks). Wages are specified by a base nominal wage rate w^* and an indexing parameter γ, where w^* is the solution of the labor-market equilibrium conditions:

$$L^d = f(v/\alpha), \quad v \equiv w/p \quad \text{(labor-demand function)} \quad (10.37)$$

$$L^s = g(v) \quad \text{(labor-supply function)} \quad (10.38)$$

$$L^d = L^s \quad (10.39)$$

at $\alpha = \beta = 1$. That is, w^* is obtained by solving (10.37)–(10.39) for v for $\alpha = 1$ and then multiplying v^* by the p that satisfies (10.34)–(10.36) for $\beta = 1$. The indexing parameter $\gamma = 0$ means that nominal wages are fixed at w^* (irrespective of what happens to α and β), whereas $\gamma = 1$ means that the real wage rate is fixed in contracts at v^*.

Let us consider monetary shocks first, ignoring real shocks. From the preceding equations, we have

$$(1 + \xi)\overline{M} = k(w/v)G[f(v)] \tag{10.40}$$

If $\gamma = 0$, $w = w^*$. Thus any shock ξ affects w and hence employment and output. In this case, monetary disturbances have real effects. If $\gamma = 1$, on the other hand, $v = v^*$, and clearly the real sector is insulated from monetary shocks. Next, consider real shocks. In this case we have, instead of (10.40),

$$\overline{M} = k(w/v)(1 + \mu)G\{f[v/(1 + \mu)]\} \quad \{G'(f) < 0, \quad f'[\quad] < 0\} \tag{10.41}$$

It is readily seen that the real sector remains undisturbed by real shocks only if $\gamma = 0$, exactly the opposite to the case with monetary shocks, for then and only then can $v/(1 + \mu)$ remain constant. Thus, "while indexing is an effective means of insulating the real sector from monetary shocks, it exacerbates the real effects of real disturbances" (Gray 1976, p. 229). Gray then illustrated, in terms of a log-linear model, that there is indeed an optimal degree of indexing in an economy that is subject to both real and monetary shocks.[1]

10.6   Is there really a trade-off between inflation and employment?

Can the monetary authority create more jobs by increasing the rate of monetary expansion? The proponents of the Phillips curve say it can, whereas the proponents of the "natural-rate hypothesis" tend to be pessimistic. Even in the short run, they argue, the trade-off may well be quite small, especially when people form expectations "rationally." The closer the expected inflation is to $\dot{p}/p$, the less significant will be the trade-off. In general, economic policies work precisely because people are ignorant of them, because they come as a surprise, or because people are temporarily constrained by existing contracts. If people are very well informed of the behavior of the government and act rationally, there will be no surprises, and hence no effects, barring various constraints. Sargent and Wallace have carried this point to the extreme and argued that if people had a correct notion of the probabilities of various policy measures that might be taken, the authority would be left with no degrees of freedom to control the economy, and thus automatic rules might be more sensible than dis-

cretion. As Lucas (1972) showed, a Phillips-curve-like statistical relation may exist in such a rational economy, but such a curve may not
represent a usable trade-off between employment and inflation.
Moreover, the universal failure of policies aimed at exploiting the
trade-off during the early seventies raises serious doubt about the significance of such an empirical relation.

10.7   Inflation in open economies

During the seventies, inflation has become a familiar phenomenon.
This inflation has had two peculiar features. One is its worldwide
prevalence. The other is its coexistence with high rates of unemployment. At the present time, there is no clear sign of the problem disap-
pearing in the near future. But why are there no easy solutions available for this problem?

Let us consider a typical Western economy suffering from inflation
and unemployment at present. The government has by now tried all
the conventional fiscal and monetary measures and even some form
of direct wage-price controls. But these efforts have not had much
success. As for fiscal policy, the government has recently been
plagued by a shortage of revenues due primarily to the dismal performance of the economy. And this is in the face of mounting needs
for spending. The resulting budget deficits have given rise to a sharp
increase in its debt, both internal and external. Interest payments on
these debts are posing a serious threat to its financial capacity. These
financial difficulties are forcing the government to adopt a variety of
economy measures whose effect on the economy is rather dismal.
What this means is that the government, like the public, is rather constrained in its fiscal choices as a result of the decade-long economic
slump. Another problem, and a potentially more important problem,
associated with deficit financing is its implications for intertemporal
reallocation of resources and welfare. Let D be the deficit. Then, by
definition,

$$D = G - TX - rV$$

where G is government spending on goods and services, TX is taxes,
and V is the government debt outstanding, all measured in real terms.
The term rV is, of course, the interest paid on the debt. Now we may
assume that the aggregate real domestic product depends on $G - TX$.
The real national income is then the real domestic product less rV (to
be precise, that portion of rV that is paid abroad; but here we assume
that the debt is entirely external debt). We write the real national in-

come as $Y(G - TX) - rV$ and regard it as the measure of current social welfare. Clearly, in the very short run, V is fixed; hence, by run-
ning a larger deficit, the welfare of the nation can be increased temporarily. But, over time, a larger deficit results in a larger debt outstanding, which requires a larger stream of interest payments (out of the
real income of the future generations). In view of such intergenerational transfers implicit in deficit financing, it is not clear if the government, even if it is capable of doing so, should always pursue such a
policy to attain full employment now, especially at a time when the future outlook is dim.

Next consider monetary policy. Textbooks tell us that a flexible
exchange-rate system insulates an economy against shocks from
abroad, restores the autonomy of national monetary policy, and
hence enables monetary policy to pursue domestic objectives. This
argument may be quite right when the shock is not too great and iso-
lated. But, again, in the presence of a major prolonged difficulty like
the present one, the force of such an argument is considerably dimin-
ished. Suppose a tight monetary policy is adopted in an effort to reduce the rate of inflation. Home currency tends to appreciate, and
this tends to hurt the export-goods industries and hence employment.
The magnitude of this latter effect appears to depend on the relative
efficiencies of these industries and on the behavior of domestic wages
and prices. If these industries are efficient relative to their foreign
competitors, and if domestic wages and prices are well-behaved, the
undesirable effects of currency appreciation on production and employment can be minimal (as in the cases of Germany and Japan). If
not, an attempt to curb inflation through a tight monetary policy will
be accompanied by a substantial decline in employment and hence
will not be practical. An expansionary monetary policy, too, is not
without problems. The depreciation of home currency temporarily
provides more competitive power to the export-goods industries and
stimulates production and employment. The success of such a policy
depends on how long the economy can maintain the competitive edge
produced by the currency depreciation. If this edge is quickly eroded
by higher prices and wages, continual depreciation will be the only
way to maintain the higher level of production and employment. But
because a currency depreciation means higher prices of imports, domestic consumers always suffer from it. The desirability of currency
depreciation therefore depends on the trade-off between increased
production and employment on the one hand and higher inflation on
the other. Moreover, in the case of a nation consisting of regions with
widely different structures, like Canada, the incidence of the benefit

and costs of currency depreciation tends to be very uneven across regions and sectors, which tends to reduce the virtue of flexible exchange rates (Mundell 1961). Besides, one must never forget that the textbook argument for flexible exchange rates assumes that the home economy is sound and that troubles always come from abroad. But if the domestic economy has problems of its own, such as inefficiency in production, unstable labor, and aggressive wage and price hikes, one should not expect these internal problems to be solved by adjustments in exchange rates. In any case, for a high-cost economy with a high degree of openness, there seems to be little choice other than to keep pace with the world rate of inflation. Monetarists say that inflation is always a monetary phenomenon—caused by too rapid a rate of monetary growth. This appears to be always true ex post; a period of high inflation is always accompanied by a rapid rate of monetary expansion. But it seems more reasonable to argue that the causes of the current inflation-unemployment problem are, to a large extent, real—the breakdown of the Bretton-Woods system and the resulting uncertainty about the future of the international monetary system, the energy crisis and the sudden dwindling of the future growth potential and the general loss of confidence in the business world.

10.8 Toward a behavioral theory of inflation

The high rate of inflation in the face of sizable and persistent unemployment during the seventies put macroeconomics to a hard test. The conventional inflation-unemployment trade-off no longer seemed to exist. The money-supply control did not seem to be working, for reasons never explained by the monetarists. Their old cliché that monetary authorities failed to cut the growth rate of the money stock sounds rather empty. Macroeconomics has simply failed this test.

The fundamental reason for this failure is the lack of an adequate behavioral theory of price formation. Recall our earlier remark that static-price theory is not a theory of price formation at all and that the equilibrium relationships among prices stated in that theory are established by contradiction, without any input of knowledge as to how prices are formed in realistic markets, especially in a changing environment. Unfortunately, macroeconomic theory, too, has mostly dodged this important question. What is needed is a theory of optimal pricing behavior on the part of sellers in response to changes in the market data. Such a theory, though hardly existent at the present time, will again point to the fact that price-setting decisions are complex capital-theoretic decisions. We attempted to model such price-setting behavior in Chapter 7, but this model was limited in scope for a number of reasons. First, it dealt only with very short run hoarding decisions in response to expected future prices and interest rates. Although we believe that the model is an essential part of the theory of price formation, it is not a full description of an inflationary process that goes on in the economy. Second, the model abstracted entirely from an analysis of the behavior of the final demanders. Third, it assumed competitive behavior in the markets for stock of goods, and as a consequence, it failed to bring out the price-setting strategies on the part of sellers. In reality, however, it is probably more accurate to treat sellers as a set of (more or less) monopolistic sellers.

The scenario we have in mind for a typical monopolistic seller is as follows: During the two decades after World War II, the seller enjoyed a rapid (by historical standards) growth in business, with a high average rate of return on his investment. During this period, prices remained fairly stable, for the high rate of growth in volume secured a rapid turnover of capital and consequently a comfortable profit rate. Raising prices in such an environment did not seem to the seller to be a wise strategy because of his usual concern about market shares and growth of the firm. Such a prosperity came to a close toward the later part of the sixties. The U.S. economy began to falter, and its condition was further aggravated by the Vietnam War. The postwar IMF system came to an end, and it was followed by the formation of the OPEC and the beginning of the era of high-cost energy. The occurrence of these events in quick succession shattered the optimism that had prevailed in the economy during the previous two decades. Both consumers and investors became cautious in their spending decisions, and many turned to inflation-proof assets. Faced with a sudden downturn in the future growth potential, the seller felt the need for some defensive strategy to keep his profit rate from falling. The key determinant of profit rates is the turnover rate of capital, but the turnover rate of capital depends on the net revenue (price times sales volume) from a given dollar value of the fund invested. If the volume cannot be expected to grow as fast as before, it must be made up for by higher prices. In ordinary circumstances, the seller's perceived cost of raising prices in an oligopolistic market is considerable. But in a period in which asset inflation has already been set in motion and energy prices are predicted to increase continuously, such a perceived cost is reduced, and the seller becomes more ready to raise his price than in ordinary times. In the meantime, aggregate demand in real terms remains low, which encourages similar defensive price increases in general. As more sellers take such strategies, individual sellers find it increasingly difficult to maintain their profit rates and are led to further price hikes. The consequence is a self-sustaining inflation without noticeable improvement in production and employment.

According to the preceding scenario, the cause of the present inflation is more real than monetary. True, money has been generally accommodating rather than restraining throughout the seventies. But a tighter monetary policy would not have been able to remove the fundamental source of inflationary behavior. Sellers will rely on price increases as long as their profit rates are "below normal" and their future prospects of economic expansion remain dim. The major implication of the preceding argument is that, contrary to popular analysis, inflation has not been the cause of all the troubles but rather has been a consequence of the gloomy future prospect that has dominated the world scene. Direct wage-price controls would not have provided an ultimate solution either, for at best they could have converted an explicit inflation into a latent one for a limited period of time.

The discussion in this section is highly speculative. Nor is it suggested as a general theory of inflation. Inflation may come from various other causes. However, many will, we hope, agree that there is a need for a plausible theory of price-setting behavior.

Questions

10.1 Perform an analysis similar to that presented in Section 10.3 using an income tax [i.e., a tax on $f(k)$] rather than commodity taxes. How do your results differ from those in the text?

10.2 For an increasing concave utility function $U(x)$, the quantity $-U''(x)/U'(x)$ is called a measure of absolute risk aversion. Why? What is the general form of utility functions having a constant absolute risk aversion?

10.3 One of the peculiar features of Gray's model is the absence of a Keynesian aggregate-demand function. How are Gray's analysis and conclusions affected when an aggregate-demand function is introduced into her model?

10.4 In the recent inflation, certain capital assets (e.g., homes) have risen in price much more sharply than other consumer goods. Is this a norm or an anomaly? Consider a capital asset capable of producing a stream of net output. Suppose the price of this output was originally expected to remain constant. Then inflation started, and the price of the output is now expected to increase at a proportionate rate $\pi > 0$. What will the time path of the capital asset look like? Is the asset price likely to increase at the same rate as the output price? Or is a sudden once-and-for-all jump of the asset price more likely? (Hint: Start with the case of perfect foresight.)

10.5 Monetarists have maintained the proposition that inflation is a monetary phenomenon. The basis for such a claim seems to be that the excess demands for all other goods can be summarized as an excess supply of money and that therefore inflation can always be attributed to the excess supply of money. Comment on the logic and the significance of the monetarist proposition.

CHAPTER 11

The economics of social security

11.1 An overview

Social security is probably the single most popular policy of governments today. In 1975 the U.S. old-age security and disability insurance program promised a sixty-five-year-old single individual a maximum benefit of $580 per month, and the Canadian old-age security program provided maximum individual benefits amounting to $140 per month. (The corresponding figure for the Canada Pension Plan, which was started in 1966, was $155.) These benefits are certainly not very high, but even so, the social security expenditure for the United States in 1976 was running at about $80 billion. In Canada, federal expenditures for the old-age security program, Canada Pension Plan, and veterans benefits alone amounted to $6 billion, almost half of the total federal expenditure on social welfare (which includes expenditures for unemployment insurance $4 billion, family allowance $2 billion, and Canada Assistance Plan $1 billion).

Social security refers to that part of social welfare programs that concerns income security for retirees, their spouses, and dependents. As such, social security is a compulsory savings program for retirement intended to supplement private pension schemes. But this is not all. Social security also functions as an income-redistribution scheme from high to low income earners. How to reconcile the two functions (i.e., the savings function and the redistributive or welfare function) has been one of the basic problems since the inception of the social security program. The 1935 Social Security Act in the United States stressed the principle of a fair rate of return to each contributor (the principle of "individual equity"), which was to be secured by maintaining a trust fund for such savings. In this sense, the system originally was closer to a private pension than the social security as we know it today. Over the years, however, the principle of individual equity was gradually deemphasized, giving way to the notion of "social adequacy." According to this latter principle, benefits are to be determined not by lifetime contributions but rather by a minimum standard of living, as determined by the society. The 1939

Table 11.1. *Formula for basic U.S. social security benefits (1976)*

137.77% of the first $110 of AME
+ 50.11% of the next $290 of AME
+ 46.83% of the next $150 of AME
+ 55.04% of the next $100 of AME
+ 30.61% of the next $100 of AME
+ 25.51% of the next $250 of AME
+ 22.98% of the next $175 of AME
+ 21.28% of the next $100 of AME

Source: Munnell, A. H., 1977, *The Future of Social Security* p. 28, New York: Brookings Institution.

amendments to the Social Security Act resolved the conflict in favor of social adequacy, and since then the minimum benefits have become very high relative to minimum contributions.

Roughly speaking, the present U.S. system operates in two tiers. Since 1972, the pure welfare component of social security has been handled by the supplemental security income program, and the savings component has been handled by the old-age, survivors, and disability insurance (OASDI) program. Both programs are administered by the federal government. The supplemental security income program is financed out of general revenues, whereas the OASDI program is financed by social security taxes. This, nevertheless, does not mean that the latter is free from redistributive components. The benefits from this program are determined by first calculating the individual's average monthly earning (which is the simple mean of his earnings over the past 20 years) and then applying the formula of Table 11.1 to the average monthly earning (AME). This shows that the OASDI benefits increase with AME at or below $1,275 in a very regressive fashion to a maximum of $578. In Canada, the rate of contribution to the Canada Pension Plan was set at 1.8 percent of annual earnings up to $8,400, equivalent to a maximum "tax" of $150.20 with the maximum basic benefit of $154.86, as mentioned earlier.

Today, after years of comparatively trouble-free operation, the social security programs of the United States and Canada are said to have serious difficulties. The nature of the problem is financial. In 1975 the U.S. OASDI program disbursed $69.2 billion, while collecting only $66.7 billion in taxes and interest on reserve-fund bonds. Even larger deficits are expected in the near future, such that the pro

Table 11.2. *U.S. OASDI reserves*

Year	Reserves (billion dollars)
1977	41.4
1978	35.5
1979	28.6
1980	20.7
1981	11.6
1982	0.1
1983	−14.8

Source: Heilbroner, R. J., and Thurow, L. C. 1977.
The Economic Problem Newsletter 8(2). Englewood
Cliffs, N.J.: Prentice-Hall.

gram's reserve fund, which stood at some $40 billion in 1977, will be
wiped out completely by 1982 if the same rules of operation are maintained (Table 11.2). Canada's social security problem is similar but
smaller in magnitude. Canada's old-age and survivors (OAS) plan also
started to record deficits in 1972 and continued to do so until 1976,
when it was merged into the general account.

A number of factors account for these difficulties. First, there is the
effect of the economic recession in the 1970s. Stagnant wages and
high unemployment decreased tax revenues. Second, the number of
people over sixty-five years of age as a proportion of the total population has doubled since 1935, and the number of benefit recipients has
doubled over the past decade, an increase averaging to 7 percent per
annum. Third, there has been a series of excessively generous increases in benefits in the past–too generous in the sense that the resulting benefits have exceeded what a correct actuarial calculation
warranted. Notwithstanding the difficulties of correctly predicting future economic conditions and demography, the present difficulties
are undoubtedly largely due to mismanagement. We do not need
growth theory to understand that a small initial error in an exponen-
tially growing variable spells disaster over a long period of time. In
the case of the social security program (which, incidentally, takes
thirty to forty years to reach a steady state), a mistake committed at an
early stage tends to go undetected for a long time while deficits accu-
mulate, and when the mistake is finally detected, it is often too late for
an easy remedy. It is no coincidence that after forty years of operation
financial difficulties have suddenly become acute. There is something
counterintuitive about exponentials. Consider this old story: Once

upon a time, there was a man of great wit. The king hired him for entertainment. One day the king was so pleased with the man's witty responses that he told the man he could choose his own reward. The man thanked the king and humbly revealed his request, which was that he would be given one cent on the first day, two cents on the second day, four cents on the third day, and so forth, just for thirty days. The king could not understand why a man of such intelligence would make such a modest request when he could choose anything. It took the king two weeks to realize that the request was anything but modest. He had to stop payment to avoid bankruptcy (the monthly total for the man's request comes to more than $10 million).

Now back to the social security program. In the early stages of the program, contributions naturally exceeded benefit payments. Membership grew faster than the population, and there were relatively few recipients. This resulted in phenomenal growth of the social security fund. This, however, did not indicate that the social security tax was too high or that the benefit level was too low; it was merely a transient phenomenon. It is understandable, however, that the social security planners were alarmed by the rapid growth of the fund and consequently were tempted to accelerate benefit payments over and above what a correct actuarial calculation warranted. Thus a certain Ida Fuller, a legal secretary, who became the first social security retiree in the United States on January 1, 1940, eventually drew $21,000 in benefits for a total of $22.54 in payroll tax payments (*U.S. News and World Report*, November 21, 1977, pp. 31–2).

Further ad hoc increases in benefits were gradually adopted up to 1972, culminating in a final "gross error" in the same direction in that year. The U.S. Congress instituted a consumer price index (CPI) indexing of social security benefits in 1972. This piece of legislation resulted in a "double indexation" of benefits, according to Munnel (1977, p. 25) and Feldstein (1975, pp. 6–7). According to the new rule, the AME, on which benefits are based, were first indexed. In addition, the percentage rates applied to various portions of the AME as shown in Table 11.1, were indexed to the CPI. This, Munnell and Feldstein claimed, along with many others, is double indexation. The cumulative effect of such ad hoc policies over the long run is staggering. By the time the mistake became apparent, it was beyond repair, resulting in the problem we face today.

11.2   The economics of social security

From the point of view of economic theory, designing a social security program means instituting an intertemporal social welfare policy. A such a social security program is capable of influencing both intergenerational and intragenerational distributions of income. However, in this section we shall focus our attention on the former, that is, the intergenerational distributive effects of social security systems.

Consider an economy made up of a succession of generations of mortal individuals. Each individual lives for two periods. The first period is a working period; the second period is a retirement period. In the absence of government intervention, individuals earn a certain wage income during their working period, which they allocate for consumption during their lifetimes. The first question we ask is this: Does such a decentralized allocation mechanism generally lead to an intertemporally efficient allocation of resources in the sense of Pareto? The answer turns out to be negative, which implies that there is, in general, room for government intervention. Consequently, the second question arises: What is the optimal mode of government intervention? In this section we shall attempt to provide an answer to this question using a simple intergenerational mode of savings.

Let us begin with Samuelson's classic pure-consumption-loans model (1958). Assume that all individuals have identical preferences, denoted by $u(c^1,c^2)$, and that each individual earns real income equaling unity (measured in terms of a single consumption good). In this economy no capital goods exist, and hence there is no opportunity to earn interest on savings. Therefore, the best each individual can do is to allocate his first-period income between c^1 and c^2 so as to maximize $u(c^1,c^2)$. His budget constraint clearly is

$$c^1 + c^2 \leqq 1 \tag{11.1}$$

with equality holding only if the commodity keeps perfectly well at no cost. This is the situation facing each individual when there is no government intervention.

But now suppose that the population is growing at a positive rate n per period. In each given period there is a flow of savings generated by the young generation, equaling sL, and a flow of dissavings due to consumption by the old generation, equaling sL_{-1}, where s is the amount of savings by each individual in his working period and L is the number of individuals currently in the working period. Because $L = (1 + n)L_{-1}$, by assumption, the net aggregate savings during each period is $S = sL - sL_{-1} = sLn/(1 + n) > 0$. But these savings serve no useful purpose; they actually imply inefficiency, as can be seen from the following argument: Suppose a central agency, called the government, collects individual savings by offering savers a rate of return equaling n and transfers these collected savings to the old generation. Because the old generation simply consumes these transfers and then dies, the government cannot expect repayment. But its liabilities to the younger generation, amounting to $(1 + n)sL$, remain. In other words, the government has incurred a debt of this size that becomes due after one period. In the next period, however, the government again collects savings from the new young generation that it can use to pay the debt. Thanks to the population growth, the amount of savings collected in this period is $sL_{+1} = s(1 + n)L$, which is exactly sufficient to repay the principal and interest on the old debt. From this discussion it should be obvious that so long as the population grows at a nondecreasing rate and successive generations follow the same pattern of behavior, no problem concerning the repayment of the debt will arise, although the government debt grows at the same rate as the population.

The welfare effect of the preceding government policy can be assessed by considering the opportunity sets of the individuals. With a positive interest rate n, the budget constraint of a typical individual under this policy is

$$c^1 + \frac{c^2}{1 + n} \leq 1 \tag{11.2}$$

Clearly, the feasible consumption set determined by (11.2) is larger than the set determined by (11.1). Thus, this centrally coordinated pension policy results in a Pareto-superior allocation. That the policy is indeed Pareto-optimal can be readily seen by recognizing that n is the highest feasible interest rate the government can pay. Note that the economy's net aggregate savings under this policy are zero in each period. It is clear that the preceding policy involving intergenerational transfers is a social security program. The particular way of financing transfer payments (social security benefits) in this program, namely, financing current payments entirely by current revenues, is called a pay-as-you-go scheme. The preceding exercise has shown that a pay-as-you-go social security program can be beneficial to the society. An intuitive explanation for this success is the following: Before the government becomes involved, each individual is forced to rely on his own storage activities for intertemporal reallocation. The implied rate of return on his savings is, at best, zero. He is unable to lend his savings to anyone at a positive rate of interest because the older generation, having no income, will never be able to repay, his contemporaries' tastes and income are identical with his, and the succeeding generation has no desire to borrow. On the other hand, the society as a whole has a built-in marginal productivity over time given by the "biological interest rate" n. This interest rate is there to be exploited, but this is possible only by means of an institution with a permanent life, such as the government. By exploiting the biological interest rate, the previously described social security program has made every present and future individual better off.

Diamond (1965) studied a model similar to the preceding one, but he included productive capital. Productive capital provides individuals with an income-earning asset, thus relaxing the budget constraint (11.1) without the help of a government. Is it still true that government can increase intertemporal efficiency in this more realistic case? Diamond assumed that all the capital is owned by the old generation and rented to the young at the marginal-productivity rental rate. The aggregate amount of capital available in a given period is given by $(w_{-1} - c_{-1}^1)L_{-1}$, where w_{-1} is the wage rate in the preceding period and c_{-1}^1 is the per-capita consumption during the working period of the generation born in the preceding period. The young generation in the current period rents this capital, produces with its help a homogeneous output according to a production function $F(K,L)$, where $K = (w_{-1} - c_{-1}^1)L_{-1}$, earns wages, and pays back K (principal) and rK (interest) to the old generation. If we assume the usual neoclassical properties of constant returns to scale and diminishing returns to substitution for the F function, we can write $F(K,L) = LF(K/L,1) = Lf(k)$, $k = K/L$, and

$$w = f(k) - kf'(k), \qquad r = f'(k) \tag{11.3}$$

where $k = (w_{-1} - c_{-1}^1)/(1 + n)$. Suppose the economy is in a steady state in which k is stationary. In such a state, the values c^1, c^2, and k are determined by the following three equations:

$$c^1 + \frac{c^2}{1 + f'(k)} = f(k) - kf'(k) \tag{11.4}$$

$$\frac{\partial u(c^1,c^2)/\partial c^1}{\partial u(c^1,c^2)/\partial c^2} = 1 + f'(k) \tag{11.5}$$

$$(1 + n)k = f(k) - kf'(k) - c^1 \tag{11.6}$$

The question is this: Is this decentralized intertemporal resource allocation efficient in the sense of attaining the maximum $u(c^1,c^2)$ for the individuals? The answer, unfortunately, is no. Full efficiency in the preceding sense is attained

$$f'(k) = n \tag{11.7}$$

But the amount of steady-state capital stock implied by (11.4)–(11.6) does not generally satisfy (11.7). In this sense, decentralized intertemporal decisions lack an Invisible Hand.

In this situation the task of a benevolent government is to find ways to correct the dynamic inefficiency due to decentralized decisions. Following the theory of Samuelson (1975), let us introduce a social security program involving three parameters: per capita social security tax t, per-capita benefits b, and per-capita social security capital k_s. We write privately owned capital as $k - k_s$. Again concentrating on a steady state, we first have the three equations corresponding to (11.4)–(11.6):

$$c^1 + \frac{c^2}{1 + f'(k)} = f(k) - kf'(k) - t + \frac{b}{1 + f'(k)} \tag{11.8}$$

$$\frac{\partial u(c^1,c^2)/\partial c^1}{\partial u(c^1,c^2)/\partial c^2} = 1 + f'(k) \tag{11.9}$$

$$(1 + n)(k - k_s) = f(k) - kf'(k) - t - c^1 \tag{11.10}$$

Additionally, we have the budget constraint of the social security program. From the obvious accounting relation

$$K_{s,+1} - K_s = f'(k)K_s + tL - bL_{-1} \tag{11.10'}$$

we obtain

$$\frac{b}{1 + n} = t + [1 + f'(k)]k_s - (1 + n)k_s$$
$$= t + [f'(k) - n]k_s \tag{11.11}$$

The efficiency condition in this model is, of course, still (11.7). From (11.11) we therefore see that in an efficient steady state, the social security benefit must satisfy

$$b = (1 + n)t \tag{11.12}$$

That is, the benefit is exactly equal to the social security tax plus its biological rate of interest.

Let us now consider how the social security parameters can be used to direct the economy to an efficient steady state. Suppose first that the technology and tastes of the people are such that their decentralized decisions lead to a steady state in which $f'(k) > n$, implying that the amount of capital falls short of the efficient level. Hence the government must encourage capital accumulation. In this case there is a simple rule the government can follow. If it just pays benefits according to (11.12) and invests remaining balances at the market rate of return, it is easy to see, from equation (11.10'), that the social security fund grows according to

$$\Delta k_s = \frac{f'(k) - n}{1 + n} k_s \tag{11.13}$$

Thus, as long as $f'(k)$ exceeds n, the social security capital keeps rising in per-capita terms. But because aggregate capital is the sum of privately owned capital and social security capital, aggregate capital per capita will at least eventually start to increase, lowering the rate of return $f'(k)$ until the efficient steady state is reached. But then $f'(k) = n$, and social security capital stops accumulating. In such a steady state, the amount of social security capital is positive, and the fund is self-financing. This type of social security program is called a "funded scheme," in contrast to the pay-as-you-go scheme mentioned earlier. Although we have not performed an explicit dynamic optimization, and hence we cannot claim to have identified the optimal policy, this simple policy is at least asymptotically efficient.

Next we consider the case in which decentralized decisions result in "too much" capital, in the sense of driving the steady-state marginal productivity of capital below n. In this case the solution is more difficult. From (11.13) it is clear that the previously described funded scheme will not work, because whatever positive level of k_s we have initially, the fund will eventually become depleted. Because the problem here is oversaving and overinvestment, the government should attempt either to reduce private savings by taxation or to divert part of private savings from capital accumulation by borrowing. The reader should recall the national accounting identity:

private savings + taxes = private investment
+ government spending (including transfer payments)

or

private savings = private investment + government budget deficit

This last equation suggests that if the social security program is to correct the inefficiency due to overinvestment, the benefits must be set in such a way that the social security system incurs a deficit as long as $f'(k) < n$. Taking this and the formula (11.12) into account, a reasonable rule may be the following:

$$b = (1 + n)t + \theta[n - f'(k)] \qquad (\theta > 0) \qquad (11.14)$$

In words, (11.14) states that a "bonus" proportional to the difference between the biological rate and the market rate is added to the long-run social security benefits $(1 + n)t$. According to (11.14), the government debt V follows a path described by

$$V_{+1} = \theta[n - f'(k)]L_{-1} + [1 + f'(k)]V$$

or, in per-capita terms,

$$v_{+1} = \frac{1 + f'(k)}{1 + n} v + \theta \frac{n - f'(k)}{(1 + n)^2} \qquad (11.15)$$

A more revealing way of writing (11.15) is

$$\Delta v = \frac{f'(k) - n}{1 + n} \left(v - \frac{\theta}{1 + n} \right) \tag{11.16}$$

which implies that the long-run equilibrium is going to be either the efficient state or one in which $v = \theta/(1 + n)$. It is our hope that by setting θ sufficiently large, we can force the long-run equilibrium to the efficient state.

In order to complete this analysis, we now look at the dynamics of the capital stock. We know that private savings in per-capita terms, s, can be written as

$$s = f(k) - kf'(k) - t - c^1$$

where we take c^1 to be a fraction of the per-capita lifetime income, $f(k) - kf'(k) - t + b_{+1}/(1 + f_{+1}')$. The total savings will be held in k and v. Thus we can write $s = (1 + n)(k_{+1} + v_{+1})$. Finally, using (11.15) to substitute for v_{+1}, we arrive at a dynamic equation for k of the form

$$(1 + n)k_{+1} = (1 - \alpha)(f - kf' - t) - \alpha \frac{(1 + n)t + \theta(n - f_{+1}')}{1 + f_{+1}'}$$

$$- (1 + f')v - \frac{\theta(n - f')}{1 + n} \tag{11.17}$$

where α $(0 < \alpha < 1)$ is the fraction of lifetime consumed in period one. Because k_{+1} appears on both sides of the equation, (11.17) is a little more complex than the corresponding equation for v. From (11.17) we obtain

$$\partial k_{+1}/\partial v = - \frac{1 + f'}{(1 + n)D} \tag{11.18}$$

$$\partial k_{+1}/\partial k = - \frac{f''[(1 - \alpha)k + v - \theta/(1 + n)]}{(1 + n)D} \tag{11.19}$$

where

$$D = 1 - \alpha f_{+1}''(\theta + t)/(1 + f_{+1}')^2 > 0 \tag{11.20}$$

The easiest way to study the dynamics of this model is to approximate the difference-equation system with a differential system. To do this, we define $x = (k,v)$, set $\dot{x} = \Delta x$, and investigate the local properties of the differential system around its equilibria (in particular, around the efficient equilibrium). Equation (11.16) yields an expression for $\dot{v}$, and from (11.19) we have

$$\partial\dot{k}/\partial k = \partial k_{+1}/\partial k - 1 = -\frac{f''[(1-\alpha)k + v - \theta/(1+n)] + (1+n)D}{(1+n)D}$$

$$(11.21)$$

whereas $\partial\dot{k}/\partial v$ is given by (11.18).

Now we consider the efficient equilibrium. Expanding around this point, the coefficient matrix becomes

$$\begin{bmatrix} \partial\dot{v}/\partial v & \partial\dot{v}/\partial k \\ \partial\dot{k}/\partial v & \partial\dot{k}/\partial k \end{bmatrix} = \begin{bmatrix} 0 & \dfrac{f''}{1+n}\left(v - \dfrac{\theta}{1+n}\right) \\ -1/D & \partial\dot{k}/\partial k \end{bmatrix} \qquad (11.22)$$

where $\partial\dot{k}/\partial k$ is, of course, given by (11.21). A sufficient condition for a local stability of the efficient equilibrium is that the following two inequalities be simultaneously satisfied:

$$\partial\dot{k}/\partial k < 0 \qquad (11.23)$$

$$v < \theta/(1+n) \qquad (11.24)$$

By inspection of (11.21), we see that the condition (11.23) is satisfied if the bonus coefficient θ is sufficiently large, a sufficient value being $\theta = (1-\alpha)(1+n)k$, provided that the condition (11.24) is already met. But the condition (11.24) is itself dependent on the choice of θ, since the value of v in the efficient equilibrium does not depend on θ. So we see that a large enough θ will make the model stable around the efficient equilibrium.

The preceding analysis can be depicted graphically as follows: First, from (11.16), we see that the two lines $k = k_{GR}$ and $v = \theta/(1+n)$ constitute the $\dot{v} = 0$ loci. Next, from (11.17) the $\dot{k} = 0$ locus is given by

$$\left.\frac{dv}{dk}\right|_{k=0} = \frac{f''[(1-\alpha)k + v - \theta/(1+n)] + (1+n)D}{1+n}$$

which is negative if θ is large enough to satisfy (11.23). Figure 11.1 shows that E_1, the efficient or Golden Rule equilibrium, is a stable focus, whereas E_2, the other equilibrium, is a saddle point.

To summarize: The formula (11.14) leads an overinvesting economy to an efficient steady state if the policy parameter θ is chosen sufficiently large. However, this prescription is not the optimal policy in the true dynamic sense; it is only asymptotically efficient. On the other hand, a true optimal policy would require full knowledge of individual preferences and technology and hence would not be practical.

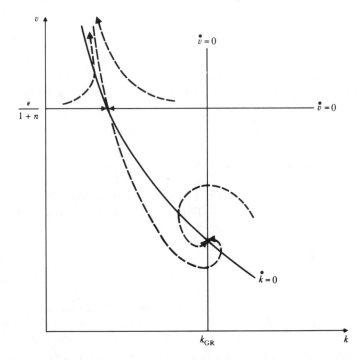

Figure 11.1. Attaining a Golden Rule equilibrium in an overinvesting economy.

11.3   Some observations about the present social security problems

The purpose of this concluding section is to briefly assess the present state of the North American social security programs in the light of the preceding theoretical analysis and point out some problems that were not considered here.

Point 1: As we argued in the first section of this chapter, the financial difficulties of the North American social security systems are, to a large extent, due to the adoption of "wrong" levels of benefits. But how could such gross errors have occurred? Munnell attributed them to the existence of the two competing goals imposed on our social security programs, namely, the goals of individual equity and social adequacy. As mentioned in Section 11.1, both the U.S. and Canadian old-age security programs began as funded schemes (which fitted the original concept of individual equity), but the subsequent emphasis on social adequacy led to the notion of the guaranteed minimum income for retirees and their dependents. These minimum benefits have, over the years, grown very high relative to the minimum contribution. The consequence is erosion of funds and increasing reliance on general revenues. Probably a better strategy would have been to draw a clear distinction between the savings component and the welfare component and keep the former in a funded scheme, while financing the latter by general revenues from the outset.

In 1977 the U.S. Congress raised the social security payroll tax, corrected a serious error in the way pensioners' benefits are adjusted to inflation, and increased the amount a pensioner may earn without forgoing benefits. These steps were, of course, designed to help avert the predicted exhaustion of the social security fund. But some long-run problems still remain. One of the most serious recent threats to the social security program is its declining public support. The analysis in the previous section showed that the sustainable "rate of return" on contributions is n. It also concluded that even if the prevailing $f'(k)$ is higher than n, n should be the rate of return on social security contributions. However, when $f'(k) > n$, a problem arises. To the contributor, and especially to a high-income earner who because of the regressiveness of the present benefit formula in fact subsidizes his poorer comrades, contributions to social security seem an inferior way of saving. With n expected to stay near zero, people are strongly tempted to drop out of the social security program and save for themselves at the $f'(k)$ rate of return. Very substantial clerical costs of staying in the program have also caused many (small) firms to withdraw from it, preferring their own private pension programs. This appears to be a major threat to the future of the social security program.

Point 2: The social security program is causing a "capital shortage." This feeling seems quite prevalent in business circles. To the extent that individuals regard payment of the social security tax as savings in return for the promised benefits, such taxes compete with private savings, leaving less for private capital formation, especially since these taxes are immediately paid out as benefits and do not, at least not directly, constitute investment funds. Feldstein (1975, pp. 14–15) estimated the order of magnitude of this effect on the U.S. economy:

In 1974, total social security taxes were $89 billion or 9 percent of total disposable personal income. If individuals think of these taxes as equivalent to savings and reduce their own personal savings accordingly, the effect on total savings would be very substantial. More specifically, in 1974 personal savings were $77 billion or 8 percent of disposable personal income. An $89 billion reduction in personal savings induced by social security would thus cut personal savings to less than half of what they would otherwise be. Of course not all private savings are personal savings. Corporate retained earnings account for nearly half of all private capital accumulation. In 1974, these corporate savings were $53 billion and total private savings were $130 billion. If social security reduced savings by $89 billion, the total potential private savings of $219 billion were reduced by about 41 percent. In the long-run, this implies that the U.S. capital would also be about 41 percent less than it would otherwise be.

Feldstein's estimate, however, must be modified in a number of ways. First, individuals may not regard the social security tax as being equivalent to savings. For high-income earners, especially, the expected benefits are not commensurate with contributions; furthermore, the benefits are possibly far too small to affect their savings behavior systematically. If so, the social security tax will not reduce private savings dollar for dollar. Second, Feldstein seemed to equate private savings with capital formation. But the effects of social security on capital formation are not restricted to the effects of taxes on private savings. If taxes reduce savings, the deficit in the social security program also reduces the amount of after-tax savings going into (private) capital formation. Third, governments also invest. That part of governmental capital formation made possible by the social security loans must be taken into account. This third factor is admittedly rather insignificant in the United States, where the social security fund has all but dried up, but in Canada it remains important. The Canada Pension Plan (CPP) is a fully funded scheme, and because it is young, the fund is growing rather rapidly. At present, the fund provides loans to provincial governments in proportion to the amounts paid into the fund by contributors from each province at an interest rate not less than the long-term federal borrowing rate. On the other hand, there are no restrictions on the uses to which the provinces may put their loans. Judging from the substantial capital formation made by provincial governments, however, it seems reasonable that at least some portion of the CPP loans is directed to capital formation. At any rate, the so-called capital-shortage problem may be interpreted in terms of our model as the situation in which private savings are not large enough and the social security program is further chewing away at the investible resources, a situation that resembles the doomed path diverging upward in Figure 11.1.

Point 3: The social security program, not surprisingly, seems to have a significant negative effect on people's work incentives and especially

Table 11.3. *Increase in early retirements of eligible persons, U.S.*

	Year	Men (%)	Women (%)	Both sexes (%)
Percent of eligible insured aged 62–64 years receiving OASDI benefits	1957	—	16	16
	1960	—	44	44
	1965	32	47	38
	1970	34	46	39
	1973	41	52	46
	1974	44	54	48
	1975	46	55	50
Percent of total OASDI benefits received by early retirees	1956	—	31	12
	1960	—	59	21
	1965	43	59	49
	1970	49	66	56
	1973	56	70	61
	1974	58	73	64
	1975	59	72	65

Source: Munnell, A. H., 1977, *The Future of Social Security* p. 174, New York: Brookings Institution. Copyright © 1977 by the Brookings Institution.

on their choices of retirement dates. As Table 11.3 shows, since the 1960s increasing numbers of people are opting for early retirement. Thus two-thirds of the benefits paid out by the U.S. OASDI program in 1975 were to early retirees. Even if the present value of the stream of benefits received by early retirees is the same as that given to regular retirees, early retirees put a lot of financial pressure on the program by reducing the number of taxpayers.

We must conclude that the future of our social security programs, although not entirely hopeless, seems very difficult.

Questions

11.1 Show why (11.7) is the efficiency condition.

11.2 Referring to the discussion following equation (11.2), do you think a private corporation could and would have done what the government did in the model? If so, why and how? If not, why not?

11.3 Samuelson has recently proposed a "two-part Golden Rule" in which the individual's lifetime utility is maximized first with respect to the choice of k, as in (11.7), and then with respect to the demographic parameter n.

Using the simple functions $u(c^1, c^2) = b \ln c^1 + (1 - b) \ln c^2$ $(0 < b < 1)$ and $f(k) = k^a$ $(0 < a < 1)$, obtain the two-part Golden Rule condition. Illustrate your solution graphically.

11.4 In Samuelson's pure consumption-loan model, suppose the government issues debts denominated in money rather than in commodities, so that the old person holds sp_{-1} dollars' worth of "bonds" to finance his second-period consumption, where p_{-1} is the money price at which his savings were purchased by the government. Suppose further that the government attaches a nominal interest rate on bonds equaling i percent per period.

(a) Show that as long as the bonds are issued only in exchange for savings, the real interest rate on the savings of each individual remains at n, irrespective of the amounts of bonds issued to subsequent generations.

(b) Suppose, in contrast, that the government buys up the entire output in each period in exchange for such bonds so that the young generation, too, must buy their first-period consumption goods from the government using part of the freshly issued bonds. How does this policy change affect individuals' allocation decisions?

CHAPTER 12

Much ado about nothing?

12.1 The capital-theory controversy

In this chapter we shall survey two issues that have been prominent in the recent writings on macroeconomics, namely, the Cambridge controversy on capital theory and the monetarist–Keynesian policy debate. We shall begin with the controversy on capital theory.

What are the issues between the two Cambridges? Despite the impressive body of literature turned out by both factions, it is not easy to explain the issues clearly and exhaustively, especially from an analytical point of view. Therefore, in what follows, we choose to look at what seem to be the two central issues: the concept of aggregate capital and the theory of distribution.

The concept of aggregate capital

The usual exposition of the neoclassical growth theory postulates an aggregate-production function relating the value of real GNP to the amounts of two inputs: capital and labor. With the aid of the marginal-productivity theory, this function is then used to explain and forecast the long-run trends of the rates of return on the two inputs and their relative shares. What are we really doing in this exercise? Are we justified in postulating such an aggregative relationship? Are we explaining something? Or is it really just a measurement without theory?

Suppose that the economy consists of n sectors (firms), each of which produces an output using a combination of labor and a set of heterogeneous capital goods. We write the production function as

$$Y^i = F^i(K_1^i,...,K_m^i,L^i) \qquad (i = 1,...,n)$$

where i is the index for the sector or the firm. Suppose for simplicity that labor services and outputs are homogeneous. Then we can put $Y = \Sigma_i Y^i$ and $L = \Sigma_i L^i$. Also, let $K_j = \Sigma_i K_j^i$, and put $J - J(K_1,...,K_m)$. Under what conditions can we represent the aggregate technology by an aggregate-production function

$$Y = F(J,L)$$

for some function $J(K_1,...,K_m)$? Unless such a jelly capital J can be defined precisely and consistently, the use of capital aggregates is unwarranted, not to mention the validity of speaking of the "marginal product" of such an aggregate capital. This was the first point made by Joan Robinson (1953) and others at Cambridge, U.K., and when it was subsequently learned that the existence of J depended on the stringent condition of weak separability between capital goods and labor (and other) inputs, they thought they had won the argument. Indeed, this was one of the glorious moments for the Cambridge School.

However, Robinson's criticisms of the neoclassical theory did not stop at the aggregation issue. She went on to question the value of the concept of capital in general. Capital, she argued, is, after all, cumulated labor, so that the value of a piece of capital goods may be written as

$$K_t = \sum_{\tau=t-n}^{t} (1 + r)^{t-\tau} L_\tau w_\tau$$

But, if so, the value of capital depends on r and w and hence cannot explain r and w. This is a point that goes beyond the definability of aggregate capital and its marginal productivity; it refers to the question of causality.

In the meantime, Samuelson (1962) came up with what appeared to be a satisfactory answer. Let the state of technological knowledge be given by a set of "blueprints," α, β, γ,.... We refer to these blueprints as technology α, technology β, etc. Each technology uses a specific type of capital good in fixed combination with labor. Technology α uses, for example, a_α units of capital good of type α with l_α units of labor to produce one unit of output, which can be either consumed or invested. It is further assumed that the outputs forthcoming from the various technologies are homogeneous as far as consumption is concerned.

Let w and r be the wage and interest rates measured in units of the consumption good. In a steady state of a competitive economy, the zero-profit condition prevails, and we have, for any technology,

$$1 = l_i w + k_i r \quad \text{or} \quad w = \frac{1 - k_i r}{l_i} \qquad (i = \alpha,\beta,\gamma,...) \tag{12.1}$$

This equation, when plotted in the (r,w) space, is called a factor-price

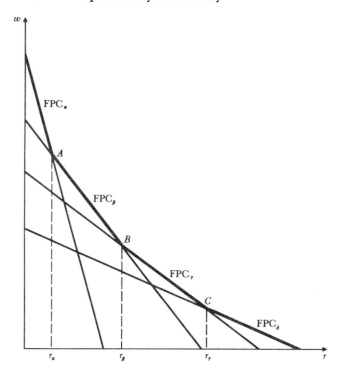

Figure 12.1. FPF under linear FPCs.

curve (FPC) associated with individual technologies. Under the preceding assumptions, an FPC is a downward-sloping straight line in the (r,w) space. All the technologies can now be represented in a single diagram (Figure 12.1). In Figure 12.1 four technologies are represented. The outer envelope of the four FPCs may be called the factor-price frontier (FPF). It tells us, for each range of the interest rate r (i.e., $[0,r_\alpha]$, $[r_\alpha,r_\beta]$, etc.), which technology is the most efficient.

Let us now move on to Samuelson's "parable." Suppose we approximate the FPF by a smooth (everywhere differentiable) curve. Such a smooth curve could have been derived from a "surrogate production function" in which a homogeneous aggregate output is produced by two homogeneous inputs J and L subject to constant returns to scale. That is, the smooth curve could be interpreted as having been derived from a production function $Y = F(J,L)$ by relating $w \equiv \partial Y/\partial L$ to $r \equiv \partial Y/J$. This J is called surrogate capital. The quantity of the surrogate capital is calculated as follows: From the linear homogeneity of the F function, $Y = LF(J/L,1) \equiv Lf(J/L)$, $w = \partial Y/\partial L = f(J/L) - $

$(J/L)f'(J/L)$, $r = \partial Y/\partial L = f'(J/L)$. From this,

$$-\frac{dw}{dr} = -\frac{dw/d(J/L)}{dr/d(J/L)} = \frac{J}{L}$$

or

$$J = (-dw/dr)L \tag{12.2}$$

That is, the quantity of J is obtained by multiplying the amount of homogeneous labor by the absolute slope of the smooth approximate FPF, evaluated at the prevailing pair of values (r,w). Conversely, using the surrogate production function $Y = F(J,L)$, one can interpret r as the marginal product of J. The degree of approximation will improve as more detailed knowledge of the book of blueprints is employed.

An alternative way of calculating (or verifying) the magnitude of J, as suggested by Samuelson, is to take an observed market interest rate, an observed total output, and an observed labor share and use them to calculate the residual share of property and capitalize it at the observed interest rate. The resulting national total $p_\alpha K_\alpha + p_\beta K_\beta + \ldots$ may be put as J. One trouble with such a measure J is that it generally depends on the values of (r,w) at which it is calculated. Champernowne (1953) searched for a measure of aggregate capital J independent of the values of (r,w) and such that r is given as its marginal product. The resulting formula is known as the Champernowne chain index. His method was to determine the chain of weights, p_α, $p_\beta,\ldots$ at the intersections of the FPCs. Referring to Figure 12.1, FPC$_\alpha$ and FPC$_\beta$ intersect at point A. At this fixed pair $(r,w)_A$, one obtains the ratio $p_\alpha{:}p_\beta$. Then, at point B, a similar ratio $p'_\beta{:}p'_\gamma$ is obtained. Likewise, a ratio $p''_\beta{:}p''_\gamma$ is found at point C. Combining these ratios, one finally arrives at a chain index $(\bar{p}_\alpha{:}\bar{p}_\beta{:}\bar{p}_\gamma{:}\ldots)$.

Samuelson's notion of surrogate capital and surrogate production function has subsequently met the serious criticism that this fairy tale works only for the case in which production is not joint production. To illustrate this point, let us consider a very simple model of joint production, namely, a primitive two-sector model. Consider one technology of the following type:

$$C = \min\left[\frac{K_c}{b_c}, \frac{L_c}{a_c}\right], \quad I = \min\left[\frac{K_I}{b_I}, \frac{L_I}{a_I}\right] \tag{T}$$

where C is the amount of consumption goods produced, I is the amount of investment goods produced, K_c is the amount of capital used in the C industry, and L_c is the amount of labor used in the C industry (similarly for K_I and L_I). The coefficients a_c, b_c, a_I, and b_I are all positive. Again, using C as the numeraire, the steady-state zero-profit conditions are written as

$$a_c w + b_c rq = 1 \tag{12.3}$$

$$a_I w + b_I rq = q \tag{12.4}$$

where q is the price of capital goods (in terms of the consumption goods) and rq is the rental price. Note that q is no longer identically equal to unity. Eliminating q, one obtains an FPC from (12.3) and (12.4) as

$$w = \frac{1 - b_I r}{a_c - (a_c b_I - a_I b_c)r} \tag{12.5}$$

One can readily verify that $dw/dr < 0$ and

$$\text{sign}(d^2 w/dr^2) = \text{sign}(a_I b_c - a_c b_I) = \text{sign}\left(\frac{b_c}{a_c} - \frac{b_I}{a_I}\right) \tag{12.6}$$

where b_c/a_c is the capital intensity in the C industry and b_I/a_I is the capital intensity in the I industry. Equation (12.6) shows that the FPC will be linear if and only if the two capital intensities are the same, which is nothing but the case of a single production function. In the present, more general, case, the FPC will not be linear. It will be convex to the origin if $b_c/a_c - b_I/a_I > 0$ and concave to the origin if $b_c/a_c - b_I/a_I < 0$. The condition $b_c/a_c - b_I/a_I > 0$ is known as the capital-intensity condition (CIC), and violation of the CIC is known to create difficulties. Because we are not directly interested in the CIC itself, we shall not go into details, but the nature of the difficulties may be briefly indicated as follows: Consider the problem of allocating fixed amounts of K and L between the two industries:

$$a_c C + a_I I \le L$$

$$b_c C + b_I I \le K$$

In particular, consider the case in which the amounts (K,L) permit full employment of both factors. Regarding these as equations, one can solve for (C,I) in terms of (K,L). Suppose the CIC is violated (i.e., $b_I/a_I > b_c/a_c$). Then one can easily show (the Rybczynski theorem) that an increase in K increases I at the cost of C; that is, the more capital-abundant the economy is, the more investment will be made, an intuitively disturbing case. What this means is that the equilibrium value of capital stock p^*K^* will no longer be inversely related to the interest rate.

Returning to the main argument, an FPC will be a curve in the gen-

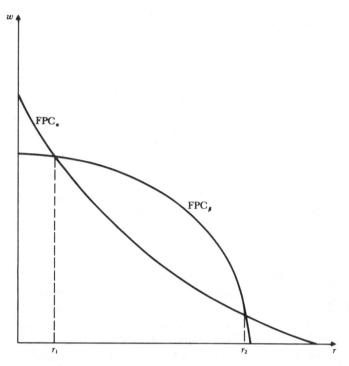

Figure 12.2. Nonlinear FPCs and reswitching.

eral joint-production case. Why is this a serious problem? To see that, suppose there is another technology similar to the one described earlier. When we plot the two FPCs, they are capable of intersecting each other more than once (Figure 12.2). The situation depicted in Figure 12.2 is known as a "double-switching." At a low interest rate $r < r_1$, technology α dominates technology β. For a higher range of r, $r_1 < r < r_2$, technology β dominates technology α. But for a still higher range of r, $r_2 < r$, technology α reappears as the superior technique. Although we have drawn one FPC convex and the other concave in Figure 12.2, it is plain that double-switching can occur even between two convex or concave FPCs. The trouble with double-switching is that the relative prices of the two types of capital vary from one intersection to another, and thus there is no longer a unique chain index by means of which to aggregate heterogeneous capital goods.

Another way of showing the paradoxical nature of double-switching is that the nice inverse relationship between the equilibrium value of capital stocks and the rate of interest (which is an important implication of fairy tales in capital theory and the major conclusion of the Austrian capital theory) is destroyed, and this may occur without violation of the CIC.

The initial reaction at Cambridge, Mass., to the double-switching problem was to deny its existence, but they have since accepted it as a possibility ("Symposium on Capital Theory" 1966). The possibility of double-switching thus destroys the theoretical justification for the use of surrogate aggregate-production functions, and the marginal-productivity theory of distribution based on them goes down the drain, or so it seems. The position currently taken by the economists at Cambridge, Mass., is that all that has been marred is their "low-brow" aggregate-capital model designed for expository purposes, whereas their "high-brow" theory with multiple heterogeneous capital goods remains perfectly intact. In the situation described in Figure 12.2, for example, the equilibrium wage rate and the two rental prices of capital goods are well defined and continuous across switch points and are capable of an exact marginal-productivity interpretation. However, this position, which is logically unassailable, represents a substantial retreat, for a large-scale Walrasian capital model is unlikely to produce the kind of sharp results that growth theory is expected to yield.

The theory of distribution

If the marginal-productivity theory of distribution is not acceptable, what alternative theory do the economists in Cambridge, U.K., have to offer? The spirit of their alternative theory is captured in this somewhat enigmatic proposition of Kalecki (1939): "Capitalists earn what they spend, and workers spend what they earn." According to Kaldor's exposition (1960), the preceding proposition is derived as follows: Take a typical Cambridge, U.K., model of macroeconomic equilibrium:

$$Y = W + P \tag{12.7}$$

$$I = S \tag{12.8}$$

$$S = S_w + S_c \tag{12.9}$$

$$S_w = s_w W \tag{12.10}$$

$$S_c = s_c P \qquad 1 \geq s_c > s_w \geq 0) \tag{12.11}$$

where Y is national income, W is wages, P is profits, and the rest of the symbols are self-explanatory. There are five equations for seven unknowns. The main feature of the Cambridgeshire theory is to leave I and income distribution undetermined. From (12.7)–(12.11) we get

$$\frac{I}{Y} = \frac{s_w W + s_c P}{Y} = (s_c - s_w)\frac{P}{Y} + s_w$$

or

$$\frac{P}{Y} = \frac{1}{s_c - s_w}\frac{I}{Y} - \frac{s_w}{s_c - s_w} \tag{12.12}$$

as the "fundamental equation." In this theory the fundamental independent variable is I/Y, which is determined by Robinsonian "animal spirit" or Harrodian G_w. The causal relation is from I/Y to P/Y. It is here that the condition $s_c - s_w > 0$ becomes the crucial stability condition in the sense that a greater I/Y entails a higher profit share and hence a higher S/Y. In particular, if $s_w = 0$, equation (12.12) becomes simply $P/Y = (1/s_c)I/Y$, the content of Kalecki's proposition. This special version of equation (12.12) was proved to hold even when $s_w > 0$ by Pasinetti (1962), and it has been named the Pasinetti paradox by Samuelson and Modigliani (1966). But why should the behavior of one group be solely responsible for the long-run state of the whole economy? Following Samuelson and Modigliani, we write $K = K_c + K_w$ by ownership. Under the assumed savings behavior, we have

$$\dot{K}_c = s_c P_c = s_c(rK_c)$$

$$\dot{K}_w = s_w[rK_w + wL]$$

or, in per-capita terms,

$$\dot{k}_c/k_c = s_c r - n \tag{12.13}$$

$$\dot{k}_w/k_w = s_w[rK_w + wL]/K_w - n = s_w\frac{f(k) - rk_c}{k_w} - n \tag{12.14}$$

where $f(k) = Y/L$. From (12.13) and (12.14) follows (12.15):

$$\frac{\dot{k}_c}{k_c} - \frac{\dot{k}_w}{k_w} \gtreqless 0 \quad \text{as} \quad \frac{k_c}{k_w} \gtreqless \frac{\alpha(k)s_c - s_w}{[1 - \alpha(k)]s_w} \tag{12.15}$$

where $\alpha(k)$ is the competitive share of capital (not of capitalists). In a steady state, we set $\dot{k}_c = \dot{k}_w = 0$ in (12.13) and (12.14), and we have

$$s_c r^* - n = 0 \tag{12.16}$$

$$s_w[f(k^*) - r^*k^*] + (s_w r^* - n)k_w^* = 0 \tag{12.17}$$

From equation (12.16),

$$r^* = n/s_c \tag{12.18}$$

which corresponds to the special version of equation (12.12) (multiply Y/K on both sides and use the fact that $I/K = n$ in equilibrium). But from (12.15) we have

$$k_c^*/k_w^* = [\alpha(k^*)s_c - s_w]/[1 - \alpha(k^*)]s_w \tag{12.19}$$

It is plain that the nonnegativity of k_c^* and k_w^* requires

$$\alpha(k^*)s_c - s_w \geqq 0 \tag{12.20}$$

Samuelson and Modigliani then argued that the Pasinetti paradox holds only if equation (12.20) holds with inequality, that is, if the workers' savings ratio is sufficiently low relative to that of capitalists. For s_w equal to or greater than the critical value $\alpha(k^*)s_c$, capitalists will have been driven out of existence, leaving only K_w as the economy's capital. In this "anti-Pasinetti phase" the long-run state of the economy is characterized by

$$k^*/f(k^*) = s_w/n \quad \text{with} \quad k_c^* = 0 \tag{12.21}$$

Thus, according to Samuelson and Modigliani, the Kalecki-Kaldor-Pasinetti alternative theory of distribution holds true in only one of the two phases. In the other phase, the economy consists in many homogeneous worker-capitalists rather than the two conflicting classes, and something like the marginal-productivity theory of distribution prevails. Should we conclude from this that both sides won?

Solow (1968) ruled that neither side won, in the sense that neither the marginal-productivity theory nor the Kaldorian theory is a complete theory of income distribution in a more general setting. Rather, the two theories are complementary. Consider an economy consisting of n goods and m factors of production. Then there is a subset of equations of general competitive equilibrium stating that the value of the marginal product of each factor in the production of each good is equal to its price. This subset of equations, whose number is nm, is usually said to constitute the marginal-productivity theory of distribution. To this subset is added a set of balance equations for the m factors of production. Unknowns, on the other hand, are the nm allocations of factors to industries, m factor prices, and the $n - 1$ relative prices of goods, or $nm + m + n - 1$ unknowns in all. If we refer to the preceding $nm + m$ equations as the marginal-productivity theory, it is plain that the theory is incapable of determining an equilibrium all by itself, unless $n = 1$. When $n > 1$, the theory must be supplemented by demand equations for commodities, but this will bring in the kind of considerations that appear in the savings-investment theory promoted by the proponents of the alternative theory. For a similar reason, the macro savings-investment theory of Cambridge-shire is also incomplete by itself. It is totally incapable of handling allocational problems.

As is evident from the preceding sketch, the disagreement between the two Cambridges is deep-rooted and multifaceted. One may describe it variously: classical versus neoclassical economics; macro versus micro; historical approach versus theoretical approach; causal approach versus simultaneous approach. But it seems fair to say that both schools suffer from some element of "schizophrenia." The Cambridge, U.K., school stresses in spirit their historical interest in capitalist economies, but their analysis is purely formal and nonempirical. The Cambridge, Mass., school, on the other hand, relies ultimately on the Walrasian general-equilibrium theory, which in its fundamental nature is abstract and nonhistorical. But when it comes to applications, they abandon it in favor of shaky aggregative parables.

Neoclassical economics is basically static in nature. It is not adequate to deal with dynamic problems such as capital accumulation, changes in technology and tastes, and other institutional evolutions. Its aim is a rigorous investigation of the structure of prices in a narrowly confined environment. The alternative theory promoted by its opponents follows the classical tradition and is supposed to be concerned more directly with these dynamic questions. But their analysis has been confined to steady states and has seen no visible improvements in the past two decades. If the goal of growth theory is to understand the central mechanisms of the growth process of capitalist systems, our conventional list of endogenous variables is probably too short for the problem at hand. It goes without saying that the distribution problem is not simply that of fighting for larger shares of a fixed pie, as Marxists often make it out to be. How to increase the size of the pie is at least as important. But the driving force for the latter, which holds the key to prosperity, still remains a mystery.

12.2   Monetarists versus Keynesians

As is evident from our discussions in previous chapters, a macroeconomy is a fairly complex general-equilibrium system. The goal of macroeconomic theory is to capture in an operational model the essential economic forces working in such a general-equilibrium system. Although macroeconomics is widely believed to be intellectually less challenging than microeconomics, this is far from the truth. The apparent crudeness and ad hockeries employed in conventional macro model building are the price paid for keeping the model operational. As we noted in the previous section, certain levels of aggregation and other simplifying assumptions are unavoidable if one wants to obtain any interesting results at all. Furthermore, as we mentioned in Chapter 1, the kinds of results established in microeconomic theory have very limited use in macroeconomics. Consider, as an example, the theory of exchange-rate determination between two currencies. If one focuses on the long run, one will arrive at a version of the purchasing-power-parity theory, for the exchange rate satisfying such a parity is the only sustainable rate. But, as we all well know, the day-to-day or even month-to-month behavior of any exchange rate cannot be explained adequately by such a theory. One might, of course, argue that the actual rate hovers around the parity rate. One might even attempt some decorating by introducing another unknown, like expectations, and thus make the story sound quite believable. However, unless these expectations are adequately theorized, the story will not have much scientific content.

The quantity theory of money, to which monetarists adhere, is much like the purchasing-power-parity theory. If one looks at the long-run relationship between the price level or money income and the money stock, one expects a fairly stable correlation between the two. Friedman (1959) reported that the long-run velocity of money for the U.S. economy during 1869–1957 steadily declined with the increase in per-capita permanent income, with an elasticity with respect to the latter equaling -0.810. From this fact comes the monetarists' much-publicized stability of the demand-for-money function. When this stability is combined with their belief in the autonomy of the money supply, money becomes the key policy tool for controlling the income level. But there are a number of loose ends to be fixed in order for this conclusion to be valid. In what follows, we shall consider the three serious loose ends: short-run effects of monetary policy; interactions between the money sector and the real sector; the autonomy of the money supply.[1]

Short-run effects of monetary policy

Given that the quantity-theory proposition is a long-run proposition, how can it be applied to the short run, where the $M-Y$ relationship is expected to be much more complex? The answer Friedman and other monetarists have offered is to introduce another variable called expectations and place the whole burden of explanation on it. Recall Friedman's distinction between permanent income and actual income, or that between anticipated inflation and unanticipated inflation. If they observe a fall in the velocity, for example, they argue that actual income is temporarily below permanent income and that the shortfall of actual income is not expected to last, which is why people have not adjusted their money holdings. But unless they provide us with a sensible theory of expectation formation, the theory is irrefutable and hence meaningless.

The Keynesian focus, in contrast, has traditionally been on the short run. In the *Treatise* (1930, Volume I, p. 229), Keynes parted with the quantity theory for the following reason:

> Formerly, I was attracted by this line of approach [i.e., the quantity-theory approach]. But it now seems to me that merging together of all the different sorts of transactions — income, business, and financial — which may be taking place only causes confusion, and that we cannot get any real insight into the price-making process without bringing in the rate of interest and the distinction between incomes and profits and between savings and investment.

Keynes's point was precisely that the simple quantity theory is incapable of explaining prices in the very short run, that even if the output level is fixed momentarily, the effect of monetary changes on prices is not straightforward. What he offered as an alternative was his "fundamental equations" (Keynes 1930, Chapters 9 and 10). The fundamental equations attempt to describe the price-making process in the very short run, in which the levels of output and employment are fixed. According to the equations, the general price level p is expressed as the sum of an average factor cost, including normal rewards to entrepreneurs, and an average level of "profits," where profits measure the excess of actual income over some normal income. In such a very short run, not all prices are likely to be flexible. If there are some rigid prices, they stay put while other flexible prices adjust to absorb profits or losses. One can see that the prices so established are nothing other than temporary-equilibrium prices in our terminology. Such temporary-equilibrium prices, in turn, induce changes in output and employment in the short run, the analysis of which was the main subject of the *General Theory*. The fundamental equation for the general price level is written as

$$p = \frac{E}{O} + \frac{Q}{O} = w_1 + \frac{I - S}{O} \tag{12.22}$$

where p is the general price level, E is the society's normal income or the total production cost, O is physical volume of output, Q is profits (i.e., the difference between the society's actual income and the normal income), w_1 is the average production cost, I is the money value of investment, and S is savings (i.e., the society's normal income less the money value of consumption). Whereas equation (12.22) is a definitional equation, Keynes brought life into it by making a pair of behavioral assumptions, namely, that I is a function of interest rates and other expectational factors and that S is a function of E. Because quantities are fixed, any excess demand for commodities, $I(r) - S(E)$, is absorbed by prices in the very short run. In this context, we recall that in the *General Theory* Keynes referred to the allocation of $I - S$ between prices and quantities in the short run.

From the point of view of money, any monetary change has its temporary effect primarily on profits or on $I - S$ through changes in the interest rate r. The average production cost w_1 might also be affected by monetary changes if they were to produce continued large profits or losses, but otherwise it is not very sensitive to monetary changes. Thus a given monetary change is expected to have its immediate effect on p through the profit term. This effect, however, is not very predictable, partly because of the instability of I as a function of r and partly because of the volatility of the speculative demand for money, or of the "financial circulation" in Keynes's terminology in the *Treatise*. In Keynes's view, such an effect could be understood only by careful examination of the asset markets. When Friedman (1956) "restated" the quantity theory, he formulated it as a theory of demand for money in the general framework of asset choice, which resulted in a quantity theory conceptually indistinguishable from that of Keynes. But as Patinkin, Johnson, and others have pointed out, the quantity theory as restated by Friedman is hardly identifiable with its traditional form, and, in any case, such a theory does not lend itself to the type of empirical propositions Friedman and his followers have conventionally asserted, especially in the short run.

*Interactions between the money sector
and the real sector*

The monetarists' approach to macroeconomics is a partial-equilibrium approach centered around the seemingly innocuous quantity equation. This means that the model is incompletely specified. An economy can be thought of as consisting of two broad sectors, the real sector and the monetary sector. The dynamics of the economy are determined by the interactions of the forces operating in these two sectors. To characterize the economy by a single market equation is to focus on one set of forces and ignore the other. The monetarists' choice is to single out the causation from the money sector to the real sector. Possible reverse causation is totally ignored.

This incomplete specification of the economy has given the monetarists several degrees of freedom to interpret and defend the quantity theory, for they can make almost any assumptions about the
behavior of omitted variables without worrying about model consistency. Working with a single money equation means assuming the
real variables to be given and stable. But the real issue is determining
precisely what generates economic fluctuations: Is it real forces or
monetary forces? In this sense, the partial approach of monetarists is
inadequate as a theory of a macroeconomy. The alleged high correlation between money stock and nominal income cannot be of help in
answering this fundamental question. No matter what the source of
economic fluctuations, this correlation is expected to remain high, for
it is a fundamental feature of a monetary economy that all spending
must be backed by money.

We must admit that monetarists are not the only macroeconomists
who use a partial approach. Macroeconomists, in general, have been
strangely attracted to partial-equilibrium models. One glorious example from the recent past concerns the Phillips curve. That the
Phillips curve should have become the treasure of Keynesians is particularly disappointing, because Keynesians had always asserted the
importance of a general-equilibrium approach to macroeconomics.
Another well-known example of partial analysis involves the so-called
Gibson paradox. It states that the observed correlation between nominal interest rate and price level is mostly positive, and quite high. In
terms of a simple IS-LM diagram, if the increase in the interest rate is
caused by a leftward shift in the LM schedule, we expect a decline in the
price level. But, of course, a rightward shift in the IS curve also can
cause the interest rate to increase, in which case we expect the price
level to rise. The moral of the story is that it ceases to be a paradox
when the two different sources of change are properly recognized.

The autonomy of the money supply

Monetarists have long claimed that the money stock is the cause of
changes in nominal income. This means much more than just a high
correlation between the two. But what evidence have they offered on
this matter? Friedman appears to have given two answers. One is that
the money stock can change autonomously. The other is that changes
in the money stock have consistently preceded changes in nominal income over business cycles. As for the first answer, the fact that the
monetary authority can take the initiative does not, of course, mean
that it does. In fact, historical evidence is hardly favorable to this view

The old real-bills doctrine implied a completely passive adjustment of money. The interest-pegging policy during the war years was also passive. The postwar IMF system, in principle, denied the autonomy of money (at least prior to 1973). The IS-LM interpretation of the Gibson paradox, moreover, indicates that the real sector has been the initiating cause of economic changes for most of the years during the past century, with the stock of money following with some lags. Indeed, this was Keynes's account of the paradox (1930, Volume II, pp. 98–208). The controllability of the money stock also faces difficulties from the practical point of view. The money stock consists of currency and demand deposits. The ratio of currency to demand deposits is of the order of 1 : 3. Suppose the monetary authority wants to carry out an expansionary policy. It does so by creating excess reserves for commercial banks through buying operations, through reduced reserve requirements, or through lower rediscount rates to facilitate member banks' borrowings. However, what the commercial banks do with the excess reserves so created is up to them. When the economy is in serious depression, as in the 1930s, banks are not likely to actively create deposit currency by new loans; rather, they tend to hold excess reserves or to buy safe assets such as government securities. When the economy is booming, banks have strong incentives to extend loans by borrowing from the central bank, if necessary. In either case, commercial banks tend to counteract the intention of the monetary authority and to make the money stock respond passively to nominal income.

The second answer, which sounds quite convincing, also has some difficulties. First, theoretically it is not possible to rule out the possibility that the money-stock change precedes the change in income, even when the real sector takes the initiative. For a concrete example, see the work of Tobin (1970). Some simulation studies based on general-equilibrium models have also shown that the chronological order of monetary changes and income changes does not provide useful information about causation (e.g., Brainard and Tobin 1968).

More recently, articles by Granger (1969) and Sims (1972) created a worldwide boom in the "causality test." Central bankers were among the most ardent followers of this new test, for it proposed a way to establish empirically the long-sought-after proposition that money determines income, rather than the converse. Simply put, the test procedure suggested by Granger and claimed by Sims is as follows: Let M and Y be two time-series variables. Denoting the past values of the two variables by $\bar{M}$ and $\bar{Y}$, respectively, let the minimum predictive-error variance of Y, given $\bar{Y}$, be $\sigma^2(Y/\bar{Y})$ and the minimum predictive-error variance of Y, given $\bar{Y}$ and $\bar{M}$, be $\sigma^2(Y/\bar{Y},\bar{M})$. If $\sigma^2(Y/\bar{Y},\bar{M}) < \sigma^2(Y/\bar{Y})$ then M is said to cause Y. Similarly, if $\sigma^2(M/\bar{M},\bar{Y}) < \sigma^2(M/\bar{M})$, then Y is said to cause M. If both inequalities hold feedback is said to occur. I both inequalities are replaced by equalities, neither M nor Y cause the other. But if $\sigma^2(Y/\bar{Y},\bar{M}) < \sigma^2(Y/\bar{Y})$ and $\sigma^2(M/\bar{M},\bar{Y}) = \sigma^2(M/\bar{M})$ then it is concluded that the causality runs from M to Y. In the actua test procedure used by Sims, future values of M are also employed i the regression of Y for the reason that "if causality runs from M to only, future values of M in the regression should have coefficien insignificantly different from zero as a group" (1972, p. 545).

The reader may have noticed the peculiar use of the term "cause in the preceding discussion. When M is said to cause Y, this mere means that $\bar{M}$ is informative or has explanatory power about the curre value of Y. Does this informativeness really represent causality in th true sense of the term? In a recent article, Jacobs, Leamer, and War (1979) have shown that Sims's test is a test of informativeness rathe than of causality. Following these authors, consider the followin simple structural model:

$$M_t = aY_t + b_{11}M_{t-1} + b_{12}Y_{t-1} + \epsilon_{1t} \tag{12.2}$$

$$Y_t = cM_t + b_{21}M_{t-1} + b_{22}Y_{t-1} + \epsilon_{2t} \tag{12.2}$$

where ϵ_{1t} and ϵ_{2t} are independent, serially uncorrelated random var ables with finite constant variances. This structural system implies th following reduced form:

$$\begin{bmatrix} M_t \\ Y_t \end{bmatrix} = [\pi] \begin{bmatrix} M_{t-1} \\ Y_{t-1} \end{bmatrix} + \begin{bmatrix} u_{1t} \\ u_{2t} \end{bmatrix} \tag{12.2}$$

where

$$[\pi] = (1 - ac)^{-1} \begin{bmatrix} b_{11} + ab_{21} & b_{12} + ab_{22} \\ cb_{11} + b_{21} & cb_{12} + b_{22} \end{bmatrix}$$

and

$$\begin{bmatrix} u_{1t} \\ u_{2t} \end{bmatrix} = (1 - ac)^{-1} \begin{bmatrix} 1 & a \\ c & 1 \end{bmatrix} \begin{bmatrix} \epsilon_{1t} \\ \epsilon_{2t} \end{bmatrix}$$

In this system there are two hypotheses that describe the extent which M influences Y. These hypotheses are

H_1: $c = b_{21} = 0$ (absence of causality)

H_2: $cb_{11} + b_{21} = 0$ (absence of informativeness)

Referring to the preceding structural equations, H_1 states that the d turbances in the M equation are never transmitted to Y. Under H

the value of ϵ_{1t} chosen by a policy has no impact, now or later, on Y. In this sense, H_1 is the appropriate hypothesis for the causality test. H_2, on the other hand, refers to the reduced-form equations and states that the coefficient on M_{t-1} in the Y equation is zero, meaning that M is not informative about future Y. Jacobs, Leamer, and Ward identified H_2 as the hypothesis involved in the Granger-Sims causality test. However, whereas H_1 implies H_2, the converse is not necessarily true; $cb_{11} + b_{21}$ may be zero even when c and b_{21} are nonzero. However, because these structural equations are unidentified, it is not possible to determine the values of these structural parameters on the basis of the estimated π matrix. In a word, the Granger-Sims test is a necessary, but not sufficient, test of causality.

Another important issue in this connection is the problem of controllability of the money supply. The money stock is usually defined as the sum of currency in circulation C and a certain category of bank deposits (e.g., demand deposits D).

$$M = C + D$$

The monetary base B is C plus bank reserves R:

$$B = C + R$$

Writing $c \equiv C/D$ and $r \equiv R/D$, we have

$$M = \frac{1 + c}{r + c} B \tag{12.26}$$

In this formula the monetary authority has direct control only over B. The variables r and c are primarily chosen by banks and the general public, and M depends negatively on each of these variables. These variables are known to move perversely over cycles; that is, they tend to fall during booms and rise during slumps. This means that these variables tend to move passively in response to income and against the intention of the monetary authority. Indeed, under the lagged-reserve requirements, as in the United States and Canada, the monetary authority has little control over the money stock in the very short run. In such a circumstance, money and income are probably "causing" each other. Moreover, the estimated values of the coefficients such as π_{21} depend on the behavior of the monetary authority. What central bankers should be doing is improving on their ability to control the money stock rather than letting a statistical test be the judge of their own usefulness.

There is, indeed, a more serious problem concerning the controllability of the money supply by the central bank. Ignoring the buildings, desks, chairs, and other nonmonetary items owned by the central bank, its balance-sheet identity (in difference form) can be written as

$$
\begin{aligned}
&\Delta && \text{Credit to the government} \\
+&\Delta && \text{Credit to the member banks} \\
+&\Delta && \text{Credit to the foreign sector} \\
\equiv&\Delta && \text{High-powered money}
\end{aligned}
\tag{12.27}
$$

Credit here means net loans and purchases of securities issued or owned by the sector in question. In the case of the foreign sector, it includes purchases of foreign currencies. Because the amount of these credits can be altered by the central bank, one may say that the central bank controls the amount of high-powered money. However, this is only in theory. Even monetarists admit this and focus on the second credit item, namely, that extended to the member banks. Their use of (net or free) reserves as an indicator of monetary policy seems to be based on the realization that this is the only item under the proper control of the central bank. Specifically, their argument is that the currency part of high-powered money cannot be controlled adequately. This leaves the reserve part, and hence their choice of the indicator. From the institutional viewpoint, however, even this is questionable. Historically, the central bank was created by the government primarily as its fiscal agent. The central bank's role as the bank of banks was secondary. This latter role gained significance as the world moved from the gold standard to a managed-currency system. Under the gold standard, an increase in high-powered money had to be supported in principle by a corresponding increase in the holdings of gold. Under a managed-currency system such as the present one, there are no such restrictions. The government's IOU is as good an asset as gold or foreign currency. Not only that. The central bank has an obligation to provide credit to the government as need arises. In short, the central bank has no control over the first credit item in list (12.27). Note that an open-market sale of government securities is merely a swap between the first and second credit items. It is a historical fact that when the first item is large, monetary control by the central bank becomes virtually nonexistent. War years provide such examples. Even in peacetime the governmental budget deficit is a serious threat to the central bank. During 1979 in Canada, for example, high-powered money increased by more than 11 percent because of the first item. In such a circumstance it would have been extremely difficult for the Bank of Canada to offset the pressure by curtailing the net credit to the member banks. Similarly, the central bank's ability to control the third credit item is also quite limited by exchange-rate considerations. It has been some years since the central bankers all over the world identified the conquest of inflation as the most urgent goal of their monetary policy. Yet the stock of high-powered money has been rising at an annual rate of over 10 percent in most countries. Would it be too naive to wonder why?

12.3   Some observations

Let us briefly reflect on the debates surveyed in the two previous sections from the standpoint of dynamic economics. As for the capital-theory controversy between the two Cambridges, the debate remained the opposition between the Keynesian and neoclassical theories and yet largely failed to focus on the fundamental issue. The gist of Keynes's theory was to recognize the limitation of the static-equilibrium approach of the neoclassical theory and replace it with a more realistic disequilibrium or dynamic theory of economic fluctuations and growth. His "monetary economy" was not an abstract model economy but a historical economy at the stage of our own economies. This oversight was quite unfortunate.

As for the monetarist–Keynesian debate, it has been made to look too much like an ideological opposition without a commensurate scientific content. Indeed, monetarism is not so much a theory of money as a laissez-faire philosophy. From a purely formal point of view, monetarism merely sums up all the excess demands for nonmoney goods, calls the sum an excess supply of money, and proposes to use the latter as the determinant of the general price level. As such, it is not at all novel or productive. Most of the results credited to monetarists are rather due to various assumptions that embody their beliefs. Because of the absence of any theoretical novelties, monetarists regard the issue as empirical. But their empiricism is strictly confined to data on monetary aggregates; they seldom, if ever, find it necessary to refer to the historical and institutional aspects of money and credit. The same analysis and prescription apply equally well to any country at any time. This is a peculiarly abstract empiricism. In this context, Keynesians, once again, should have stressed the historical empiricism of matters related to money and credit. Another, and more important, point Keynesians should have stressed is the importance of Keynes's theory as a general-disequilibrium theory built around the dynamics of capital goods. As Hahn (1980) has pointed out, the significance of Keynes's theory lies in the fact that it attempted to deal with money and credit in a framework in which they did matter. But this point has been largely avoided in the debate.

Questions

12.1 Consider an economy possessing two technologies. The first technology, say T_1, is given by equation (T) at the beginning of Chapter 12, whereas the second technology T_2 has production coefficients exactly opposite those of T_1, namely,

$$C = \min \left(\frac{K_c}{b_I}, \frac{L_c}{a_I} \right), \qquad I = \min \left(\frac{K_I}{b_c}, \frac{L_I}{a_c} \right) \tag{12.Q1}$$

Assume that the capital goods employed by these technologies are physically different, although labor is homogeneous and freely shiftable between the two technologies. Assuming that the two FPCs intersect twice, compute the equilibrium-price ratios of the two capital goods at the two intersections. Are they the same? [Hint: An optimal-growth model of this type has been studied by Nagatani and Neher (1977).]

12.2 Prove that when the CIC is violated, the equilibrium value of capital stock p^*K^* will be positively related to the rate of interest.

12.3 Solow stated that "the central concept in capital theory should be *the rate of return on investment*. In short, we really want a theory of interest rates, not a theory of capital" (1965, p. 16). What did he mean by that? What light does this view cast on the capital-theory controversy?

12.4 Comment on Mayer's items 2, 3, 7, 8, 9, and 10 (Notes, Chapter 12). (Hint: Try to distinguish between beliefs and testable hypotheses.)

CHAPTER 13

Concluding comments

We began this book with the observation that prosperity is a dynamic concept closely connected with a state of progress or economic growth. It seems fair to say that the economic difficulties experienced by many nations during the seventies are due to the slowdown in their growth rates necessitated by a number of exogenous events. The consequences have been a weakening of investment incentives and an increased unemployment rate. The sudden change in outlook has induced defensive actions on the part of the public. Firms have resorted to price increases to make up for the loss in volume, and individuals have taken flight in homes and other real assets. Savings and investment have found a low-level balance.[1] In the meantime, inflation has caused inadequate maintenance of capital and a decline in Tobin's q (the ratio of market value to replacement cost of capital assets). Deterioration in the quality and quantity of capital has resulted in a marked decline in the trend of labor productivity.

In the face of such structural difficulty, the efficacy of the traditional monetary and fiscal policies has proved to be rather limited. Fiscal authorities are plagued by revenue shortages and are eventually forced to make ends meet. Monetary authorities have discovered that they, too, are constrained. Because asset inflation has been allowed to develop for several years, any attempt to further raise interest rates will spell disaster for many householders who are up to their ears in mortgage debt, not to mention its general negative effect on employment. These considerations should remind us of the fact that policy choices, like those of the public, must be based on a solid dynamic framework. The problem faced by policymakers is not where to make the IS and LM curves intersect day by day but how to generate a desirable path of such intersections over time, with proper recognition of the dynamic constraints that bind them.

Furthermore, it should be clearly recognized that aggregate-demand policies through fiscal and monetary tools are not, in general, perfect substitutes for capital accumulation and hence are not guaranteed solutions to the question of prosperity. This point may be illustrated by means of a simple model devised by Kaldor (1940) and

227

Varian (1979). According to Kaldor, the fundamental dynamics of an economy can be described by a pair of differential equations, one for capital stock K and one for real output Y.

Following Varian, we may write these equations as

$$\dot{K} = I(K,Y) \qquad (I_K < I_Y > 0) \tag{13.1}$$

$$\dot{Y} = C(Y) + I(K,Y) - Y = I(K,Y) - S(Y) \qquad (0 < S_Y < 1) \tag{13.2}$$

Although Kaldor's original model was a pure business-cycle model without a trend, we interpret these equations as describing a growing economy net of trend. One basic property of the Kaldor model concerns the relative magnitudes of I_Y and S_Y: $I_Y - S_Y < 0$ for high and low values of Y, whereas $I_Y - S_Y > 0$ for a middle range of Y. Under this assumption, we have

$$\left.\frac{dY}{dK}\right|_{\dot{Y}=0} = \frac{-I_K}{I_Y - S_Y} \quad \begin{array}{l} <0 \text{ for high and low values of } Y \\ >0 \text{ otherwise} \end{array}$$

whereas

$$\left.\frac{dY}{dK}\right|_{\dot{K}=0} = \frac{-I_K}{I_Y} > 0$$

Thus the $\dot{Y} = 0$ curve has a "fold" in the (K,Y) space, and the $\dot{K} = 0$ curve is a positively sloped curve in the same space. The position of equilibrium, as well as the motion around it, may be depicted as in Figure 13.1. Figure 13.1 shows that for a given $\dot{Y} = 0$ curve, the position of equilibrium depends on the investment function. If investment is strong, the economy has a high Y equilibrium (E_1), and vice versa (E_3). Both these equilibria are semistable. When investment is moderate, equilibrium becomes E_2, which is an unstable equilibrium. This means that in such a case the system keeps oscillating in the direction of the dotted arrows. Imagine that our economy was at E_1 equilibrium during the sixties. As we moved into the seventies, the investment function shifted down, and in the absence of any policy intervention, this would have brought both curves down so that a stable equilibrium similar to E_1 would have been realized at a lower value of Y. But what actually happened was that policy measures were taken to prevent the fall in Y. The result was that although the $\dot{K} = 0$ curve shifted down, the $\dot{Y} = 0$ curve stayed roughly where it was during the sixties. As is evident from the figure, however, such a demand-management policy cannot maintain a high Y equilibrium unless it can shift the investment function upward at the same time.

Viewed from this angle, it is evident that the macroeconomic-policy question is a much more inclusive question than is popularly believed.

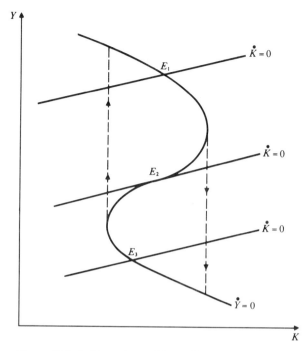

Figure 13.1. Stable and unstable equilibria.

Aggregate-demand policies have been oversold. Maintenance of prosperity requires a proper combination of aggregate-demand policy
and aggregate-supply policy. The key to successful management is
knowing how to maintain the investment–savings balance at a level
consistent with the long-run target growth rate of the economy. Specifically, the following matters require serious consideration: determination of a target growth rate for the economy; coordination, at the
national level, of investment plans for major industries and their
financing; a continuous review of the viability of existing industries,
with a view to improved efficiency in the future; appropriate policy
guidances toward these and other conventional ends.

Notes

1 A historical review

1 The word "economics" in Greek means house law, and the history of economic thought may be traced back to the writings of Plato and Aristotle. However, the term "macroanalysis" is rather new. Ragnar Frisch coined it, according to Schumpeter (1954, p. 278n).

2 The Ricardian tradition still lives in the Cambridge economics (e.g., Harcourt et al. 1975).

3 This is not to say that the neoclassical economics omits capital altogether. It has a solid body of theory of capital (e.g., Wicksell 1934). But the neoclassical concept of capital is "materialistic" (i.e., capital means a collection of physical capital goods), and the theory focuses on the explanation of the rates of return on various capital goods in equilibrium.

4 M. Kalecki is believed to have worked out the substance of Keynes's theory independently and even prior to Keynes. Kalecki's work has recently been collected and published (1971). A distinguishing feature of Kalecki's formulation is his emphasis on the different behavioral patterns of capitalists and workers. The two-class model has become the standard model of the Cambridge School.

5 See the work of Hicks (1974) for an illuminating historical account of the concept of capital. The work of Eagly (1974) is also useful. According to Hicks, the word "capital" was first used in the sense of a fund. It was a malleable, forward-looking concept; this is in sharp contrast to the materialistic, backward-looking concept of capital in the neoclassical economics. Keynes's use of the term was again "fundist." The output-capital ratio in this context must be understood in the fundist sense (i.e., as the expected turnover rate of a given fund). The output-capital ratio appears also in the writings of some neoclassical economists (e.g., Jorgenson 1963). But what it really represents is the physical marginal product of capital as determined by technology.

6 In Chapter 7 we shall discuss the meaning of "fixed prices."

3 Hicksian temporary equilibrium and comparative dynamics

1 A word of caution. In the finite-time problem, there is, in general, no justification in linearizing the system at long-run equilibrium. The preceding analysis is applicable only when the endpoints are sufficiently close to

long-run equilibrium values. Whereas the possible divergence between the impact effect and the long-run effect is disturbing in limiting the predictive power of static models for dynamic problems, Epstein (1980) has recently shown that a regularity condition due to Morishima tends to eliminate such divergence. For an exposition of the Morishima condition, the reader is referred to the work of Bassett et al. (1967).

4 Rational-expectations models

1 It is useful to recall the limitations of the conventional theory of general-equilibrium dynamics. According to the theory, prices adjust in response to the size of the excess demand, and the excess demand is specified as a given function of the current price vector p. This means that the participants' decisions are based only on current prices. But what about the expected future prices? The answer is that in the tâtonnement game there is no room for expectations, for nothing could be gained by knowing the future. No transactions can be carried out at nonequilibrium prices, and hence there are no rewards for outsmarting others. In other words, writing the excess-demand function as a function of current prices alone is logically consistent with tâtonnement. This also means that the equilibrium prices $p*$ are independent of the particular adjustment rules employed. Once we leave the artificial world of tâtonnement, however, trading takes place at "false" prices, and hence capital gains and losses become reality. In such a world, expectations constitute an essential part of the market game.

2 For a description of expectations formation during the Great Depression, see the work of Temin (1976), who argued that nobody had correctly forecast it.

3 See Question 4.4 following.

4 According to Houthakker (1959), there are only sixty to seventy well-organized forward markets in the real world.

5 See Chapter 11.

6 According to the way Lucas formulated the maximization problem of the young, there is a fixed membership rule in these markets, so that if one person participates in one market in his youth, he must return to the same market in the next period.

7 This equation is Lucas's equation (4.2). This equation and his equation (5.2) form the core of Lucas's model. The derivation of his equation (5.2) from (4.2) requires a few elementary transformations of variables. All the θ values that appear in his equation (5.2) should be interpreted as random variables and should not be confused with the realized value of the random variable (Lucas did not distinguish between them by notation).

8 Take, for example, a rectangular distribution $f(x,\theta) = $ constant, defined over $\theta = [0,2]$ and $x = [0,\bar{x}]$. Then, at least for the range of z below $\bar{x}/2$, $\Pr\{\theta \leqq \bar{\theta} \mid x/\theta = z\}$ is independent of the level of z for all values of $\bar{\theta}$. So

long as the marginal distribution of x is uniform, the same conclusion holds, irrespective of the shape of the marginal distribution of θ. But see Question 4.6.

5 Equilibrium theories of Keynesian unemployment

1 See the work of Barro and Grossman (1971). But this is only half of the rationale for the Keynesian consumption function. The other and more important half is the explanation why the marginal propensity to consume out of income is less than unity, or, alternatively, why savings constitute a leakage from the demand for currently produced goods and services. This latter fact derives from the central feature of a monetary economy in which savings take the form of acquisition of financial assets.

2 For a good survey of this old issue, see the work of Bodkin (1969).

6 Savings and investment in Keynesian temporary equilibrium

1 This brings up the problem of targets and indicators that has been much publicized by the monetarists in recent years. According to the literature, endogenous variables are classified into instrument variables, intermediate variables, and target variables. Instrument variables are those variables that are under direct control of policymakers. In the case of monetary policy, they include certain short-term interest rates, free reserves of commercial banks, and the money stock. Target variables are those variables in terms of which the performance criterion of policy is evaluated. Real income is a natural choice. Intermediate variables are all other endogenous variables that lie between instrument variables and target variables in the process of transmission. Finally, an indicator is an intermediate variable selected by policymakers that serves as a target variable for the purpose of policy. In other words, an indicator is a variable in terms of which the efficacy of policy is to be assessed. Monetarists' favorite indicator is the money stock. Their choice of instrument is usually the monetary base or high-powered money. Monetarists do not see any serious problem in the link between H (high-powered money) and M (the money stock). Nor do they recognize much noise between M and Y (real income); they see only V (monetary velocity) between M and Y, but V, they believe, is very stable after all. In contrast. Keynesians see the whole vector of r's (interest rates) between M and Y; they see even more inclusive variables, such as q. Generally speaking, an ideal indicator must meet two conditions. First, it must be sensitive to the movement in instrument variables so that the effects of policy may be assessed quickly and accurately. Second, it must be an accurate predictor of the true target, lest policymakers react to false signals. Whether or not such an ideal indicator exists for monetary policy, however, is a moot question.

2 This equation assumes that planned fixed investment is fully realized, which may not be a very good assumption at times.

7 Markets for stocks in Keynesian temporary equilibrium

1 Exceptions are those industries that produce bulky products with high engineering content, such as ships, airplanes, and buildings. These industries typically produce to orders.

2 The Keynes effect refers to the familiar progression: money stock → interest rate → investment → output channel.

3 Tobin's graphic analysis (1975, pp. 200–1) seems to contain a minor error. His p on the vertical axis should be interpreted as ln p.

4 These three figures have been constructed with data from various sources: issues of the *Statistical Abstracts of the United States* and the *Economic Report of the President;* Friedman and Schwartz (1963); Kendrick (1961).

5 K. Otani's thesis, which is in progress at the University of British Columbia, performs a rigorous stability analysis of the short-run equilibrium under several simplifying assumptions.

6 This nonnegativity constraint on sales should not be taken too seriously. There is no intrinsic reason why a seller should always be a seller. In abnormal situations a seller may become a buyer (in which case $s < 0$), as was actually observed in some markets during the 1973–4 disturbances.

7 Economists' dynamic interpretation of the so-called Le Chatelier principle falls in the same category. The principle in itself has no dynamic implications. The true dynamic relationship between short-run and long-run responses is much more complex because of possible intertemporal substitutions. See the work of Epstein (1978) for an illuminating analysis.

8 Here we are assuming that it pays for the firm to stay in business. A sufficient condition for this is that $C_y(0) < \bar{q}(z)$ for all $z > 0$.

9 The only ambiguous term is $D_{zz} + D_{sz}s_z$. Because $R_s(s) - D_s(s,z) = q$, $s_z = D_{sz}/(R_{ss} - D_{ss})$. Substituting this expression in $D_{zz} + D_{sz}s_z$ shows that it is positive.

10 This is not a very important assumption. All it does is to determine the quantitative response of the interest rate on x. One can show that $i_x \lessgtr 1$ as the term is positive or negative. Empirical studies have suggested that i_x is positive but less than unity.

11 Solow (1968) emphasized the firm's freedom to control the utilization rate of a given stock of employed workers. In his spirit, our Y becomes closer to E. There is no doubt that the burden of fluctuating demand is generally absorbed by both inventories and factor utilization rates, the exact allocation between them depending on cost considerations and expectational factors. Such a general model would contain at least two stocks. Besides, its dynamic system would be time-dependent in the context of business cycles. The difficulties involved in analyzing such a model explain the paucity of rigorous theoretical models of business cycles. For a recent empirical discussion of this subject, the reader is referred to the work of Feldstein and Auerbach (1978), who argued that the production-adjustment model, which assumes production to eliminate the difference between actual and desired inventories, produces implausibly low esti-

mates of the adjustment parameters. They proposed instead a theory that production adjusts very fast but that the adjustment speed of desired inventories to sales is rather slow. The dynamic implications of this alternative formulation are of some interest. See Question 7.3.

12 We do not draw an essential distinction between the short run and the long run. These terms are interchangeable in this chapter.

13 For a precise formulation of the adjustment of the subjective-demand function to the objective-demand function, see the work of Kanemoto (1980).

14 Recently, Drabicki and Takayama (1978) have argued that the myopic-expectation assumption is compatible with stability when the model is more properly specified to take full account of balance-sheet constraints.

15 The role of stocks has not been stressed in the existing studies of the Great Depression (e.g., Temin 1976). Once stocks are considered, it is not so much the Depression in the thirties as the general prosperity during the twenties in the face of high inventory levels that remains a riddle.

16 For an interesting empirical result on the basis of a model very similar in spirit to ours, see the work of Maccini (1978). An empirical estimation of equations (7.27) and (7.28) was performed using Canadian monthly data. Because we had not modeled financial markets in sufficient detail, our emphasis was on the price equation. The dependent variable was the manufacturing selling price, and this was regressed on stock of commodities, stock of unfilled orders, employment stock, money stock, average price of industrial shares, material prices, expected rate of inflation, and government purchase of goods and services, all in logarithmic first differences. Moreover, we postulated a distributed lag structure of temporary equilibrium. The sample period was July 1962 to August 1976, a total of 171 observations. The overall fit was reasonably good, with $R^2 = 0.69$, $DW = 1.91$, and $F_{17,154} = 63.41$ and with large and correct (signwise) coefficients on commodity inventories, unfilled orders, money stock, and material prices. Furthermore, an examination of the time pattern of the effects of these independent variables revealed that the commodity stock has the most immediate and strongest (negative) effect on the price, that unfilled orders begin to affect the price with a quarter lag, that the money stock has a significant effect on the price for about a year with a quarter lag, that material prices have an immediate and lasting effect on the selling price, that the employment stock has a slight negative effect on the price, and that the effects of share price, expected inflation rate, and government spending are neither very large nor highly significant.

8 Capital markets and money

1 This section draws somewhat on the work of Harris (1975).

2 One form of such utility functions is the so-called constant absolute risk aversion variety. This class of utility functions can be written as $U(W) =$

$a - be^{-cW}$ $(a,b,c > 0)$. Expanding $u(W)$ at $M = E(W)$ and taking a second-order approximation,

$$u(W) = u(M) - \frac{bc^2\sigma^2}{2} e^{-cM} \equiv f(M,\sigma)$$

Hence, $(dM/d\sigma)\Big|_{F=\text{const}} = 2c\sigma/(2 + c^2\sigma^2)$. If W is normally distributed, with mean M and variance σ^2, then

$$Eu(W) = \int_{-\infty}^{\infty} (a - be^{-cW})N(M,\sigma^2)dW$$

$$= a - b \exp(-cM + \frac{c^2}{2} \sigma^2)$$

Hence, max $Eu(W) \Leftrightarrow$ max $(M - c\sigma^2/2)$, so that we may regard $M - c\sigma^2/2 \equiv f(M,\sigma)$ as the utility function in the MV model. This F also satisfies (8.24).

10 Inflation

1 Recently, considerable attention has been paid to the nature of labor contracts. Azariadis (1975), for example, argued that the implicit long-term nature of labor contracts is responsible for rigid wages and unemployment. Negishi (1979), on the other hand, showed that this is not necessarily the case. Under the assumptions that firms are risk-neutral, that employees are risk-averse, and that employees always prefer some employment at some positive wages to unemployment, he demonstrated that firms will indeed choose an employment contract that ensures full employment at stable (i.e., state-independent) real wages.

12 Much ado about nothing?

1 According to Mayer (1978, p. 2), today's monetarists are characterized by the following twelve items:

1. Belief in the quantity theory of money, in the sense of the predominance of the impact of monetary factors on nominal income
2. Belief in the monetarist model of the transmission process (which is through the real-balance effect rather than the Keynesian interest-rate effect)
3. Belief in the inherent stability of the private sector
4. Belief in the irrelevance of allocative detail for the explanation of short-run changes in money income, and belief in a fluid capital market
5. A focus on the price level as a whole rather than on individual prices

6. Reliance on small rather than large econometric models
7. Use of the reserve base or similar measure as the indicator of monetary policy
8. Use of the money stock as the proper target of monetary policy
9. Acceptance of a monetary-growth rule
10. Rejection of an unemployment-inflation trade-off in favor of a real Phillips curve
11. Relatively greater concern about inflation than about unemployment, as compared with other economists
12. Dislike of government intervention

Of these twelve items, the only substantive item from the scientific viewpoint is the second item, concerning the transmission process. It is interesting to note that the monetarists have traditionally been reluctant to deal with this issue. Stein (1976) provided a good overview of the recent state of the monetarist–Keynesian debate.

13 Concluding comments

1 We have in mind the U.S. economy (see *Economic Report of the President, 1980*). For years the U.S. economy has been devoting a smaller fraction of its GNP to capital formation than have any of the major industrialized nations.

References

Archibald, G. C., and Lipsey, R. G. 1958. "Monetary and Value Theory: A Critique of Lange and Patinkin." *Review of Economic Studies* 26:1–22.

Arrow, K. J. 1959. "Toward a Theory of Price Adjustment." In Abramovitz, M. (ed.) 1959. *The Allocation of Economic Resources: Essays in Honor of Bernard Francis Haley.* Stanford: Stanford University Press.

——— 1964. "The Role of Securities in the Optimal Allocation of Risk-Bearing." *Review of Economic Studies* 31:91–6.

——— 1967. "Samuelson Collected." *Journal of Political Economy* 75:730–7.

——— 1968. "Optimal Capital Policy with Irreversible Investment." In Wolfe, J. N. (ed.) 1968. *Value, Capital and Growth: Essays in Honor of Sir John Hicks.* Chicago: Aldine.

——— 1978. "The Future and the Present in Economic Life." *Economic Inquiry* 14:157–69.

Arrow, K. J., and Hahn, F. H. 1971. *General Competitive Analysis.* San Francisco: Holden-Day.

Azariadis, C. 1975. "Implicit Contracts and Underemployment Equilibria." *Journal of Political Economy* 83:1183–202.

Bailey, M. J. 1956. "The Welfare Cost of Inflationary Finance." *Journal of Political Economy* 64:93–110.

Barro, R. J., and Grossman, H. I. 1971. "A General Disequilibrium Model of Income and Employment." *American Economic Review* 61:82–93.

Bassett, L., Habibagahi, H., and Quirk, J. 1967. "Qualitative Economics and Morishima Matrices." *Econometrica* 35:221–33.

Benassy, J.-P. 1975. "Neo-Keynesian Disequilibrium Theory in a Monetary Economy." *Review of Economic Studies* 42:503–23.

Blinder, A. S., and Solow, R. M. 1973. "Does Fiscal Policy Matter?" *Journal of Public Economics* 2:319–37.

Blinders, A. S., and Fischer, S. 1978. "Inventories, Rational Expectations and the Business Cycle." Harvard University working paper No. 220.

Bodkin, R. G. 1969. "Real Wages and Cyclical Variations in Employment: A Re-Examination of the Evidence." *Canadian Journal of Economics* 2:353–74.

Brainard, W. C., and Tobin, J. 1968. "Pitfalls in Financial Model Building." *American Economic Review* 58:(Papers and Proceedings):99–122.

Brock, W. A. 1972. "On the Models of Expectations that Arise from Maximizing Behavior of Agents over Time." *Journal of Economic Theory* 5:348–76.

Champernowne, D. G. 1953. "The Production Function and the Theory of Capital: A Comment." *Review of Economic Studies* 39:112–35.

Clower, R. W. 1965. "The Keynesian Counterrevolution: A Theoretical Appraisal." In Hahn, F. H., and Brechling, F. P. R. (eds.) 1965. *The Theory of Interest Rates.* London: Macmillan.

Diamond, P. A. 1965. "National Debt in a Neoclassical Growth Model." *American Economic Review* 55:1126–50.

238   **References**

1967. "Stock Markets in a General Equilibrium Model." *American Economic Review* 57:759–76.

Diewert, W. E. 1974. "Intertemporal Consumer Theory and the Demand for Durables." *Econometrica* 42:497–516.

1977. "Walras' Theory of Capital Formation and the Existence of a Temporary Equilibrium." In Schwödiauer, G. (ed.) 1977. *Equilibrium and Disequilibrium in Economic Theory.* Dordrecht: D. Reidel.

Drabicki, J. Z., and Takayama, A. 1978. "Endogenous Supply of Money, National Debt and Economic Growth." Unpublished manuscript.

Drèze, J. 1973. "Existence of an Equilibrium under Price Rigidity and Quantity Rationing." CORE discussion paper. Brussels: CORE.

Eagly, R. V. 1974. *The Structure of Classical Economic Theory.* Oxford: Oxford University Press.

Edgeworth, F. Y. 1881. *Mathematical Psychics.* London: Kegan-Paul.

1888. "The Mathematical Theory of Banking." *Royal Statistical Society Journal* 51:113–27.

Epstein, L. 1978. "The Le Chatelier Principle in Optimal Control Problem." *Journal of Economic Theory* 19:103–22.

1980. "Comparative Dynamics in the Adjustment-Cost Model of the Firm." University of Toronto working paper No. 8004.

Feldstein, M. S. 1975. "Toward a Reform of Social Security." Harvard University discussion paper No. 416.

Feldstein, M. S., and Auerbach, A. 1978. "Inventory Fluctuations, Temporary Layoffs and the Business Cycle." Harvard University discussion paper No. 651.

Fischer, S. 1977. "Long-Term Contracts, Rational Expectations, and the Optimal Money Supply Rule." *Journal of Political Economy* 85:191–205.

Fisher, I. 1907. *The Rate of Interest.* New York: Macmillan.

1930. *The Theory of Interest.* New York: Macmillan.

Fleming, W. H., and Rishel, R. W. 1975. *Deterministic and Stochastic Optimal Control.* New York: Springer-Verlag.

Friedman, M. 1956. "The Quantity Theory of Money: A Restatement." In Friedman, M. (ed.) 1956. *Studies in the Quantity Theory of Money.* Chicago: University of Chicago Press.

1959. "The Demand for Money: Some Theoretical and Empirical Results." *Journal of Political Economy* 67:327–51.

1968. "The Role of Monetary Policy." *American Economic Review* 58:1–17.

1969. *The Optimum Quantity of Money and Other Essays.* Chicago: Aldine.

Friedman, M., and Schwartz, A. J. 1963. *A Monetary History of the United States 1867–1900.* Princeton: Princeton University Press.

1970. *Monetary Statistics of the United States.* New York: Columbia University Press.

Goldman, S. M. 1968. "Optimal Growth and Continual Planning Revision." *Review of Economic Studies* 35:145–54.

Granger, C. W. J. 1969. "Investigating Causal Relations by Econometric Models and Cross Spectral Methods." *Econometrica* 37:428–38.

Gray, J. A. 1976. "Wage Indexation: A Macroeconomic Approach." *Journal of Monetary Economics* 2:221–36.

Grossman, H. I. 1972a. "Was Keynes a Keynesian?" *Journal of Economic Literature* 10:26–30.

1972b. "A Choice-Theoretic Model of an Income-Investment Accelerator." *American Economic Review* 62:630–41.

Grossman, S., and Stiglitz, J. E. 1978. "On the Impossibility of Informationally Efficient Markets." Stanford University technical report No. 259.

Hahn, F. H. 1960. "Equilibrium Dynamics with Heterogeneous Capital Goods." *Quarterly Journal of Economics* 74:633–46.

1980. "Monetarism and Economic Theory." *Economica* 47:1–17.

Hahn, F. H., and Negishi, T. 1962. "A Theorem on Non-Tâtonnement Stability." *Econometrica* 30:463–9.

Harcourt, G. C., Dobb, M., Hahn, F. H., and Hicks, J. R. 1975. "The Revival of Political Economy." *Economic Record* 51:339–71.

Harris, R. G. 1975. "Essays in Capital Market Equilibrium." Ph.D. thesis, University of British Columbia.

Harrod, R. F. 1948. *Toward a Dynamic Economics.* London: Macmillan.

1951. *The Life of John Maynard Keynes.* London: Macmillan.

Hart, O. 1975. "On the Optimality of Equilibrium When Markets Are Incomplete." *Journal of Economic Theory* 11:418–33.

Hawtrey, R. G. 1950. *Currency and Credit.* London: Longmans, Green.

Helliwell, J. F. 1977. "Recent Development in Policy Optimization for an Open Monetary Economy." Unpublished manuscript.

Hicks, J. R. 1946. *Value and Capital.* Oxford: Oxford University Press.

1965. *Capital and Growth.* Oxford: Oxford University Press.

1969. *Critical Essays in Monetary Theory.* Oxford: Oxford University Press.

1974. "Capital Controversies: Ancient and Modern." *American Economic Review* 53(*Papers and Proceedings*):247–59.

Houthakker, H. S. 1959. "The Scope and Limits of Futures Trading." In Abramovitz, M. (ed.) 1959. *The Allocation of Economic Resources: Essays in Honor of Bernard Francis Haley.* Stanford: Stanford University Press.

Intriligator, M. D. 1971. *Mathematical Optimization and Economic Theory.* New York: Prentice-Hall.

Jacobs, R. L., Leamer, E. E., and Ward, M. P. 1979. "Difficulties with Testing for Causation." *Economic Inquiry* 17:401–13.

Jevons, W. S. 1875. *Money and the Mechanism of Exchange.* London: Appleton.

Jones, R. A., and Ostroy, J. M. 1979. "Liquidity as Flexibility." University of California, Los Angeles, discussion paper No. 163.

Jorgenson, D. W. 1963. "Capital Theory and Investment Behavior." *American Economic Review* 53(*Papers and Proceedings*):247–59.

Kaldor, N. 1940. "A Model of the Trade Cycle." *Economic Journal* 50:78–92.

1960. *Essays on Value and Distribution.* New York: Free Press.

Kalecki, M. 1939. *Essays in the Theory of Economic Fluctuations.* London: Allen and Unwin.

1971. *Selected Essays on the Dynamics of the Capitalist Economy.* Cambridge University Press.

Kanemoto, Y. 1980. "Price-Quantity Dynamics in a Monopolistic Economy." Unpublished manuscript.

Kendrick, J. W. 1961. *Productivity Trends in the United States.* Princeton: Princeton University Press.

Keynes, J. M. 1930. *A Treatise on Money.* London: Macmillan.

1936. *The General Theory of Employment, Interest and Money.* London: Macmillan.

Koopmans, T. C. 1960. "Stationary Ordinal Utility and Impatience." *Econometrica* 28:287–309.

1965. "On the Concept of Optimal Economic Growth." In *The Econometric Approach to Development Planning.* Chicago: Rand McNally.

Lange, O. 1944. *Price Flexibility and Employment.* Chicago: Principia Press.

Laroque, G. 1978. "On the Dynamics of Disequilibrium: A Simple Remark." *Review of Economic Studies* 45:273–8.

Lerner, A. P. 1944. *The Economics of Control.* London: Macmillan.

Lipsey, R. G. 1960. "The Relation between Unemployment and the Rate of Change of Money Wage Rates in the United Kingdon, 1862–1957." *Economica* 31:1–31.

Lucas, R. E. 1972. "Expectations and the Neutrality of Money." *Journal of Economic Theory* 4:103–24.

Maccini, L. J. 1978. "The Impact of Demand and Price Expectations on the Behavior of Prices." *American Economic Review* 68:134–45.

Malthus, T. R. 1820, 1836. *Principles of Political Economy.* London: William Pickering.

Mangasarian, O. L. 1966. "Sufficient Conditions for the Optimal Control of Nonlinear Systems." *SIAM Journal of Control* 4:139–52.

Mayer, T. 1978. *The Structure of Monetarism.* New York: Norton.

Menger, C. 1892. "On the Origin of Money." *Economic Journal* 2:239–55.

Metzler, L. A. 1951. "Wealth, Saving, and the Rate of Interest." *Journal of Political Economy* 59:93–116.

Modigliani, F., and Miller, M. H. 1958. "The Cost of Capital, Corporation Finance and the Theory of Investment." *American Economic Review* 48:261–97.

Modigliani, F., and Sutch, R. 1966. "Innovations in Interest Rate Policy." *American Economic Review* 56(*Papers and Proceedings*):178–97.

Mundell, R. A. 1961. "A Theory of Optimum Currency Areas." *American Economic Review* 51:557–65.

Munnell, A. H. 1977. *The Future of Social Security.* New York: Brookings Institution.

Muth, J. F. 1961. "Rational Expectations and the Theory of Price Movements." *Econometrica* 29:315–35.

Nagatani, K. 1969. "A Monetary Growth Model with Variable Employment." *Journal of Money, Credit and Banking* 1:188–206.

——— 1978. *Monetary Theory.* Amsterdam: North-Holland.

Nagatani, K., and Neher, P. A. 1976. "Oil in the World Economy: A Dynamic Model of World Temporary Equilibrium with a Resource Constraint." Unpublished manuscript.

——— 1977. "On Adjustment Dynamics — An Exercise in Traverse." In Schwödiauer, G. (ed.) 1977. *Equilibrium and Disequilibrium in Economic Theory.* Dordrecht: D. Reidel.

Negishi, T. 1964. "Stability and Rationality of Extrapolative Expectations." *Econometrica* 32:649–51.

——— 1974. "Involuntary Unemployment and Market Imperfection." *Economic Studies Quarterly* 25:32–41.

——— 1979. *Microeconomic Foundations of Keynesian Macroeconomics.* Amsterdam: North-Holland.

Oniki, H. 1973. "Comparative Dynamics (Sensitivity Analysis) in Optimal Control Theory" *Journal of Economic Theory* 6:265–83.

Pasinetti, L. 1962. "Rate of Profit and Income Distribution in Relation to the Rate of Economic Growth." *Review of Economic Studies* 29:267–79.

Patinkin, D. 1965. *Money, Interest and Prices.* New York: Harper & Row.

——— 1976. "Keynes and Econometrics: On the Interactions between the Macroeconomic Revolutions of the Interwar Period." *Econometrica* 44:1091–123.

Phelps, E. S., and Taylor, J. B. 1977. "Stabilizing Powers of Monetary Policy under Rational Expectations." *Journal of Political Economy* 85:163–90.

References

241

Phillips, A. W. 1954. "Stabilisation Policies in a Closed Economy." *Economic Journal* 64:290–323.

Pigou, A. C. 1941. *Industrial Fluctations.* London: Macmillan.

1949. *The Veil of Money.* London: Macmillan.

Poole, W. 1970. "Optimal Choice of Monetary Policy Instruments in a Simple Stochastic Macro Model." *Quarterly Journal of Economics* 80:197–216.

Ramsey, F. P. 1928. "A Mathematical Theory of Saving." *Economic Journal* 38:543–59.

Robinson, J. 1953. "The Production Function and the Theory of Capital." *Review of Economic Studies* 21:81–106.

Samuelson, P. A. 1941. "The Stability of Equilibrium: Comparative Statics and Dynamics." *Econometrica* 9:97–120.

1955. *Economics.* New York: McGraw-Hill.

1958. "An Exact Consumption-Loan Model of Interest with or without the Social Contrivance of Money." *Journal of Political Economy* 66:467–82.

1962. "Parable and Realism in Capital Theory: The Surrogate Production Function." *Review of Economic Studies* 39:193–206.

1975. "Optimum Social Security in a Life Cycle Model." *International Economic Review* 16:539–44.

Samuelson, P. A., and Modigliani, F. 1966. "The Pasinetti Paradox in Neoclassical and More General Models." *Review of Economic Studies* 33:269–301.

Sargent, T. J., and Wallace, N. 1975. "'Rational' Expectations, the Optimal Monetary Instrument and the Optimal Money Supply Rule." *Journal of Political Economy* 83:241–54.

Schumpeter, J. A. 1954. *History of Economic Analysis.* Oxford: Oxford University Press.

Shavell, S. 1976. "Sharing Risks of Deferred Payments." *Journal of Political Economy* 84:161–8.

Shupp, F. R. 1976. "Optimal Policy Rules for a Temporary Incomes Policy." *Review of Economic Studies* 43:249–59.

Sidrauski, M. 1967. "Rational Choice and the Patterns of Growth in a Monetary Economy." *American Economic Review* 57(*Papers and Proceedings*):534–44.

Simon, H. A. 1956. "Dynamic Programming under Uncertainty with a Quadratic Criterion Function." *Econometrica* 24:74–81.

Sims, C. A. 1972. "Money, Income and Causality." *American Economic Review* 62:540–52.

Solow, R. M. 1956. "A Contribution to the Theory of Economic Growth." *Quarterly Journal of Economics* 52:65–94.

1965. *Capital Theory and the Rate of Return.* New York: Rand McNally.

1968. "Distribution in the Long and Short Run." In Marchal, J., and Ducros, B. (eds.) 1968. *The Distribution of National Income.* London: Macmillan.

Solow, R. M., and Stiglitz, J. E. 1968. "Output, Employment and Wages in the Short Run." *Quarterly Journal of Economics* 82:537–60.

Stein, J. L. 1976. *Monetarism.* Amsterdam: North-Holland.

Symposium on Capital Theory 1966. *Quarterly Journal of Economics* 80:503–83.

Symposium on Economics of Information 1977. *Review of Economic Studies* 44:389–601.

Temin, P. 1976. *Did Monetary Forces Cause the Great Depression?* New York: Norton.

Theil, H. 1954. "A Note on Certainty Equivalence in Dynamic Programming." *Econometrica* 22:346–9.

Tobin, J. 1965. "Money and Economic Growth." *Econometrica* 33:671–84.

1969. "A General Equilibrium Approach to Monetary Theory." *Journal of Money, Credit and Banking* 1:15–29.

1970. "Money and Income: Post Hoc Ergo Propter Hoc?" *Quarterly Journal of Economics* 84:301–17.

1975. "Keynesian Models of Recession and Depression." *American Economic Review* 65(*Papers and Proceedings*):195–202.

Tsiang, S. C. 1972. "The Rationale of the Mean Standard Deviation Analysis, Skewness Preference and the Demand for Money." *American Economic Review* 62:354–71.

Turnovsky, S. J. 1973. "Optimal Stabilization Policies for Deterministic and Stochastic Linear Systems." *Review of Economic Studies* 40:79–95.

1975. "Optimal Choice of Monetary Instrument in a Linear Economic Model with Stochastic Coefficients." *Journal of Money, Credit and Banking* 7:51–80.

1977. *Macroeconomic Analysis and Stabilization Policy.* Cambridge University Press.

Varian, H. 1979. "Catastrophe Theory and the Business Cycle." *Economic Inquiry* 17:14–28.

Walras, L. 1874, 1900, 1926, 1954. *Elements of Pure Economics.* Chicago: Irwin.

Wicksell, K. 1901, 1934. *Lectures on Political Economy.* London: Routledge and Kegan-Paul.

Witte, J. G. 1963. "The Microfoundations of the Social Investment Function." *Journal of Political Economy* 71:441–56.

Index